DISCARDED

The Second Chance
AMERICA AND THE PEACE

The Second Chance
America and the Peace

BY

GORDON A. CRAIG
GERHART NIEMEYER
JOHN B. WHITTON
FRANK D. GRAHAM
EDWARD S. CORWIN
JEROME S. BRUNER
GEORGE F. THOMAS

EDITED BY

JOHN B. WHITTON

Essay Index Reprint Series

BOOKS FOR LIBRARIES PRESS
FREEPORT, NEW YORK

Copyright © 1944 by Princeton University Press

Reprinted 1970 by arrangement

STANDARD BOOK NUMBER:
8369-1735-9

LIBRARY OF CONGRESS CATALOG CARD NUMBER:
77-111874

PRINTED IN THE UNITED STATES OF AMERICA

Contents

Introduction, by JOHN B. WHITTON ... 1

PART I

1. AMERICAN FOREIGN POLICY: RETROSPECT AND PROSPECT, by GORDON A. CRAIG ... 8

    Last time. Next time. Alternatives to world-wide collaboration. Conclusion.

2. WORLD ORDER AND THE GREAT POWERS, by GERHART NIEMEYER ... 30

    The end of power politics? The leadership of the "Big Three." Russia and the West. Methods of peace. The limitation of international power. International organization for what? Outlines of an international organization.

3. INSTITUTIONS OF WORLD ORDER, by JOHN B. WHITTON ... 68

    Basic principles. Nature of the new world organization. Functions—corrective measures; restrictive measures; suppressive measures. Problems—Are sanctions workable? Determination of aggressor; Do sanctions mean war?

4. ECONOMICS AND PEACE, by FRANK D. GRAHAM ... 115

    The philosophy of mercantilism. Peace must come first. The minimal economic conditions of peace—full employment; access to raw materials; control of monopolies. Protective tariffs; international monetary mechanism; international investment. Conclusion.

CONTENTS

PART II

5. THE SENATE AND THE PEACE, WITH A NOTE ON SOVEREIGNTY, by EDWARD S. CORWIN ... 143

The treaty-making authority splits into two authorities. Self-corrective powers of the Constitution. The executive agreement. President and Congress versus "the recalcitrant one-third plus one." Legislative approval preferable today to Senatorial approval. The Senate's dilemma. Summary. Note on Sovereignty.

6. PUBLIC OPINION AND THE PEACE, by JEROME S. BRUNER ... 177

The bases of opinion on foreign policy. Foreign policy: the people's version. The machinery of collective action. Dominance and sovereignty. Certain dangers. Some conclusions.

7. AMERICAN IDEALS AND THE PEACE, by GEORGE F. THOMAS ... 198

Our belief in progress. America's destiny: nationalism or internationalism? The basis of world order: justice and force. The moral basis of peace.

ACKNOWLEDGMENTS ... 225

INDEX ... 229

Introduction

By JOHN B. WHITTON

AMERICANS hate war and fervently hope that somehow the world may be freed from war and the threat of war. But they are by no means agreed on the best way of attaining this goal.

There is no dearth of plans and blueprints. Books and articles are appearing every week telling us "how to win the peace," and these are being discussed throughout the nation. The American people are giving far more serious thought to post-war problems than they did during the last war. As a result, we have achieved a somewhat clearer idea of the many obstacles that lie in our path, and of the dangerous impracticability of such oversimplified formulas as "self-determination" and "disarmament." Since a more enduring peace depends so largely upon informed public opinion, in our country and in other countries, our awakening interest in the problem of the post-war settlement is encouraging.

But interest and debate will not suffice. If America is to contribute what she can and must contribute to the establishment of a peaceful world order, American voters, in whom political power ultimately resides, must realize more clearly than they do now the basic issues of the present crisis and the advantages and disadvantages of alternative policies.

This volume attempts to clarify some of these issues and to state as realistically as possible what, in our opinion, America should do to get rid of war and the threat of war. The authors are all members of the Princeton Group for the Study of Post-War International Problems. This Group was organized in January 1943 at the suggestion of Professor Ralph Barton Perry, chairman of the Universities Committee, which has encouraged the formation of similar faculty committees throughout the country. The Princeton Group has been fortunate in having as its members representatives not only of the University but of the Institute for Advanced Study, the League of Nations Economic, Financial and Transit Department (located in Princeton since 1940), and the Princeton Theological Seminary, as well as several other scholars, unattached, living in Princeton.

We fully realize that what happens in the coming years will depend to a very considerable extent upon the other Great Powers, the smaller allied nations, and our present enemies, and that the policies of these other nations will be influenced by the United States only to a limited degree. We also realize how little any one group of American scholars can do to influence American public opinion, whether in war or in peace. Nevertheless, we have become increasingly persuaded that the chief duty of American citizens is to decide now what line this country should follow during these crucial years. We have written this book in the belief that a group of American scholars drawn from different fields ought to be able to clarify the objectives toward which a wise American foreign policy should be directed. For just as the fight against disease enlists the cooperative efforts of doctors, biologists, chemists, psychologists and social workers who can accomplish little alone but much in concert, so the fight against war, the greatest social malady, challenges the cooperation of historians, economists and political scientists, students of military strategy, experts on public opinion, theologians and philosophers. All these specialized approaches have been represented in our Group and all have made important contributions to our analysis and discussion of post-war problems and the role which America should play in the post-war world.

The Group, after several months of preliminary discussion, decided to request several of its members to prepare for publication a volume on American foreign policy, under the direction of an editor and a small editorial board. The resulting volume is not a mere compilation of unrelated essays. The

INTRODUCTION

chapters develop a continuous argument. Each has been written and rewritten in the light of the rest. Yet each contributor has been left free to express his own opinions in his own way. The several chapters differ, therefore, not only in emphasis but, on occasion, in basic belief as to what is or is not essential to world peace. The volume thus honestly records whatever differences of opinion we have not been able to reconcile. But the reader will discover that we agree far more than we differ. Above all, we agree emphatically that *the United States should, for its own sake and the sake of other nations, participate wholeheartedly in a world-wide effort to achieve an enduring peace.* The authors have not attempted to consider all the major problems that must be dealt with at the coming peace conference. We have focused our attention upon the more basic issues—the spirit in which these and other problems can most realistically be attacked, the chief methods and conditions of international cooperation, and the active role which the United States should play in the "one world" in which we now find ourselves.

Our argument falls roughly into two parts. In the first part, we study some of the most fundamental conditions both of security from war and of cooperative effort in a peaceful world. Professor Craig first reviews the Versailles Peace Conference and our eventual repudiation of the League of Nations, with an eye to the mistakes made after the last war and their avoidance after this war. He then examines the chief alternative foreign policies open to us today—nationalism (either "isolationist" or imperialistic), a policy of alliances with the other Great Powers, and participation in some form of world-wide collaboration—and assesses their respective advantages and disadvantages. Professor Niemeyer, recognizing the inevitable strength and responsibility of the Great Powers, discusses the political conditions under which alone they can cooperate efficiently and justly with each other and with other nations. Professor Whitton explores the ways in which all states, large and small, might cooperate in a world organization under a rule of law, and the principles, institutions and activities which might make such a world organization workable. Professor Graham examines the interdependence of peace and economic activity, with special concern for certain reforms in finance, industry and trade which would contribute to the abolition of war. These chapters, taken together, constitute our answer to the question, What are the minimum political and economic prerequisites to a more just and more durable peace?

The second part raises the complementary questions, How feasible are these proposals for American participation in a world order, and What moral and spiritual conditions must be met if peace is to endure? Professor Corwin describes the part the United States Senate can be expected to play in determining our post-war policy. He also discusses sovereignty in so far as it bears on the question of our participation in a new world organization. Dr. Bruner analyzes the present trends of American public opinion on the involvement of this country in world affairs. Professor Thomas discusses the extent to which our proposals conform with traditional American idealism.

Certain crucial questions have arisen again and again in our discussions, and around them the argument of this book revolves. All these questions are highly controversial and many are already being debated in Congress and throughout the nation. We have recorded our own answers to some of them. Others can be answered only in the light of information not yet generally available, or by events that still lie ahead. For still others no adequate solution is at present forthcoming because they concern a pioneering venture in human cooperation.

1. Should enduring peace be sought through a world organization with specified rules and activities, or should the United States rely primarily on the "leadership" of the Great Powers, in the hope that they will be able to reconcile their own conflicting interests and aims and, in addition, feel impelled to deal justly with weaker nations?

INTRODUCTION

2. The enforcement of peace, whether a function of a new world organization or entrusted mainly to the Great Powers, will require overwhelming force. But to prevent an abuse of power "it is necessary," as Montesquieu declared, "from the very nature of things, that power should be a check to power." How, in a society of independent states, can this collective force be effectively supervised and controlled?

3. Can measures designed to lessen the evils of unemployment, economic crises, high tariffs and trade discriminations, and the like, be taken while nations are still subject to the threat of war? And will such measures, if they are possible, lessen this threat, or must they await the establishment of security by other means?

4. What likelihood is there that American public opinion, at present favorably disposed toward active world cooperation, will shrink from the responsibilities entailed by such cooperation after the war has been won and when the cost of world peace is more fully realized? What, if anything, can be done to prevent such a reaction, should it threaten to occur?

5. Even if a majority of the American people continues to favor a policy of active international collaboration, may not Congress prevent our entrance into a world organization? What can be done to lessen this possibility?

6. May Russia embark, on her own initiative, on a policy of isolationism or even imperialistic expansion, thereby inducing the United States to adopt a similar policy? May symptoms of isolationism in the United States arouse Russian suspicion and encourage that country to consult only its own interests? Can the United States dissuade Russia from isolationism by adopting soon and wholeheartedly a policy of collective security?

7. Is there an essential conflict between what would be acceptable to our own and other nations and what would effectively dispel the threat of war? Would any central organization powerful enough to maintain peace and order have to

require of all participating nations "sacrifices" which they would almost certainly refuse to make? Is it likely that any plan to which all these nations would subscribe would be ineffectual? How can we best follow Aristotle's advice that "the true legislator and statesman ought to be acquainted with that which is best in the abstract but also with that which is best relatively to the circumstances?"[1]

8. Are "power politics" and moral obligation necessarily incompatible? If they are, must the world continue to rely on power politics in view of inescapable national self-interest?

Implicit or explicit in the foregoing questions is clearly discernible the underlying theme of the book—the reconciliation of power and law, of might and right, of "realism" and "idealism." A glance at Dr. Bruner's analysis of American public opinion reveals apparently inconsistent beliefs: a strong trust in power, whether military or political, together with an equally profound faith in what Jefferson called "the laws of nature and of nature's God," whether economic or moral laws. Apparently the American people are convinced, with Machiavelli, that "the chief foundations of all states ... are good laws and good arms." Americans pride themselves on being hardheaded; at the same time they are less afraid than most peoples of being called soft-hearted. Thus it is entirely in accord with our highest traditions that our soldiers and sailors should today be risking their lives overseas not only for national self-preservation but also for sincere humanitarian motives. Americans seem unwilling to believe that the realm of what is and the realm of what ought to be are as sharply distinguished as Machiavelli

[1] The necessity of acceptability has been admirably phrased by Secretary of State Hull, as follows: "It is obvious, of course, that no matter how brilliant and desirable any course may seem it is wholly impracticable and impossible unless it is a course which finds basic acceptance, not only by our allies but by the people of this country and by the legislative branch of this government which, under our Constitution, shares with the Executive power and responsibility for final action." *New York Times*, April 10, 1944.

INTRODUCTION

said they were. They believe rather with Max Lerner that there is a third realm: "the realm of what can be."[2] This is the realm which the present book explores. It may be that right and might are eternally irreconcilable, but Americans from the Constitutional Convention to the present have never been willing to think so. Some medieval states have been described as "all law and no government." Some modern states might be described as "all government and no law." Neither conception is in line with the tradition from which this book draws its inspiration, a tradition brilliantly illuminated by Abraham Lincoln when he spoke—almost casually, and as if his hearers knew instinctively what he meant—of *firmness* in the *right*."

Equally evident throughout the book is our belief that a victorious peace will certainly have to be a total peace. Peace, like war, can be won only by a coordinated effort in which all forces are mobilized against the scourge of war. To depend upon only one mode of attack would be as foolish and disastrous as to let the infantry storm a beachhead without the aid of planes, tanks and artillery. Political agreement among the Great Powers will be essential, but not sufficient. International laws and institutions will be essential, but we dare not rely on them alone. Peace can be ensured only with the aid of force, but force must be supported by economic readjustments and social changes. All these methods—military, political, legal, economic, and social—will be ineffectual if they are not directed and inspired by spiritual forces. Military victory will be the prelude to a tragic defeat if we and other nations are not wise enough and determined enough to do *all* that is necessary to ensure peace throughout the world.

[2] Max Lerner, ed., *The Prince and the Discourses by Niccolo Machiavelli* (New York: Modern Library, 1940), p. xlvi.

1. American Foreign Policy: Retrospect and Prospect

BY GORDON A. CRAIG

Ever since the United States became actively involved in the present war, the foreign policy of the nation has been guided by two major objectives. The first of these, stated clearly in the United Nations Declaration of January 1, 1942, and confirmed in the Moscow Declaration of October 30, 1943, is the complete defeat of those nations presently engaged in war against us. Our second objective—and the one with which this book is largely concerned—is that of securing the fruits of victory by continued collaboration with our Allies and other peacefully disposed nations in the years which follow the cessation of hostilities.

In pursuing the second of these objectives, the government of the United States has been attempting, in Mr. Cordell Hull's words, "to focus and direct" the will of 135,000,000 people living within the borders of this nation. Each step forward, from the United Nations Declaration to that of Teheran, has been based upon a major assumption—namely, that the American people has turned its back upon isolationism and the pursuit of unilateral aims and has recognized the ideal of international collaboration as the only feasible foreign policy for the United States in a changing world. In his speech of April 9, 1944, Secretary Hull gave clear expression to this assumption. In the last three years, said the Secretary, the American people "have moved from a deep-seated tendency toward separate action to the knowledge and conviction that only through unity of action can there be achieved in the world the results which are essential for the continuance of free peoples." Determined to press ahead toward the complete defeat of the enemy, the people of this nation are determined also "to go on, after the victory, with our Allies and all other nations which desire peace and freedom to establish and maintain in full strength the institutions without which peace and freedom cannot be an enduring reality."[1]

Secretary Hull's faith in the people's will to continued international collaboration after the war seems, at the moment, to have a solid foundation of fact. Both Houses of Congress have gone on record as being in favor of United States membership in some post-war organization to preserve the peace, and the public reaction to the congressional resolutions has been overwhelmingly favorable. Moreover, as is pointed out elsewhere in this book, public opinion polls taken throughout the nation indicate that the tide is running strongly in favor of internationalism. It was undoubtedly in response to this sentiment that both Democratic and Republican parties, at their recent national conventions, adopted planks in their platforms favoring our entrance into a world organization.[1a]

Lest these facts, however, engender an unwarranted and unhealthy optimism, it should be remembered that we have not yet devised any dependable means of gauging the intensity of public conviction at any moment. We have as yet no way of telling how durable the public desire for continued international collaboration will be when the American people is confronted with the actual costs and sacrifices involved. And we have, in the story of the reception of the Versailles Settlement in the United States, an example of the fate of commitments made during a war in the name of the American people.

If the United States is to do its share in the task of forging an enduring peace after this war, we must avoid a repetition of the experience of 1919 and 1920. In the foreground of all thinking and planning of American foreign policy, therefore, there must be a clear understanding of the reasons for the

[1] *New York Times*, April 10, 1944.
[1a] At this writing (September 1, 1944), public response to the Dumbarton Oaks negotiations appears very favorable.

American withdrawal from the international community after the last war. Only with that understanding will we be able to recognize the beginning of a similar post-war reaction and to take the necessary steps to avoid it.

LAST TIME

There can be little doubt that, during the last war, the majority of the American people supported the main tenets of the Wilson program, including that part which called for continued cooperation with other nations for the maintenance of peace. Then, as now, public opinion polls showed that a clear majority of the American people favored the acceptance of the Versailles Treaty and the League of Nations. Early in 1919, when the first attacks were launched against the League in the Senate, the "irreconcilables" themselves admitted that they represented a very small part of the people. Senator Lodge admitted later that "the vocal classes of the community, most of the clergymen, the preachers of sermons, a large element in the teaching force of the universities, a large proportion of the newspaper editors, and finally the men and women who were in the habit of writing and speaking for publication ... were friendly to the League as it stood and were advocating it."[2] The Republican Senators who congratulated Senator Borah after his attack on the League on February 21, 1919 said: "That was great; that was fine; we agree with you; but we got to have some sort of league; everybody is for it."[3]

Despite this large measure of public support, however, the Versailles Settlement and the League were defeated. Why were they defeated? Most authorities agree that, in large part, the defeat was caused by the shrewd tactics of the Senate opponents of the settlement. Protected by the two-thirds rule, Senator Lodge and his colleagues employed all of the weapons

[2] Henry Cabot Lodge, *The Senate and the League of Nations* (New York: Scribners, 1925), pp. 147-148.
[3] Thomas A. Bailey, *A Diplomatic History of the American People* (New York: Crofts, 1940), p. 669, n. 6.

in the constitutional armory to delay and amend the treaty. In the end they smothered the document with reservations which the President considered inadmissible, shifted the onus of responsibility onto his stubborn shoulders, and defeated the treaty out of hand.

Granted the truth of these facts, they are insufficient in themselves to explain what happened in 1919. To lay the full responsibility for the defeat of the treaty at the door of the Senate is to oversimplify, if not to falsify, the record. In a democracy it is the mass of the people which decides what will, in the last analysis, be done. If the American people had been united, and if they had desired the acceptance of the Versailles Settlement with sufficient intensity, they could have compelled the Senate to ratify it. Indeed, after the first defeat of the treaty in November 1919, public opinion was strong enough to force the Senate to reconsider its decision.[4] When, however, the treaty was defeated for a second time, in March 1920, that volume of public support for the treaty had largely disappeared. And in November 1920—in a presidential election which Mr. Wilson himself considered a solemn referendum on the treaty—the American people gave 404 out of a possible 531 electoral votes to a man who had obliquely repudiated the Wilson interpretation of international collaboration by stating, in his speech accepting nomination, that it was not the duty of the United States to attempt "to purge the Old World of the accumulated ills of rivalry and greed."[5] In the 1920 election the Democratic candidate clearly advocated acceptance of both treaty and League; the Republican candidate's position on internationalism was so equivocal as to be meaningless. Yet it was the Republican who got the votes. It is true, of course, that many of those who voted for Warren Gamaliel Harding may have done so in the belief that, after election, he would support a broad program of

[4] Bailey, *op. cit.*, p. 676.
[5] Charles and Mary Beard, *The Rise of American Civilization* (New York: Macmillan, 1927-42), Vol. II, p. 674.

international collaboration. If so, they bore their disappointment with equanimity. Certainly there was remarkably little protest when, in his inaugural address, the new President said: "The administration which came into power in March 1921 definitely and decisively put aside all thoughts of entering the League of Nations. It doesn't propose to enter now by the side door, back door, or cellar door."[6]

It seems clear, in short, that in the two years between the Armistice and the election of 1920 the American public itself had weakened in its desire for the kind of international program outlined by President Wilson during the war years. Lip service was still being paid to the idea of international collaboration, but the American public by 1920 had begun to desire other things more intensely. They now wanted "not heroics but healing, not nostrums but normalcy, not revolution but restoration"; and, if the attainment of those goals involved the repudiation of Wilson's program, they were now ready to allow such repudiation.

Three things contributed to this swing from Wilsonism to the isolationism of the Harding administration.

In the first place, the American people were weary of the war and the very thought of the war. Even before the fighting had stopped this feeling was general in the United States. Once the Armistice was signed, the American people wanted one thing above all else—namely, a quick liquidation of the war and a speedy realization of the benefits they had been led to expect would flow from the peace. As he sailed for Paris in December 1918, Wilson was profoundly disturbed by the popular temper. He is reported to have said to George Creel: "All of these expectations have in themselves the quality of terrible urgency. There must be no delay. It has always been so. People will endure their tyrants for years but they will tear their deliverers to pieces if a millennium is not created immedi-

[6] Samuel F. Bemis, *A Diplomatic History of the United States* (New York: D. Appleton-Century, 1935), p. 657.

ately. Yet you know and I know these ancient wrongs, these present unhappinesses, are not to be remedied in a day or with the wave of a hand."[7]

The American people saw no reason why they should not be so remedied. Only a few realized that the organization of the peace might be both a difficult and a lengthy process. The majority seemed to believe that peace could be declared, much as war is declared, in a moment, and that immediately all troops would be demobilized and peaceful intercourse would be resumed among the nations. When the negotiations at Paris were continued for seven months, during which time American troops were kept in the field, there was widespread dissatisfaction in the United States. The cry "Bring the boys home" was loud enough to disturb the negotiators at Paris and was proof in itself of the fact that, when confronted with the sacrifices necessary to make international collaboration a workable ideal, the American people were not sure they approved of them.

When, after the long negotiations in Paris, the Senate insisted upon talking about the treaty from July 1919 until March 1920, the weariness of the general public tended to degenerate into boredom. By the end of 1920 the American people were heartily sick of the whole business. It is significant that in choosing a slogan for their campaign, the Republicans steered carefully away from any reference to the international problem and chose the cheerful but meaningless phrase: "Let us be done with wiggle and wobble."[8]

Had the supporters of the League made a concerted attempt to convince the American public that membership in a world organization was essential for the protection of their own vital interests, war weariness and boredom might not have taken such a powerful hold upon the popular consciousness.[9] Most

[7] J. Fred Rippy, *America and the Strife of Europe* (Chicago: Chicago University Press, 1938), p. 213.
[8] Bemis, *op. cit.*, p. 656.
[9] What attempts were made to portray the price of abandoning the League were, however, singularly ineffective. Throughout 1919 and 1920

of the arguments for the League were impregnated with the moral idealism which had been so effective in 1918 but which was now losing its force. Indeed, the second factor which weakened popular support for the international cause was the very real slump in idealism which set in in 1919.

Even before the Armistice was signed, the American people were beginning to react violently against the ideals which had sustained them in the dark days of the war. For this reaction the President himself was partly to blame. As Frank P. Chambers has said: "Wilson's high-sounding war-time watchwords dropped to a sudden chilly bathos when in October 1918, before the congressional elections, he appealed for the return of a Democratic majority, and at a stroke injected party politics into the entire post-war settlement. In such an atmosphere, the hard-headed matter-of-factness which always belonged to the American political character quickly leavened the old missionary zeal, symbolized by the Fourteen Points."[10] The electorate responded to the President's appeal by returning a Republican majority, and for many loyal Republicans from that time on the arguments for international collaboration seemed merely examples of Democratic electioneering.

The slump in idealism continued when disgruntled newspaper reporters, barred from the sessions at the Peace Conference, began to send to American papers exaggerated ac-

Secretary Daniels of the Navy Department argued that unless the United States entered the League, the armaments load necessary for national security would be overwhelming. On January 31, 1920, Franklin D. Roosevelt, Assistant Secretary of the Navy, warned that the Navy would cost the American people a billion dollars a year in case international relations went "back to what they were before" the war. These public pronouncements did not check the drift away from internationalism. See Harold and Margaret Sprout, *Toward a New Order of Sea Power* (Princeton: Princeton University Press, 2nd ed., 1943), p. 76.

[10] Frank P. Chambers, C. P. Grant and C. C. Bayley, *This Age of Conflict: A Contemporary World History 1914-43* (New York: Harcourt, Brace, 1943), p. 437. In his speech of May 18, 1944, Sumner Welles spoke of the injection of party politics into the discussions of 1919-20 as "the gravest mistake" made in those years. *New York Times*, May 19, 1944.

counts of the differences among the Allies at Paris. The American public was encouraged to believe, first, that the President was freely sacrificing all of his much advertised ideals and, second, that our former allies were engaged in a frenzied pursuit of private interest. The natural difficulties of multilateral negotiation were so distorted as to suggest that we could no longer trust our allies, and this feeling had its inevitable effect in the Senate debate on the treaty.

Moreover, the relaxation of war censorship soon produced in the United States the first of a great horde of "debunkers." Men like Sir Philip Gibbs proceeded to demolish all of the arguments formerly used to justify the fighting of the war—branding the Belgian atrocity stories as war myths and portraying the Allied leaders as incompetent or cynical gamblers with human life. Even more startling material was released to the public as the Russian, German and Austrian archives were forced open by revolution. "The secret negotiations, conversations, agreements and treaties by which the Entente Powers had planned to break Germany and divide the spoils of war according to the ancient rules were exposed to the public gaze. In all its naked horror the sordid and grimy diplomacy which had precipitated the bloody conflict was revealed; and, by way of supplement, memoirs, papers, treatises and articles on the background of the war began to flow from the presses."[11] By the end of 1919 the belief that the war had been fought to end all war had begun to weaken and the public desire for continued collaboration with European nations was at very low ebb.

Finally, there can be little doubt that much of the earlier popular support of the League was based upon lack of understanding of the cost involved. During the war and the first months thereafter, when the ideal of international collaboration was a mere abstraction, it was easy to support the League. As it threatened to become an actuality, and as it became apparent

[11] Beard, *op. cit.*, pp. 672-673.

that pursuing it would involve certain sacrifices on the part of the United States, many of the men who had cheered Wilson's Fourteen Points began to have misgivings. After Wilson's collapse, his supporters were without leadership, and there was no one capable of explaining to the doubtful, in terms which would convince them, that the necessary sacrifices were small in comparison with the advantages to be gained. As a result, many people changed their minds, confused by the arguments put forth by the Senate critics and by the Hearst press, fearful that entrance into the League might really mean the end of American independence, and worried because international collaboration, upon closer examination, seemed to violate American practice and tradition. Irritated already by the necessity of keeping American troops in Europe during the peace negotiations, these people proved readily susceptible to the argument that cooperation with other nations in any world system would involve the sending of American troops abroad at any time. The chaos into which the German defeat had plunged central and eastern Europe—the Spartacist uprising in Germany, the disorders which followed the Bela Kun regime in Hungary, the bitter fighting between Poland and her neighbors—seemed to prove that peace could be secured for America only by complete abstention from entanglements with that unhappy continent.

In his speech of April 9, 1944, Secretary Hull said: "Under our constitutional system the will of the American people in this field (i.e., foreign policy) is not effective unless it is united will. If we are divided we are ineffective."[12] That is an apt summary of our experience in 1919 and 1920. At the end of the war, the majority of the American people favored the execution of the international program expounded by President Wilson in 1918. But they were not united in this desire long enough. Wearied by the war and irritated at the delay in liquidating it, suspicious of their former allies, distrustful of the slogans which

[12] *New York Times*, April 10, 1944.

had inspired them during the conflict and ignorant of the true necessity of continued sacrifice, the American people wavered uncertainly, and in the end not only allowed the Senate to have its way but gave their stamp of approval to Harding's policy of isolationism.

NEXT TIME

The record of 1919-1920 has a profound relevance for our own time. In an article in the *New York Times* in December 1943, Senator Claude Pepper pointed out that, despite the fact that both Houses of Congress had voted overwhelmingly in favor of United States participation in a broad scheme of postwar international collaboration, there were still enough "irreconcilables" in public office to block the effective implementation of that vote. Addressing himself particularly to the situation in the Senate, Senator Pepper said: "In any task of statesmanship so large in import, so broad in the scope of interests involved, so burdened with almost endless ramifications [as the drafting of an effective peace settlement], the odds that one-third of the membership of the United States Senate present and voting will find one reason or another for opposing it are almost overwhelming."[13] The Senator then appealed to the American people to exert sufficient pressure upon the Senate to prevent any repetition of the 1919 pattern.

In trying to avoid the dangers outlined by Senator Pepper, we dare not count too heavily upon such public pressure. It would be well to remember that, as the war approaches its end, American public opinion will be subject to the same disruptive forces which weakened it in 1919-1920.

In the first place, since the burden of the war effort has been heavier during this war than during the last, so will the accumulating weariness with the war be stronger. The eagerness with which American newspapers have given prominent

[13] Claude Pepper, "A Summons Against the 'Kiss of Death,'" *New York Times Magazine*, December 12, 1943.

space to any and all predictions as to "when the war will be over" has been in itself evidence of the growth of that feeling. This desire for the end of the war is quite natural; it may, however, become dangerous. For this war, already so different from previous world conflicts, may not come to an end in the traditional manner. As E. H. Carr has pointed out: "The end of the present war may not be so much a single event as a series of disintegrations—a gradual transformation of organized warfare into local fighting by armed bands. . . . It should not be assumed without question that an armistice at the end of the present war will be either possible or desirable. It would be still rasher to make the same assumption about a peace conference. In 1919 the conception prevailed of peace-making as a single historical event limited in time and place—the drafting and signing of a diplomatic instrument or series of instruments —which would settle the destinies of the world for half a century or for all time; and impatience was expressed that the performance of these necessary acts had not been completed within six months of the armistice. After the present war it will be wise to recognize that peace-making is not an event, but a continuous process which must be pursued in many places, under varying conditions, by many different methods and over a prolonged period of time; and anyone who supposes that it will be complete within six years should be regarded with the utmost suspicion."[14]

Mr. Carr's view of what lies ahead is possibly exaggerated, but it is probably closer to the truth than that held by the majority of the American people at the present time. Despite current optimism, the formal collapse of the governments leagued against us may not permit an appreciable relaxation of the present intense war effort. The task of negotiating peace settlements will certainly take longer than it did in 1919. And while we are in the twilight zone between peace and war,

[14] E. H. Carr, *Conditions of Peace* (New York: Macmillan, 1942), p. 245.

American troops will in all likelihood be forced to garrison large sections of the world. The American people have not yet become fully aware of these unpleasant facts. When they do become aware of them, there will be danger of the same kind of irritated reaction which swept the country in 1919.

It is still impossible to say whether, in addition to this danger, there will be anything like the slump of idealism which came in 1919. But one of the factors contributing to the slump of 1919 was a growing distrust of our allies, and to this we are not even today wholly immune.

In every coalition of sovereign powers it is natural that there should be frequent differences of opinion. The history of past wars of coalition shows that such differences become more acute as the allies become more certain of victory. Thus, the Grand Alliance against Napoleon threatened to fly to pieces after the great victory at Leipzig, and at the Vienna Congress there were moments when the allies seemed ready to engage each other in war. So, too, the differences between the Allied and Associated Powers of the last war were more serious in the months following the Armistice than they had ever been in the critical days of 1917.

As the United Nations move closer to victory it is possible that their differences, too, will multiply. There is no reason, however, that they should become irreconcilable. In 1814 the Allies were able to compose their quarrels and to lay the basis for a peace which lasted for forty years. We should be able to do as well if, as Mr. Hull points out, we realize that "agreement can be achieved only by trying to understand the other fellow's point of view and by going as far as possible to meet it."[15]

The danger is that the natural differences rising from negotiations among sovereign powers will be exaggerated or misinterpreted in such a way as to convince large sections of the American public that we are being cheated by our allies or to sow doubts as to the validity of such declarations of united

[15] Speech of April 9, 1944, *New York Times*, April 10, 1944.

purpose as those of Moscow and Teheran. The Anglo-American negotiations over post-war air routes caused one candidate for high national office to announce in 1944 that we "must not be cheated at the peace table,"[16] a statement which bears implications scarcely flattering to our allies. Repeated statements of this kind may well swell the tide of distrust and suspicion and weaken the sound basis of public confidence essential to collaboration in the interest of lasting peace.

Finally, as in 1919, the American public still favors international collaboration as an abstraction and has yet to view it in terms of actual cost. When the average citizen is confronted with the necessary cost, he may very well be both startled and dismayed. In the first place, as has been already mentioned, the winning of the peace may necessitate the presence of American troops on foreign soil for a considerable period after the war. This may entail continued military conscription, an unpleasant prospect even to the most ardent advocate of international collaboration. In the second place, it is already apparent that, if we wish to lay the basis for a working international order, the United States will have to play a major role in relief and rehabilitation projects after the war. Not until the victory is won will we be able to gauge the extent of this effort and its financial cost. The cost may well be so great, however, that a considerable strain will be placed upon the domestic economy of the United States—or, at least a strain great enough to compel us to continue and even extend some aspects of the present rationing program. Again, many authorities believe that, in order to avoid the resurgence of dangerous economic nationalism, we shall have to agree to the establishment of some international authority to supervise foreign investments, allocation of raw materials, and competition for world markets—in

[16] Gov. John W. Bricker of Ohio in a speech before the Union League Club of Chicago, reported in *New York Times*, April 8, 1944. See also speech of James P. Richards of South Carolina in the House of Representatives, reported in *New York Times*, April 19, 1944.

FOREIGN POLICY RETROSPECT

short, a system of controls scarcely compatible with our time-honored policy of unlimited free enterprise.[17] All in all, the costs of permanent peace promise to be great, greater than most Americans realize at the present time; and it is this unawareness which may be our most fertile source of trouble.

The establishment of an ordered and peaceful world will depend to a large extent upon whether the American people's desire for such a world can withstand the pressure of the forces mentioned above. Impatience at the unavoidable difficulties which will delay the peacemaking process, failure to understand the differences which will rise among the Allies, and reluctance to pay the heavy costs of enduring peace may quite possibly confuse and divide the American people. If this happens, the ever-present enemies of true international collaboration may be able to repeat their performance of 1919 and block the effective implementation of the present declared policy of the nation. In such circumstances, we should be forced to abandon wholly or partially our present intentions and our present hopes.

ALTERNATIVES TO WORLD-WIDE COLLABORATION

The disruptive forces outlined above must be checked before they seriously weaken the nation's will to peace. They can be checked if the nation's leaders realize their potency and move swiftly against them. In this respect, two things should be done. In the first place, the government should repeatedly and emphatically stress the difficulties that lie ahead, the sacrifices necessary to overcome them and the real advantages that will accrue when they are overcome.[18] In the second place—and this

[17] For an excellent discussion of the probable cost, to the American people, of a working international economic order, see William Adams Brown, Jr. *The Future Economic Policy of the United States* (Boston: World Peace Foundation, 1943).

[18] In this connection it would be well for the government, while outlining our post-war obligations, to dissociate itself from such grandiose and

is even more important—it must convince the American people that national security for the United States will be attained only if we follow the line plotted at Moscow and Teheran, and that an attempt to retreat and follow an alternative policy would certainly be disastrous.

At Moscow and Teheran the United States indicated its determination to continue its working union with Great Britain, Russia and China after the war and to use this as the nucleus for a wider union of free peoples working in common to preserve peace.[18a] What are the possible alternatives?

The first alternative is a return to isolationism. This would be the most likely result of a sudden public revulsion from internationalism. Isolationism has in the past appealed to large sections of the American public. It may very well become popular again, either because it appears less expensive than a policy of full-scale international collaboration or because it seems a healthy return to the basic traditions of the nation and to the policies of its founding fathers.

It should not be difficult, however, to prove to the American public that isolationism cannot work under modern conditions. Indeed, it is possible to show that it has never worked in the past. Certainly, if avoidance of war is the test of its validity, isolationism has been completely ineffective. We have fought in every world war from the eighteenth century to the present.

The golden age of isolationism, the age in which the isolationist tradition was developed, was the period stretching from 1815 to 1917.[19] If the United States was ever immune to attack from abroad it was in that period. Yet that immunity was due not so much to the inherent values of a policy of isolationism as to the existence of a number of factors completely outside our

essentially unworkable projects as those calling for the "re-education" and "mass-psychoanalysis" of the enemy peoples.

[18a] A similar determination was shown at the Dumbarton Oaks Conference in 1944.

[19] Whitney Griswold, in Allan Nevins and L. M. Hacker, *The United States and Its Place in World Affairs* (Boston: Heath, 1943), p. 586.

control. A balance of power in Europe and the Far East, British control of the Atlantic sea lanes, and a relatively static military and naval technology were the basic conditions of our security in the nineteenth century.[20] When those conditions threatened to break down in 1917, we went to war to restore them. When they broke down completely in 1941, we were denied even that freedom desired by our first President, the freedom to "choose peace or war, as our interest, guided by justice, shall counsel."[21] In 1941, we had war thrust upon us.

These facts in themselves should be enough to discourage a return to isolationism, if isolationism means merely the refusal to make any political commitments or enter into any international agreements in the hope that this refusal will persuade the world to leave us alone. The world has insisted upon intruding on us in the past; there is no reason to suppose that it will refrain from doing so in the future.

The impracticability of complete isolationism has of late been admitted even by the most extreme advocates of a unilateral policy for the United States in the post-war period. Realizing that a purely negative policy will no longer maintain the nation's security, they now advocate a positive, realistic, hard-boiled policy—an armed isolationism which would be not so much a withdrawal from as a defiance of the rest of the world. They urge that the United States must take advantage of the temporary armed superiority which it will enjoy after this war to make its world position impregnable, and they claim that, having done so, it will be able to follow its own course without interference from other nations.[22]

[20] See especially Edward Mead Earle, "American Security—Its Changing Conditions," *Annals of the American Academy of Political and Social Science*, Vol. 218, November 1941, and *Against This Torrent* (Princeton: Princeton University Press, 1941), pp. 39ff.

[21] Washington's "Farewell Address." *The Writings of George Washington*, Sparks, ed. (Boston: American Stationers' Company), Vol. XII, p. 231.

[22] Sumner Welles, in his speech of May 18, 1944, rightly remarked that our choice will be, not so much between isolationism and international

The benefits which would accrue from such a policy are by no means apparent; its disadvantages are only too manifest. In the last analysis, armed isolation means arming ourselves to the teeth and holding the rest of the world at bay, a task which staggers the imagination. Even if we assume that the United States can consistently outbuild its power competitors, the cost of maintaining such armed superiority would be prohibitive. In 1796, George Washington urged abstention from European affairs as the only means by which we could "avoid the necessity of those overgrown military establishments, which, under any form of government, are inauspicious to liberty, and which are to be regarded as particularly hostile to Republican Liberty."[22a] That argument has now been turned upon itself. If there is any hope of lowering the load of armaments after the war, it must be found in international political agreements. Armed isolation would doom the American people to a permanent war economy which could not fail to jeopardize social progress in this country.

Moreover, once we had embarked upon a policy of armed isolation, we would certainly drift slowly but surely in the direction of imperialism. This is implicit, for instance, in the statement which appeared in the *New York Daily News* in November 1942, declaring that the United States "should have an air force big enough and good enough for the defense of this continent, or, preferably, of this hemisphere; and a Navy of such size as the final lessons of this war may indicate we need to armor-plate this continent by sea."[23] But what if our continental neighbors did not wish to be armor-plated by the United States? What if the Latin American nations, for instance, should be less amenable to the delights of isolationism

collaboration as between true world organization and "a policy based upon military alliances, the indefinite piling up of armaments, and their inevitable adjunct, stark imperialism." *New York Times*, May 19, 1944.

[22a] *The Writings of George Washington, op. cit.*, Vol. XII, p. 220.

[23] Quoted in Raymond Leslie Buell, "Draftsmen of the New World," *Fortune*, February 1943, p. 161.

than the United States? What if they should insist upon maintaining traditional—but in our eyes dangerous—contacts with the outside world? It is possible, indeed likely, that we should then feel called upon to revert to something like the Theodore Roosevelt interpretation of the Monroe Doctrine—insisting that each of the Latin American nations have a government sympathetic to ourselves, compliant with our desires, and, in the last analysis, subject to our veto. We have already had sad experience with the difficulties of enforcing such a policy; in all probability we should find them magnified ten-fold after the war.

Let us, however, make two additional and highly unlikely assumptions: first, that by a series of economic miracles we were able to continue to maintain and increase our military establishment without serious domestic repercussions and, second, that by a series of diplomatic *coups* we were able to convince our continental neighbors to join us, as equals or subordinates, in a policy of armed isolation against the rest of the world. There is no reason to suppose that our position in the post-war world would even then be secure. As an American geographer has pointed out, the western hemisphere is surrounded by land masses which possess two and a half times the area and ten times the population of the Americas. "Even though at the present time the industrial productivity of the New World would almost balance that of the Old, the United States would still find herself irresistibly encircled by a superior force if she should ever be confronted" by a union of the other major powers.[24] It should be clear, moreover, that if we insist upon withdrawing from the rest of the world and upon attempting to outbuild it in military strength, we shall be inviting just such a union. "We cannot," as Secretary Hull has pointed out, "move in and out of international cooperation and in and out of participation in the responsibilities of a member of the family of nations," without

[24] N. J. Spykman, *The Geography of the Peace* (New York: Harcourt, 1944), p. 45.

paying the cost of such a policy. The cost in this event might very well be joint economic, political and eventually even military action against us.

The course of isolationism offers us, therefore, only great sacrifices and no tangible benefits. The time has gone by when our oceans protected us against the world. The advance in military technology and the impending growth of polar air routes have seriously weakened our strategic position. For the United States to try to stand alone in the world today would be most hazardous, even if it were possible.

It is conceivable, of course, that the United States could retreat from the high ideals announced at Moscow and Teheran without being forced to fall back on a strictly unilateral policy. For the past two years there has been in this country considerable discussion of an Anglo-American alliance in the post-war period; and the eagerness with which this policy has been embraced by public figures not especially noted for their international sympathies would seem to indicate that it might be supported not as a preliminary to a broader scheme of world order but as an alternative to it.

But, if we should base our policy entirely upon an Anglo-American alliance, how effective would this policy be in maintaining the national security? On the surface, many arguments would seem to support it. A formal union of the English-speaking peoples would be in every sense a union of natural allies. Great Britain and the United States have a common heritage of language and religion, of law and justice, of political and economic institutions. There has existed between them also, since the end of the last century, a tradition of common action which is being strengthened by their joint effort in the present war. Moreover, since the deep-seated desire of both peoples is for peace and security, there will in all probability be a fundamental identity in aim between the two powers.

In addition to this, the strength of an Anglo-American combination would be formidable. With roughly 90 per cent of the world's sea power and most of the world's important bases at their disposal, the two powers would control the sea lanes of the globe, and they could use that control, backed by the tremendous economic strength afforded by their joint resources, to defend their joint national interests.

Yet despite the obvious attractions of an Anglo-American alliance, it would surely defeat its own purposes. For, in the last analysis, this combination is unnecessary if there is to be a wider union of powers; and it is highly dangerous if it is taken as an alternative to such wider union.

The very unity of purpose which makes Great Britain and the United States natural allies makes it unnecessary for us to formalize our association by a bilateral pact. There is no reason to suppose that the mutual cooperation which has so much to do with winning the war will collapse with the coming of the peace; and unless there were danger of such a collapse, or of Great Britain joining a combination directed against us, it is hard to see what additional advantages we would derive from a formal treaty.

On the other hand, the dangers of an Anglo-American alliance, in the absence of wider undertakings, would be very great. Aside from the unpleasant historical truth that dual alliances have rarely, if ever, operated to the advantage of both parties, a post-war Anglo-American alliance would arouse the fear and suspicion of all other powers, great and small. To Soviet Russia it would almost certainly appear to be a combination inspired by distrust of Communism and one which might in the future attempt to do in a different way what the capitalist powers tried to do to Russia between 1918 and 1920. To China it would almost certainly appear to be a combination designed to protect and promote Anglo-American imperialism in the Far East. To the smaller powers it would appear as an objectionable attempt to impose upon them a strictly Anglo-Saxon conception of world order.

The most likely result of a formal Anglo-American alliance would be the formation of rival blocs and alliances, and the world would be involved once more in the kind of political, economic and military competition which has so often produced major wars. In such a world, the strength of the Anglo-American combination would afford no real assurance of peace. It is not inconceivable that that strength in itself would compel the other nations to join in a desperate assault upon the Anglo-Saxon powers. The prospect of such a war will scarcely be comforting to anyone disposed to strategical thinking. We need only remember how different the outcome of the present war might have been had the Nazi-Soviet pact remained in force, and had it enabled Germany, Russia and Japan to join forces against the two sea powers.

The deliberate choice of an Anglo-American alliance in preference to a wider union of nations would be a gratuitous insult to the other powers and an invitation to them to take adequate steps against us. It would usher in the kind of world aptly described by George Canning—a world of "every nation for itself and God help all of us"; and in this respect its results would not be markedly different from those involved in a return to isolationism. As in the case of isolationism also, it would bring to the American people no real and lasting security. Emerging from the long and trying struggle which was precipitated in 1941, the American people would find themselves once more living in a state of constant apprehension and confronting a future in which growing armaments and mounting taxes encroached increasingly upon the freedom for which they had fought.

"The true measure of nations," said Winston Churchill in 1919, "is what they can do when they are tired."[25] As we move ahead to the transition period which will follow the cessation of hostilities, the American people will be tired, and it is likely

[25] Quoted in E. H. Carr, *op. cit.*, p. xxiv.

that they will be appalled at the enormity of the task that awaits them. If they falter, and if they embrace unilateral or bilateral expedients in preference to a genuine policy of world association, the hopes with which they took up the war burden will be grievously disappointed. They will be far less likely to falter or retreat if they are told in convincing terms what the consequences of retreat from the goals set at Moscow and Teheran will be. For, as John Jay wrote in 1787: "It is not a new observation that the people of any country (if, like the Americans, intelligent and well informed) seldom adopt and steadily persevere for many years in an erroneous opinion respecting their interests."[26]

[26] *The Federalist*, No. 3. Earle, ed. (New York: The Modern Library, 1937), p. 13.

2. World Order and the Great Powers[1]

BY GERHART NIEMEYER

THREE main factors seem likely to dominate the post-war situation: inequality of might between the Great Powers and the other nations of the world; a fanatical desire, in all countries, for national independence; and a popular demand to be rid of power politics. No policy that fails to give adequate consideration to these phenomena stands much chance of success.

The position of the Great Powers will be unique in modern history. Of the seven pre-war world powers, four will have been decisively defeated. The three remaining powers will possess not only armies but raw materials, productive capacity, consumer goods, transportation facilities, and other national wealth setting them off so markedly from the rest of the world as to be without parallel since the days of ancient Rome. No other nation will be at all comparable in strength to any one of the "Big Three."

The trend toward nationalism is not only a Nazi-stimulated revival of nineteenth century ideas in Europe, but it is likewise a development of hitherto incipient movements in what were once considered "backward areas." Both types of contemporary nationalism blend into a wave of nationalistic feeling, strong enough to inspire immense sacrifices in both war and peace.

To judge by the tone of the diary found on a captured Hitler youth leader in Italy, disillusionment is leading to new ways

[1] The position defended in this chapter differs in some important respects from that defended by Professor Whitton in Chapter III. The authors of these chapters have reconciled their differences as far as they honestly could, but still disagree in their estimate of international legal rules and procedures.—THE EDITORIAL COMMITTEE.

of thought on human relationships. This youngster, reared entirely in the Nazi religion of hatred, arrogance, and force, wrote during a retreat, "I have now finally broken with all my former life. Nothing remains but a deep hatred for the bestiality of Germany. After all, one is still a human being." If even the devil's disciples are thus converted, men must have a deep and fervent desire to have done with the kind of policies from which international conflicts arise. Peoples seem to be ready for leadership in a new spirit, and, above all, are waiting for statesmen who will heed their overwhelming desire for peace.

From these facts three conclusions may be briefly drawn. *First*, this is not the time to bring the entire world under the control of a single government. While the only certain guarantee against further international wars is the formation of a world state, global unity is not feasible at the present time. It will require much patient preparation before the nations begin to develop a sense of community such as pervaded the thirteen original colonies when they decided to form the United States of America. *Second*, the full responsibility for leadership in the future will rest on the three Great Powers which hold in their hands all the material prerequisites for this role. They cannot possibly avoid this task. But where there is responsibility there is creative opportunity. In all modern history there has been no such opportunity for exercising effective leadership in a world still divided into numerous autonomous nations. *Third*, the nations of the world will prove responsive to leadership only if they develop a spirit radically different from that of the mutual distrust, fears, rivalries, and power competition characteristic of international relations of the past three hundred years. The present moment is crucial. Men are spiritually ready for change, and change is feasible. Here is a challenge to great leaders and to great peoples; the situation calls for bold vision and courageous action.

GERHART NIEMEYER
THE END OF POWER POLITICS?

Some writers maintain that a criminally-minded nation will commit aggression whenever it sees a chance of doing so with success and impunity. The motive for aggression, these authors contend, will always be found in one or another dissatisfied nation. The prevention of aggression is thus a matter of piling up the adverse odds until the prospect of success is negligible. This argument neglects the fact that the motives for aggression arise in, and are conditioned by, a general pattern of international politics which is by no means immutable. In a world in which, according to everybody's standards, material power determines the rank, prestige, and opportunities of states, giving reality to specious claims of right and shaping both international law and inter-state treaties, every nation aspires to the advantages of a position of power.[2] If security and independence have been attained by all major nations in the past through resort to force, less privileged nations will feel that they, too, are entitled to these benefits, and will follow the established method of gaining them. The moral issues of this war should not blind us to the fact that the political climate of world relationships has put a great premium on national power, and that all the Great Powers have, at one time or another, contributed to the maintenance of that climate.

This kind of world political pattern involves a standing invitation to aggressive policies. In such an environment national expansion can only too easily be justified by a national government. By invoking the example of other nations, the latter is

[2] "It is essential to remember that, in a system of power politics, war is neither a misfortune nor a supernatural event, but only the culminating point in an ascending scale of pressure; and whatever form it may take, the functions of pressure are essentially the same as those of diplomacy." G. W. Keeton and G. Schwarzenberger, *Making International Law Work* (London: Peace Book Company, 1939), p. 40. This admirable little book discusses with keen perception the general nature' of a system of power politics, and the perversion of morality, justice, and law, for national ends, which is characteristic of such a system.

in a position to enlist the support both of its own citizens and of foreign countries which feel that, in the world as it is, the only way to gain attention is to meet power with power. It is the absence of an adequate moral basis for an international "order" founded on superior power that gives aggression a plausible cause. Aggression, within the system of power politics, is not criminal in the eyes of those who perpetrate it. This constitutes a fundamental difference between the act of the private criminal and the act of an aggressor nation. An aggressive government can often enlist the most lofty sentiments in favor of its policy by presenting it as a justifiable revolution against a *status quo* issuing merely from past conflicts of power and, as such, not deserving respect or moral acquiescence. Putting it differently, the aggressor simply feels that it is taking a turn at the game which all are playing. It thus experiences no moral compunction in challenging, by resort to force, an international order which owes much of its present outlines to past actions of force in a world in which national rank is a mere function of power.

The lack of genuine moral justification of the *status quo* tends to justify aggressive policies not only in the eyes of the people at home; it may even impel the prospective victims to condone preparations for the contemplated war. Armaments, the mobilization of the national economy, military training of the population, the jockeying for diplomatic positions, alliances and other foreign support—all more or less fully practiced by the beneficiaries of the *status quo*, cannot fairly be refused to others. Aggression is, in consequence, nothing but the violent course of change encouraged by a system of power politics which puts universal emphasis on national power as the main title to world rank and world respect.

In all this I do not seek to minimize the moral guilt of the Axis countries, or to justify their policies of self-aggrandizement at the expense of other nations. We must nevertheless recognize that this, like past aggressions, has sprung from conceptions of international politics to which all nations, through their own practices, have at one time or another made a contribution. What state can claim to be guiltless of divorcing foreign policy from justice, reason, and morality, or of trusting in the "realistic" conception of national power as the criterion of international relations?

If this analysis is correct, the only way to end aggression is to eliminate the system of power politics. Most people will consider this impossible, for it is commonly assumed that power politics is of the very essence of international relations. But history teaches us otherwise. There have been periods when relations between the peoples of certain civilizations were governed not so much by the interaction of power as by principles and rules, both legal and moral. Thus, just preceding the era of power politics, a period of more than five hundred years was relatively free from large-scale war, and was governed by an impressive legal system founded on religious authority. The period of modern power politics began when this central authority of Papacy and Empire gave way to a fragmentation of power (at first in northern Italy), and when nations of approximately equal strength began to contend for survival, sovereignty, and supremacy. Each of these contending nations had good ground to hope for superior or supreme power. Each felt at the same time that its power was at least sufficient to ensure its survival, if necessary with the help of allies.

Given a military technology based mainly on iron, wood, leather, and handicraft, even the smaller countries could be powerful, provided they properly mobilized their human resources. Though unable to attain the state of absolute security which some Great Powers enjoyed, the small nations, while living under a balance of power, could look forward to a precarious survival and, in some circumstances, to considerable independence. The balance-of-power system thus was conditioned by a fragmentation of international power into many nations approximately equal in strength and rank, plus a war technology that made for open military competition. In such a system power considerations, power changes, and power calculations became the daily bread of foreign policies, with all governments equally eager to improve their own position at the expense of others. As an inevitable result, power came to be the supreme arbiter of international relations, law, and order.[3]

For the first time in many hundred years these conditions have now ceased to exist. Instead of many nations able to play the game of power politics, there will soon remain only three. New techniques of warfare have made it impossible for any small nation to survive on the basis of its own resources. Open competition for power has given way to a quasi-monopolistic concentration of power—and if, in economics, competition is possibly the essence of progress and productivity, in politics the main condition of order and of peace is concentration.

There is, of course, no assurance that concentration of power in the hands of three great states will lead to a period of true international order. But the chance of establishing such an order is better now than at any time since the thirteenth century days of Pope Innocent. No one can question the fact that the key to the system of power politics lies in the hands of the Great Powers; their intentions and practices, their examples and policies, can maintain or undo the present political system.

The Great Powers have now been so reduced in numbers

[3] "Our investigation into the social background of international law has led us to the conclusion that force is the 'supreme law' of the international society. . . . Experience has shown that the function of international law as actually practiced . . . is hardly to condition the rule of force or even to achieve priority in case of conflict between the two systems. . . .

"The international law of peace has for three centuries stabilized the equilibrium which had been achieved by force in the fundamental peace treaties concluded between 1648 and 1919. The same function is performed by the treaties of guarantee and neutralization destined to supplement and maintain a balance system and by the other agreements such as alliances and treaties of mutual assistance which are generally classified as political treaties." G. W. Keeton and G. Schwarzenberger, *op. cit.*, pp. 45, 48-49.

that an entente between them is feasible and desirable, but whether this works out for the benefit of the world will depend on how it is conceived and operated. "If this new distribution, or rather, concentration, of power is not to provide the basis of future titanic struggles, it will be because each of the three agrees that in collaborative effort for international security there is a 'powerful, evident and continuous solidarity of interests' which surpasses the possible gains to be made by a policy of individual action unhampered by any international commitment."[4] If, on the other hand, the Great Powers continue to make national strength the yardstick not only of their foreign policies, but of international law and order in general, then this criterion of power will determine the policies of all the other states. No nation outside the select circle will then be content with its lot; each will continue to regard the increase in its power at the expense of others as the only practical objective of its foreign policy. Thus it will attempt to play each of the "Big Three" against the other two and by every means to break up their solidarity, sowing among them distrust and hostility. If history runs true to its past the "Big Three," having thus trained the world in power politics, will eventually themselves fall victims to their own methods.

As the Great Powers go, so goes the world. Sooner or later the world will be unified. The major question now is whether it will be unified by the military force of a single dominant power or by the gradual growth of a common spirit and common institutions among the peoples of the earth. The process of world unification may be spread over centuries, but it is today that the die will be cast for or against the technique of militarism. The fundamental meaning of the present war is the struggle of western civilization against a general militarism which a single country threatens to impose upon it, while the

[4] Grayson L. Kirk, "International Politics and International Policing," memorandum privately distributed by the Yale Institute of International Studies.

WORLD ORDER AND GREAT POWERS

East, likewise, strives to remain free from the suffocating clutch of a militaristic order. The fight against militarism as the instrument of unification cannot be won unless we ourselves avoid the spirit we are combating. Should the present conflict be followed by a period of intense power rivalries, militant nationalism, high-pressure armaments, and serial wars, we might just as well let Hitler have his way here and now. The final effect will probably be scarcely distinguishable from the rule of the Nazis. For in such a "period of contending states," all the present "peace-loving nations" would either turn into ferocious militarist societies or they would perish and our western civilization would be borne down under the crushing weight of lasting and cumulative armaments. If we really fight for democracy, victory will be won only in the hour that sounds the end of power politics.

THE LEADERSHIP OF THE "BIG THREE"

It lies in the very nature of things that the "Big Three," in order to offer leadership to a war-weary world, must remain in close accord. This is no utopian goal; in fact, the stage is admirably set for such an understanding. The three powers are widely separated by geography, and their relations are not troubled by any very strong conflicts of interest. They will have emerged from a war fought jointly against tyranny and aggression, each having helped to save the others by tremendous sacrifice of life and material goods. Their peoples and leaders have a common dread and abhorrence of war. They share the background of a Christian civilization, with its emphasis on human welfare, its dynamic conception of history, and its promise of equality and freedom. But they still fear one another.

If the Great Powers are to lead the world, these fears must be removed. Leadership is above all a matter of spiritual guidance. History shows again and again that strength of soul and a clear mental vision are the qualities which make leaders among men.

It is not different with nations. The sheer weight of material power is indispensable as a condition, but it is scarcely the substance of leadership. To lead is to inspire trust, confidence, and loyalty, and thereby to elicit allegiance. It is no accident that kings of every epoch have considered generosity as their most essential virtue. For generosity, disinterestedness, courage, and foresight—these qualities cause soldiers to follow their captain as well as nations to follow a Great Power. Such qualities can grow only in those whose position has placed them beyond ordinary fears. Kings could afford to be generous because power and wealth were theirs. By the same standard, we lift judges and other persons of responsibility above the ordinary worries of men, assuring them office "during good behavior." Leadership that inspires confidence can be expected only from someone who has managed to be fearless.

The inequality between the Great Powers on the one hand and the rest of the world on the other contributes in many ways to the possibility of true leadership among the nations. Above all, it enables the "Big Three" to create a situation in which they may be free from fear—a situation of which no Great Power has been able to boast since the days of the Caesars. It is essential to world leadership as well as to world peace that such a situation be created. Therefore the foreign policies of the Great Powers should above all aim at this goal.

The causes of the mutual fears which still prevail are not easily defined. Britain's anxieties, formulated in 1943 by Marshal Smuts, are apparently inspired by her limited manpower and inadequate production, the lack on metropolitan soil of many vital raw materials, the insecurity of her communications and other factors which may leave her permanently weakened. But she withstood the full might of a Nazi-organized Europe, thereby proving that there is, both in her geographical position and in her spirit, a strength which renders her unconquerable. Despite this proof of might, her anxiety in the company of the two "adolescent giants," Russia and America, is easily understandable. But while these fears are comprehensible, policies inspired by fear alone cannot remedy the situation. Modern history knows of no example of a power whose attempt to compensate for declining strength by adding satellites and alliances did not end in complete disaster. Whether we take Germany, Italy, France in the inter-war period, Austria-Hungary, Turkey, or any other power frantically seeking to break the circle imposed on her by nature and history, we find that fear of insufficient strength is the worst possible counsel for such a nation's diplomacy. Moreover, Britain's position is determined not so much by what she has as by what she is—a center of world trade, world transportation, and world colonization; a bond among autonomous nations; a mediator between continents; a watchman at the nations' crossroads; a teacher of political wisdom and of social harmony. Britain has no reason to fear, for neither the world order nor the two other Great Powers can dispense with her cooperation and co-leadership. Britain is also the only one of the three Great Powers equally familiar with, and acceptable to, both European and extra-European areas. In this matter Russia has occasioned too much suspicion among her European neighbors to rival England, and America's lack of interest in Europe is traditional. Given this situation, both Russia and America will require England's help whenever the affairs of western Europe become of general concern.

Of the "Big Three," Russia has the least ground for fear. Once Germany and Japan have been defeated, what power would dare attack her? Yet Russia is full of apprehensions, as her policies toward Poland, her alliance with Czechoslovakia, and her subtle intervention in Yugoslavia amply demonstrate. The causes of Russia's present fears can be traced back to the days of the civil war, when other powers—allies and enemies alike—attempted to injure her. Even after the close of that period, Russia was separated from the rest of the western world by France's policy of the *cordon sanitaire,* and by England's reluctance to have any political dealings with the Soviets

—policies that were not unprovoked, especially during the period of Russia's double dealing via the Third Internationale. All this, however, lies in the past; the vital task today is to gain Russia's full confidence. The Russians have a keen appreciation of blunt sincerity, and a hearty contempt for "leftist sentimentality." We should, therefore, not pretend that we are their blood-brothers in political philosophy, or that we like their system. But if we wish to make our way into their hearts we must show a genuine concern for Russia's troubles, fears and problems, especially since we have done so much to create them. Looking at the problem through Russian eyes, we must realize that they have great difficulty in understanding the outside world with which they have had so little connection. We should therefore refuse to become alarmed when Moscow shows signs of continued anxiety and distrust. If we keep faith with Russia, the time will come when our words will be trusted because our deeds justify such trust, and she will begin to lose her suspicions.

Russia's collaboration in a concert of Great Powers is indispensable and cannot be replaced by that of any other comparable nation, such as Germany for example. Germany would be merely another European power, one of several possible leaders of Europe. Russia is the connecting link between Europe and Asia. The swelling tide of Asiatic nationalism, plus the rapid growth of national strength among the peoples of the East, is bound to become one of the most difficult problems of international relations. While she cannot play the role expected of China in this matter, Russia is nevertheless the only power with historical and spiritual roots both in Europe and in Asia. Moreover, her unique policy toward her many nationalities constitutes a novel approach to one of the major problems of this region, a policy worthy of application on a universal level. If Russia is freed from her present burden of perpetual suspicion, the realism which she has often manifested in her international relations should have a refreshing influence in international councils. But before Russia can bring these contributions to full fruition, we must explore with her the entire map of potential conflicts, from Finland to the Persian Gulf. On the basis of specific agreements thus reached, we must then be ready to offer her general guarantees of military assistance. The diplomatic spadework needed here resembles the type of arrangements reached between England and France after Fashoda, and between Russia and England prior to the First World War. If, through such agreements, a general system of world order is assured, the smaller powers need not fear that sacrifice of their interests will be the price of a "Big Three" accord.

The anxieties of the United States are not much more firmly grounded than those of Russia. As a result of the war, the United States will be freed of her only rival in the Pacific. As for the rest of the world, the American combination of sea power, air power, manpower, and productive capacity surpasses anything any other nation can muster. In peace, she can outproduce any other single competitor in the world. In spite of this comfortable margin of strength, the United States is afraid of both England and Russia. This fear is unrealistic. To attack America would be, for Britain, suicide, and, for Russia, political folly and military madness. Thus America's distrust of the other powers is actuated more by emotion than by reason. Although we are economically stronger than Britain, we still fear the wiliness of the British trader. Russia is now far removed from Communism, and doctrinaire Communists actually berate Stalin for his betrayal of the Revolution. Nevertheless, Soviet Russia is still regarded in this country with fear and trembling, as the home of "Reds" and a danger to our most cherished traditions. This lingering suspicion may be inspired entirely by Russia's revolutionary past, but it may also spring from the strangeness of Asiatics. In the American distrust of un-American ways some remnants of frontier parochialism may still survive. Since such fears reflect more a subjective state of mind than objective facts, they cannot be completely overcome by anything the other powers could do or promise. A rising awareness, on the part of Americans, of their country's gigantic material and moral strength will gradually eliminate such anxieties. There may be some concrete steps which would contribute to that end. But in the last analysis the problem of American fears can be solved only by Americans themselves.

In the effort toward a general accord of the "Big Three," the crux of the matter is to arrive at a point where each would feel assured that neither of the others was seeking to weaken it. Such confidence having been created, each power should find it logical to renounce policies such as alliances or other arrangements with smaller nations designed to strengthen one power in relation to the other. Existing agreements of this kind should be allowed to lapse when the treaties expire, for the practice of seeking support among secondary nations, with the quarrels resulting therefrom, has more than once led to conflict and to war.[5] The chief aim of "Big Three" diplomacy should be to create an atmosphere in which such secondary supports would become meaningless. Otherwise it would be vain to expect harmony among them or leadership from them for the world at large. Only when the policies of alliances and counter-alliances have been discarded can nations assume the statesmanship of the "Big Three" to be free from self-interest to an extent sufficient to justify their confidence in it. This does not rule out the possibility of spheres of influence. They are in fact

[5] "If a country could be imagined whose foreign relations were so favorably disposed that, in the defence of its legitimate interests, it could always count upon the sympathy of its most powerful neighbors, such a country would never . . . need to entertain those fears and misgivings, which, under the actual conditions of dominant international jealousies and rivalries, only too often compel the abandonment of a just cause as the only alternative to the more serious evil and risk of giving suspicious and unfriendly neighbors a welcome opportunity for aggression or hostile and humiliating interference." Sir Eyre Crowe, in his memorandum of January 1, 1907. G. P. Gooch and H. W. V. Temperley, *British Documents on the Origin of the War* (London: 1926-38), Vol. III, p. 398.

inevitable. Spheres of influence, however, are vicious only when used as a link in a system of outright alliances and protectorates. Properly conceived, they can be as harmless as the administrative divisions within a nation.

A further result of the diplomatic deck-clearing among the "Big Three" should be the reduction of armaments. The example of both Britain and America has proved that great nations are strong not because of the arms they already possess but because of those that they can produce. The combination of raw materials, industrial machinery and organization, and educated and intelligent manpower is what makes for the ultimate military strength of a nation. In view of this fact, the "Big Three" would profit greatly from a considerable reduction in armaments. In the first place, the national economy would be relieved of the immense burden of a great yearly output of arms. Each power could depend on a small, highly mechanized, military force continuously developing its methods and weapons. Such a force is essential to that self-assurance of the "Big Three" which, as we have already insisted, is the condition of their effective leadership. Contingents of these forces might be stationed at bases strategically distributed throughout the globe. With respect to war production, the provision for stockpiles of vital materials and the maintenance of a skeleton armaments industry should give the "Big Three" all the security they could desire. Furthermore, it might be advisable to prohibit the export from the big nations of any but small-caliber arms. All in all, such a reduction of armaments would have immeasurable psychological benefits, and would enhance rather than impair the capacity of the "Big Three" to cope with any situation that might arise. Even with a greatly reduced army, navy, and air force, the big nations would still enjoy an almost complete monopoly of military power.

If the "Big Three" should attain, and maintain, the position here outlined, they could establish a leadership which, properly exercised, would become the foremost instrument of a future world order. The power of the "Big Three," however, would be founded on no constitution, no legal instrument. It could be ultimately effective, therefore, only so far as the policies of the Great Powers succeeded in evoking the confidence and assent of the other nations. The latter, even when weak, have many ways of resisting an unwanted hegemony. Thus the power of the "Big Three" would have the character not of government but of leadership, resting ultimately more on consent than on authority.

RUSSIA AND THE WEST

Sceptics may point to the present unsatisfactory relations between Russia and her allies as a grave obstacle to harmony requisite among the powers for their joint leadership. There are, of course, reasons for distrust on both sides. On the other hand, there are many grounds for optimism. This should become evident if we examine more fully the bases of the present Russian policy.

Russia's main objectives are two-fold. First, there is the program of industrialization—a long-range undertaking which is both the object of an official plan and the substance of a fundamental social promise, a promise, in fact, on which the political power of the present regime is based. Second, as the *sine qua non* of this policy, the Russians have sought national security, thus far relying on military power, political organization, influence in neighboring countries, and possession or control of strategic territories.

The first and main objective of Russian policy is not only thoroughly acceptable but definitely reassuring to us. The second has been motivated by a deep-seated suspicion of the outside world. Russia was invaded by western armies at the time of her greatest weakness; for fifteen years her government was left outside the circle of diplomatic dealings; her attempts to bolster up the system of collective security were not appreciated; and her offer to come to the aid of Czechoslovakia during the Munich crisis was rejected. Moreover, Russia distrusts not only the Great Powers but certain of her small neighbors which have allowed themselves to become the spearhead of anti-Soviet activities. Regimes such as those once established by Pilsudski, Mannerheim and Horthy are feared as sources of further trouble. Russian statesmen believe that the precarious and unstable existence of such regimes will foster political trepidation in these regions and a resulting hostility toward the Soviet Union. Russia does not feel this way towards Czechoslovakia, because its democratic regime obviates the threat of internal revolutions which would endanger Russo-Czech relations.[6] Finally, a certain residuum of anti-western feeling remains in Russia as a result of her age-old separation from western culture. Russia, as center of the Greek Orthodox Church, has for centuries lived in a world of her own, and this tradition of aloofness has been accentuated since World War I by the general ostracism occasioned by her political and social doctrines.

The feelings of the outside world toward Russia are similarly inspired by dark anxieties. The Russian Revolution has left a deep imprint on the West. Furthermore, Russia's connection with Communist parties in other countries has given rise to lively apprehension. Whether well founded or not, this fear cannot be dissipated so long as political parties in western democracies look to Moscow for a lead. More recently, new misgivings have been added to the old suspicion. We now fear that Russia may continue, with enhanced power, to play a lone hand, and even attempt to establish a dominion over Europe, succeeding where Hitler failed. Every move of Soviet diplomacy toward its neighbors is thus watched with nervous apprehension. We seem always disposed to expect the worst when-

[6] This analysis of Central European regimes and their policies is shared by non-Russian authorities. See, e.g., Dinko Tomašić, "Reconstruction in Central Europe," *American Political Science Review*, Vol. XXXVII, October 1943, pp. 888ff.

ever some friction arises, and this alarmism tends only to aggravate such situations.

A policy of accord among the "Big Three" must strike boldly at the roots of such mutual suspicions. Particularly important is an agreement on those issues whose solution would be jeopardized by the pursuit of independent policies. Such issues are likely to arise over Poland and other political regimes in Central Europe. Since a hands-off policy of non-intervention is clearly impossible under the circumstances, a solution might be sought through practical concessions made by each power to the national interests of the others. But this would only sharpen the conflict. Thus the only possible answer is a common policy of the "Big Three," superseding their various separate policies. Such a common policy might be realized by setting up, for example, criteria of democratic government in disputed regions, and by agreeing on a favorable treatment of social groups that could be expected to honor democratic principles and procedures.

Similarly, fears of subversive agitation under Russian influence can be met by a "Big Three" agreement according to which Communist parties affiliated with the now defunct Third Internationale would be dissolved. Russia might well be expected to accept such an arrangement, for Communist parties, as Professor Niebuhr has emphasized,[7] are no longer the most effective spearheads of the proletarian cause, while Russia's connection with Communist parties in other countries has failed to pay her political dividends from the nationalistic point of view. All countries concerned would profit by such a move.

Of all the common policies to be agreed on by the Great Powers, the most important is a mutual pledge to safeguard world peace. Such an agreement must be concluded in close connection with a world organization; otherwise it would operate as a policy not of world peace but of world exploitation. Given the many reasons for distrust among the Great Powers,

[7] "Russia and the West," *The Nation*, January 16 and 23, 1943.

mutual confidence can never be established among them on the basis of sharing the world's spoils, but only on the basis of a common concern for world peace.

Another problem to be met by such mutual accord is presented by areas likely to constitute political vacuums. No arrangement among the "Big Three" can last long unless it succeeds in establishing a working political order in Europe. Against the background of Russian military strength and western political influence it might be possible to set up a number of European "special purpose federations."[8] This would serve to meet the greatest cause of disturbance in Europe, namely, the fear among European nations of being engulfed by some great neighbor. If the more important economic, financial, technical, social, and humanitarian services in Europe were internationalized, a considerable *détente* would result, with most beneficial results to the relations among the three Great Powers.

A program of this kind will not be easy to achieve. But if no common policy concerning these problems emerges after the war, each Great Power will surely pursue self-seeking policies of narrow nationalism. Europe, the Far East, the Middle East, and the Mediterranean will then become areas of sharp conflict, and the resulting disorder, particularly in Europe, will breed continuous upheavals, aggressions, and wars. Hence a common policy among the "Big Three" must not be left to chance but made a goal for our diplomacy, a goal which should not be abandoned even if our partner nations present us with disappointments. Repeated setbacks must not discourage us. On the contrary, we must face prolonged difficulties with a quiet determination to achieve ultimate harmony. Instead of asking anxiously "Can we trust Russia?" we should have the courage to repeat, "We *must* trust Russia!" By such a policy we may run certain risks, but they will surely be negligible as

[8] Proposed by Professor Arnold Brecht, in "Limited-Purpose Federations," *Social Research*, Vol. 10, May 1943, pp. 135ff.

compared with the danger we shall run if once again we stake everything on the fortunes of war.

METHODS OF PEACE

In discussing the problem of peace, many people invoke the analogy of the criminal and the policeman. Wars are compared with burglary, arson, and murder, and the prevention of war with the system of criminal justice which protects the individual citizen. On the whole, this analogy was the basis of the League of Nations. I believe it to be erroneous. If we wish to draw a comparison between the order within a nation and order among nations, war should be compared not with crime but with revolution. Grave civil strife is not avoided by police and courts, but through adjustments between classes by disposing of their differences and grievances before they lead to high emotional tension and open violence. Such a moment calls for the statesman, not the judge or sheriff; it is the statesman alone who, through foresight and political acumen, can prevent such a situation from arising, and thereby preserve domestic peace through continuous adjustment, compensation, conciliation and balance. Legal machinery helps to preserve the stability thus attained, but it does not in itself constitute the main condition of social peace.

The prevention of war, like the prevention of revolution within the state, does not depend on legal procedures, but on the art of adjustment. None of the great conflicts of modern times could have been settled by judicial process, even if backed by sanctions. Whatever success attended the war-prevention procedures of the League of Nations must be attributed largely to the political weight thrown into the scale by the Great Powers. The latter, however, did not always support the League when faced by its crucial tests. They tended to follow established national policies that led each nation in its own separate direction. The League machinery could scarcely have been otherwise devised but this only goes to show that the key to peace will be found not in machinery alone, however well planned, but primarily in the policies of powers capable of leadership. Any scheme which distracts attention from this basic truth should be suspect.

The most important field for policies designed to promote world peace lies in the settlement of differences among the Great Powers themselves. It is here, if anywhere, that the inadequacy of mere legal procedures becomes evident. What international organization could undertake to coerce Russia, the British Empire, or the United States in matters they deem of vital concern? Conflicts among them will be avoided not by some formal decision of law but by methods whose supreme objective is the maintenance of harmony and confidence. Through such methods, the "Big Three" would do much more than merely settle their own affairs. They would establish a pattern of international politics from which smaller nations would find no reason to deviate. Just as the rivalries of the Great Powers incite other nations to seek petty advantage, often providing the concrete occasion for open conflict, so a continuous practice of policies of confidence and community would exercise a beneficial influence on the policies of most of the smaller nations.

On the other hand, discontent is bound to arise here and there, and unreasonableness is always with us. But since judicial methods are not designed to deal with a problem until the conflict has become acute, joint political leadership of the "Big Three" would be more effective than any kind of legalized procedure in bringing about an adjustment before tension rises. Pressure and even force must of course be used if the leading nations are to implement their assumption of responsibility for world peace, but if there is the will to peace it should not be difficult to submit such cases to a council of world opinion before drastic action is taken or even seriously contemplated. Even so, the methods employed in the effort to preserve peace must be those of the statesman rather than those of the criminal court.

If the foregoing analysis is correct, we have the solution to a number of problems which plagued the League of Nations. The sharpest attack on this institution was the contention that its main object was to preserve a *status quo* which happened to suit the dominant powers. While it was frequently pointed out that the only reasonable alternative to war was to be found in methods of peaceful change, the League Covenant, largely a matter of legal rules and procedures, failed to face this problem adequately. This is understandable enough, for no system of law has ever made provision for peaceful change by other than political methods. Change takes place outside of contracts and established rules, and the law, far from encouraging change, inevitably emphasizes stability, routine, and precedent. The courts have no choice but to apply the law that already exists and that may be the very basis of the conflict. Neither the methods nor the standards of the law are flexible enough to meet a need for change. True, legislation is a method of change, but it is clearly not a legal but a political process, and its operation is not yet assured in international relations, as no legislative body exists able to decide whenever a demand for change arises, and endowed with commanding authority over courts and individuals. Thus, if we find that even in domestic society the nature of change is political, this must apply in even higher degree to international relations. In short, in the community of nations peaceful change can come not through law but only through the political leadership of the Great Powers acting jointly to preserve order.

A very delicate feature of peaceful change remains to be considered. Leadership must not be conceived as a monopoly for all time. Yet to discover a principle to govern the qualification for leadership would be most difficult, especially so since we have not even succeeded in setting up a standard for leadership in domestic government. A change in leadership, like any other change, must be determined by wisdom, skill, and a feeling for the fundamental common interest. It would not be possible, for example, to predict under just what conditions China could join the "Big Three" as an equal bearer of responsibility. Whether a state can exercise the functions of leadership depends on a number of factors—the size of its armed forces, its productive capacity and war potential, but also the absence of national fears and a willingness to renounce expansionist policies. Furthermore, it must be prepared to commit itself to an active policy even in remote regions. When and how such conditions of leadership will be fulfilled, it is impossible to foretell. The problem must be solved by political wisdom rather than by any fixed procedure. It should be our goal to provide for necessary changes in leadership before such changes are forced on us. We should endeavor to have the kind of farsightedness shown by the British ruling classes when they decided to institute reforms which spared them an experience like the French Revolution. This example proves that change of leadership depends primarily on the enlightenment of those in power.

If we are correct in our appraisal of the methods of peace, the responsibility for world order rests squarely on the shoulders of the Great Powers. The aims they have in mind, the policies they pursue, the methods and the spirit of their actions will contain the seeds of either world conflict or world harmony. The example which the "Big Three," in their mutual relationships, set for the world will be of crucial importance. The art of politics is the realization of concord among different groups obliged to live together. The primary aim of the foreign policies of the "Big Three" must therefore be to live in harmony with each other, and their secondary aim to help other nations to do likewise. Respect for the nationhood of other peoples is the prime prerequisite of such policies. Moreover, the leaders of the "Big Three" should realize that national weakness is accompanied by extreme sensitiveness. Having nothing to fear for their own existence, they should be able to treat small nations with special consideration and understanding. If, by any sacrifices they may make to the recurrent fears of small nations, they can manage to restore international confidence, they will have solved the most difficult task of international statesmanship.

THE LIMITATION OF INTERNATIONAL POWER

It is imperative to think of world power in terms of limitation. We have learned that unlimited power is the essence and the goal of power politics, and that power politics is the road to destruction of cities, countries, wealth, and the human soul. Power, it is true, is a condition of world order, as the League's experience has taught us. But if we rely on the power of great nations as an institution of world order, we must also think of such national power not as an end in itself, or even as a means to mere nationalistic purposes, but as an instrument toward universal ends which lie beyond political expediency. Moreover, since an instrumental view of power gave rise to the system of checks and balances in our system of national government, it is important to consider a similar limitation of international power.

One type of limitation resides in the very nature of the leadership of the three Great Powers. If they exercise this leadership together, they can lead only so far as they succeed in solving their own conflicts. Some may object that most triumvirates in history have ended in the triumph of one of the triumvirs as dictator. The analogy, however, is not well drawn. A co-ruler may be eliminated by murder, but a nation cannot be thus removed. In this matter it is significant that nations are geographically confined to a fixed location in which they fulfill functions of regional order. This circumstance prescribes both a territorial and a functional division of power among the leader nations, and this means that, so long as its inner strength persists, each of the "Big Three" will be indispensable, as a co-ruler, to the others.

However, unless their leadership is also visibly limited, for instance by institutions and principles embodying the common interest, the "Big Three" may still appear to other nations to resemble a gang organized to exploit the weak. As this impression would defeat any attempt to create a world order, the "Big Three" should find it expedient to carve out a wide niche in which the smaller powers can enjoy a share of authority over world affairs. This matter is discussed later in the chapter. Yet we must recognize that there is little chance of balance between weak states on the one hand and those with formidable military and economic resources on the other. The problem among nations is very different from that which obtains among individuals who, as Thomas Hobbes rightly observed, are on the whole on an equal footing. Some individuals are stronger and more intelligent than others, but so far as the general picture is concerned these differences cancel out. This very fact makes democratic government feasible. Nations, however, are fundamentally unequal. They differ so widely in population, territory and resources that they cannot be reduced to an average representative type. Thus a number of smaller nations cannot be matched against the might of a Great Power. Some may suggest a federation of small powers as an answer to this problem. It is doubtful, however, whether this would be a solution. Any new federation would immediately lay claim to the title and position of a Great Power although its actual strength might not place it in this category. Such a claim would be bound to run the test of conflict and war, recommencing the vicious circle, all without any benefit to the members of the federation. Thus it is clear that in international relations many a mickle does not make a muckle. The small nations can find some ways of counterbalancing the "Big Three," but only on secondary issues. This type of balance cannot, therefore, be counted on as an effective safety device.

Despite their fundamental weakness, the secondary and small nations occupy a position of vital importance in a world order based on "Big Three" leadership. With all their strength, the Great Powers would have great difficulty in preserving order in the presence of widespread dissatisfaction and opposition. It is no small matter to coerce a small nation in peacetime, as Professor Wolfers recently pointed out.[9] Public opinion may not favor mobilization of force unless it is felt that a really grave issue is at stake. Moreover, convinced of the virtue of their cause, some small nations may choose a course of suicidal defiance rather than submit to what they consider enslavement by a big power. Such an event would have dire consequences not only for the small nation concerned but also for the great country, which might thereby be placed in the unenviable position of the big bully. For these and other reasons, more fully explained in Professor Wolfers' article, not only moral laws but also political expediency would dictate the necessity of obtaining the full consent of small nations to a system characterized by an unequal distribution of power among the states. What could be done to obtain such consent?

A promising way of reconciling the small nations with "Big Three" leadership would be to reserve for them a substantial share of responsibility and international prestige. The new system should provide ample opportunities for smaller nations to prove their worth and win the respect of the world, thereby convincing them that their military weakness does not rob them of influence. The new international organization, which will have to be set up for other reasons as well, would be the most logical framework for such participation of the smaller countries. On the one hand, the secondary powers should, in this organization, be drawn continually into the council of the "Big Three," sharing with the latter the responsibility for political decisions. This would be particularly feasible on the regional level. On the other hand, smaller nations should be given the leading role in most of the administrative agencies

---

[9] "In Defense of the Small Countries," *Yale Review*, Winter 1943, p. 203.

likely to be established within the international organization. It would seem wise to institutionalize a monopoly of the small powers in this field in the same way in which Switzerland, for example, has enjoyed the sole privilege of organizing and administering the International Red Cross. Not only should the seat of such agencies be in the smaller countries; their citizens might be given the exclusive right to executive positions in these institutions. There are many tasks for which the world might come to rely completely on the services of the smaller nations, as it will rely for its peace on the harmonious leadership of the "Big Three."

It is most important of all, however, that the small nations should be convinced that they will receive fair treatment. The criteria of fairness in international relations have not been crystallized in the form of anything like legal rules. In the absence of judicial precedent, such standards are still, for the most part, in the realm of morals. The problem of applying such moral principles to the policies of leadership is discussed below. While the prevailing notions of international justice are still vague, however, an international organization might become a forum in which legal criteria governing the relationship between large and small powers could evolve. Such principles, possibly growing out of specific regional conditions, would be indispensable to any stable political order. For greater effectiveness, however, they should not be laid down *a priori*, but should be formulated only in the light of proved political experience.

There is another way to balance and limit the power of nations, one which is, in fact, more promising than the attempt to oppose small nations to Great Powers. This is the opposition of private individuals to governments. In international as well as in domestic politics the only real check on governments issues from individuals acting in private associations and with a view to non-political ends. Though a private individual is both a citizen and a "political animal," he also looks beyond politics and conceives ends and values which he deems at least as important as national interests. Thus he is capable of transcending the realm of political conflict and finding motives for union where governments must clash. In fact, such sense of world community as has developed during the last three hundred years did not spring from any affection of governments for one another but from the fact that individuals in the several countries held in common many values and interests which were conceived apart from power politics and which cut across national boundaries.

Moreover, individual man is the agent for the moral truths of mankind and therefore the ultimate guide for the policies of nations. It is thus imperative that the voice of the individual be heard above the noise of politics. The common interests of the world, above all, must be formulated by private individuals who can look beyond national interests. The values which individuals all over the world jointly recognize must be given expression as a guide for policies of governments.

This is the only fruitful way to approach the thorny problem of the limitation of sovereignty. If the state is a compact entity, founded on the fervent allegiance of its citizens, performing for them indispensable services and constituting the main frame of reference for their moral judgments, then state sovereignty can be limited only by war and subjugation. Sovereignty depends on what the power of national government means to the people living under it. The way to limit it is to loosen gradually the tight fabric of the state, by making the people look beyond it, by gradually extending and expanding the scope of community feeling, and, finally, by creating universal agencies capable of providing services that had previously been discharged by national governments alone. Sovereignty is not only a conception; it is likewise a real fact, which can be overcome only by making the wider-than-national community an equally real phenomenon in the experience of individuals.

WORLD ORDER AND GREAT POWERS
INTERNATIONAL ORGANIZATION FOR WHAT?

Leadership among nations, even more than in domestic societies, depends on confidence and voluntary acceptance.[10] Confidence among the smaller nations cannot be created merely by a simple statement of self-limitation on the part of the "Big Three." It is necessary that international institutions be set up to organize a variety of international relationships. Here the important question arises: For precisely what purposes should international organizations be created?

Little help can be obtained from the analogy of domestic government. So long as there is no single government for the entire world, no legislative, executive, and judicial functions, in the ordinary sense, can be performed by international organizations. And since we plan no superstate, the purpose of the international organization should not be to create power sufficient to coerce its members. Any international organization presupposes the continued existence of a number of states maintaining their own governments, their own systems of law administration, and their own military and economic resources. Obviously, such a situation is by its very nature fraught with dangers. Thus an international organization should be conceived in terms not of an insurance against the risk of war but rather of a concerted effort by all nations to banish the demons of international conflict. In the last analysis, even though an international organization comes into existence, the real responsibility for peace must rest with the peoples and govern-

[10] "It would . . . be but natural that the power of a State supreme at sea should inspire universal jealousy and fear, and be ever exposed to the danger of being overthrown by a general combination of the world. Against such a combination no single nation could in the long run stand. . . . The danger can in practice only be averted—and history shows that it has been so averted—on condition that the national policy of [that] State is so directed as to harmonize with the general desires and ideals common to all mankind, and more particularly, that it is closely identified with the primary and vital interests of a majority, or as many as possible, of the other nations." Sir Eyre Crowe, in his memorandum of January 1, 1907. Gooch and Temperley, *op. cit.*, Vol. III, p. 402.

ments of the various states. International organization cannot be set up as machinery that will automatically remove the threat of war. It is rather a device to coordinate and realize national policies of peace.

How can an international organization make its contribution towards a peaceful world?[11] The first and possibly the most important method is to foster the spirit and promote the more and more concrete formulation of world community. It is unrealistic to blame all wars on rational and deliberate schemes which national leaders choose to realize by force. War is not so much the pursuit of rational ends by force as it is the breakdown of rationality in the foreign relations of a country. A custom reported to exist among the Chinese may serve as an illustration. It is said that when a dispute breaks out between two coolies, a crowd gathers to watch the development of the argument. As soon as either resorts to his fists, he is declared the loser, for his wits gave out first. Similarly, war is not so much the pursuit of a conscious purpose but rather a desperate attempt to find a solution by force when all attempts at a reasonable solution have failed. Hitler's speech of June 22, 1941, gives eloquent expression to this truth; he declared that, in consequence of an unsatisfactory development of relations with Russia, he "had put the destiny of Germany once more into the hands of the armed forces."

War is thus invoked as an ordeal by battle mainly because nations in dispute fail to find a common frame of reference for a solution. Within any country there are always central in-

[11] At the risk of encroaching upon the following chapter by Professor Whitton I believe that I ought to sketch at least the outlines of an international organization as I see it from the point of view here taken. Professor Whitton's chapter deals with the type of international organization in which the security of nations is expected to flow from their voluntary submission to legal procedures. Since I have, in this chapter, rejected this assumption and have argued that peace is essentially dependent on a certain type of politics and policies, it is obviously incumbent on me to state what role I attribute to international organization. I have limited myself to the briefest suggestions.

stitutions, such as the government itself or the higher courts, which, considering the whole and not the parts, continuously interpret and formulate the community interest. This process of articulation is important, for without such a formulation of the common interest each conflicting party would have to fall back on some *ex parte* interpretation of community values, which is not likely to be acceptable to the other side. In the international community, similarly, a world authority could make a great contribution to peace by expressing the point of view of the international community whenever such an expression in concrete terms is called for. This task, however, cannot be properly performed by the official representatives of governments, as their ideas about world community are always likely to be tainted with national self-interest. Such rational guidance, supremely important for the elimination of conflict, can be provided only by a group of individuals acting in a private capacity.

The second major function for an international organization is the prevention of conflicts by adjusting and coordinating national policies. As I have pointed out,[12] wars are only the last phase of a period of friction and hostility, and when the stage of violence is finally reached the conflict is already too far advanced for any other solution. For this reason, any international organization which undertook merely to prevent actual force would be bound to fail. By the time actual conflict ensues, contrary national beliefs not only will have created an insoluble antagonism between the parties but frequently will have drawn other nations into the conflict, thus lining up most nations into two camps. Any attempt merely to avoid resort to arms is then too late. In other words, it is easier to organize procedures to lessen international friction than to establish methods of stopping war once an impasse has been reached.

An international organization, even if powerless to stop a conflagration once under way, is nevertheless in a position, if

[12] See footnote 2 above.

it acts in time, to deal with national policies which might engender conflict. For instance, it could procure information concerning the repercussions which such policies would have among other nations, and the consequences they are likely to produce. It could provide the makers of national policies with such information, and in addition could suggest different ways and means of persuading a nation to desist from a policy likely to create serious disturbance. While the full responsibility for policies will still lie with national governments and peoples, such efforts should prevent a situation in which nations blunder into war through blindness as to the results of their actions.

Third, an international organization can perform important administrative services which no other agency can discharge. One of these is the arbitration of disputes between states. An international court is hardly in a position to settle vital conflicts and thus prevent war, but it has an important function as a forum for the solution of secondary issues. International adjudication, as the history of the Permanent Court of International Justice demonstrates, is a matter of free agreement between states. Yet the contribution of judicial settlement to peaceful relationships must not be underestimated.

Another service that an international organization could properly perform lies in the field of administrative regulation. In many ways the peoples of the world are linked by material interests which would profit greatly from central administration. Air transport is an example; the production and conditions of sale of certain raw materials is another. Whatever regulation is needed here can be undertaken only by international agencies. But it is important to note that such agencies cannot relieve national governments of their individual responsibilities. An international administrative agency has no direct powers over individuals, cannot impose fines or other penalties, and cannot subpoena violators of regulations. The operation of international administrative agencies must, therefore, be different from that of national institutions. The former must seek to influence national policies while they are still in process of formulation, by disseminating information, gathering and distributing statistics, suggesting alternatives, and pointing out the international effects of national actions.

Lastly, an international organization should undertake certain promotional functions, notably in the fields of science, education, charity and welfare, where a world agency could accomplish more significant results than could national governments acting individually.

An international organization, though unable to shoulder the main responsibility for keeping the peace, could thus do much to guide national policies in the right direction. It should not be compared with a government, however, as it does not have any of the resources of power that governments possess. It has no authority over individuals, nor does it enjoy their allegiance. It does not institute courts, nor can it pass laws that bind national tribunals. It has no power over individuals and property within the nations. It does not have an armed force and, if it did, it could not command the means of mobilizing a great community for its support and supply. In fact, a world organization is quite unlike anything that can properly be called government, and it would be disastrous to impose on it tasks which only a government can discharge. So long as nations exist as separate entities, our only hope for peace is to make them peacefully disposed toward each other and to foster in them the consciousness of the community of men in which they all partake. Toward this end international organization can make an indispensable contribution.

OUTLINES OF AN INTERNATIONAL ORGANIZATION

What sort of international organization would be able to discharge the functions outlined in the foregoing pages? What would be the general nature of an organization adjunct to, and depending upon, the Great Powers for political leadership, but attempting to coordinate national policies in the general interest?

If the preceding analysis is correct, such an organization must take account of a number of different purposes and conditions if it is to function successfully. *First*, a framework must be provided for political decisions and actions taken by the Great Powers in the interest of world leadership. *Second*, the political responsibility of secondary and smaller nations must be organized and given full scope on a regional level. *Third*, spiritual leadership should issue from a non-political body capable of giving concrete expression to the interests of the world as a whole. *Fourth*, all countries, large and small, should join so as to constitute a common legal authority and a general forum for discussion. *Fifth*, adequate machinery should be set up to handle disputes between nations. *Sixth*, administrative agencies must be provided to promote welfare, regulate certain matters of general concern, and help adjust national policies. These six points will now be discussed.

1. The Great Powers, it is clear, must assume the primary responsibility for the maintenance of international order. They must be ready to act promptly so as to forestall serious friction and maladjustment. On occasion they might find themselves under the necessity of doing so without waiting for a more or less divided and distracted world to make up its mind. The Great Powers acting jointly constitute the nearest approach to an executive power that is possible in a world still divided into separate nations. The Great Powers, in respect to this quasi-executive function, must be given a certain measure of independent initiative. Hence, within a general international organization, they must form a nucleus which might be called the *Central Conference*. This would consist of the political leaders of the "Big Three" (plus whatever other powers might later join them), who would meet regularly and publicly. The Central Conference would lay down the main lines of policy for the "Big Three" to follow in the interest of world order. It

would thus serve the same ends that the great conferences of the Allied leaders have served during the war.[13]

2. To supplement the Central Conference, there should be *Regional Conferences*. In these bodies, the regionally leading powers would play a great role. China, for example, is an important power, but she has no world-wide interests except with respect to general peace. Her place is primarily in the center of a Far Eastern Regional Conference. France might play the same role in Europe. It would be advisable to have two of the "Big Three" represented in each of these Regional Conferences, thus achieving a modicum of balanced power.[14] It is in these regional organizations that the "Big Three" would have an excellent opportunity to allow substantial authority to devolve on the secondary powers, and to compensate the smaller states generously for whatever subordinate part might fall to them in the general scheme.

3. These policy-making organizations should be supervised by two bodies of general representation. The first might be called

[13] In this connection it is interesting to note how the future conditions of world peace are pictured in the mind of a leading representative of a "small" nation. Sir Girja Shankar Bajpai, Agent General for the Indian Government, stated those conditions in a speech made at Princeton on May 9, 1942, in the following terms: "First, 'an overwhelming' force must be created; second the nations that create it must agree to consult themselves constantly regarding world developments that may necessitate the use of such a force. Third, for its effective use, there should be not only consultation but agreement to entrust decisions to those nations which bear the main burden of its maintenance and have the requisite resources to reinforce it. For the smaller nations, such an arrangement would involve a surrender of sovereignty in the sense of an equality of voice; in return those accepting such a limitation of sovereignty will escape the burden of armaments beyond their capacity and the dangers of devastation inflicted by the sudden assault of more powerful neighbors. The major powers which may enjoy greater authority to use the international police force of which I have spoken will also be accepting a limitation of sovereignty in that they would be committed to placing the common good of their associates above their own strictly national interests. The exchange will, therefore, be fully equitable" (mimeographed text of the speech).

[14] The case for regionalism is upheld by Walter Lippmann in his latest book, *U.S. War Aims* (Boston: Little, Brown, 1944).

the *World Council*. It would consist of individuals who are not representatives of governments but sit on the council merely as persons of high wisdom, capacity, and moral stature. There might be one or two from each nation, but there should not be more than one hundred in all, since a larger council would be unwieldy. This Council would have, as it were, the keeping of the world's common interest and of the world's political conscience. It would keep its eye on the policies of particular nations, or the disputes between nations, and offer advice and suggestions. If two nations differed on a political issue, the Council could propose what from the world's point of view appeared to be a fair solution. If this solution were enforced by the "Big Three," no state would have a moral basis for opposition, because the proposal would have been made by individuals representative of universal moral standards and spiritual criteria.

A Council with this kind of authority would also solve one of the problems over which the League of Nations persistently stumbled. It would give a moral sanction to a *status quo* brought about according to its suggestions. No longer could a nation contend that the *status quo* owed its existence merely to the action of pressure and counter-pressure, force and counter-force, and that it therefore deserved to be challenged in the same way. A *status quo* recommended by the majority of highly respected individuals has on its side a moral authority which no situation born of power politics could ever command. Once the *status quo* had been established on a moral basis, national policies could be judged in a universal frame of reference. Not only would condemnation or approval of a given policy be more nearly unanimous, but the greater clarity of the moral issue would act as a powerful deterrent to the statesmen of a would-be rebel nation. For it is the moral anarchy of international relations far more than the absence of organization and government that encourages the nations to risk the gamble of war.

This World Council would be in a position to express the interest of the world community as distinct from that of particular nations. I have already attempted to show how important it is to have an agency ready, in every situation, explicitly to state the higher interest. The continuous and repeated formulation of world interest by a group of individuals, representative of the best in their respective nations, would also make possible the growth of an international law divorced from the vicissitudes of power politics which have so often in the past been the main instruments for the development of law among the nations.

4. The second supervisory body might be called the *Assembly of Governments*. Here each nation should have one seat and one vote. This body might convene once a year. It would serve as a general forum in which grievances could be aired, general discussions held, and international conventions debated. It would be the official center of power of the international organization, i.e., it would rule over whatever international territory might come into existence, or such other resources as the international organization might command. From this body any title would be derived, as held in the name of the international organization. It might well decide questions by majority vote, since it would not have the power of imposing obligations on the member states. Such obligations must obviously be reserved for the free agreement of the nations. But the Assembly would exercise supervision over all those branches of the international organization which require centralization in some international agency.

5. Besides the Central Conference, the Regional Conferences, the World Council, and the Assembly of Governments, there should be also a *Court of Justice*. Little need be said of this proposal, since the existing Permanent Court of International Justice is a well-tested institution of great value and considerable tradition. Nothing should be added to or subtracted from it.

6. The same is true of the *Secretariat* of the League of Nations, which was a well-functioning institution and might be revived without much alteration. Undoubtedly there will be a number of additional administrative agencies, each with its specific field and function, its own staff, directorate, and budget. These administrative agencies are bound to become very important, if for no other reason than as a practical demonstration of what the world can do by common action. The usual method of procedure of such agencies is to elaborate draft conventions which nations are expected later to ratify. This method has not been very successful, as many nations found it difficult to comply with international recommendations after they had already committed themselves to a different policy. It might be well to avoid such obstacles by putting these international agencies in direct contact with the policy-making powers within each government. This might conceivably be done by appointing an attaché of the international agency to the various governmental departments and national legislatures. Such a person would have the function of bringing to the attention of national policymakers all the international viewpoints and facts bearing on their intended policies, and of pointing out to them the dangerous repercussions certain policies might entail. Only after preliminary action designed to coordinate national policies should recourse be had to draft conventions.

An international organization, including all of the six agencies above described, should be called into existence before the final peace settlement is reached. Its *raison d'être* would be the substitution of a new spirit of foreign policy for that of power rivalry and nationalistic self-centeredness. It should not, therefore, be burdened with a peace that has been concluded under the old methods of power politics. Much of the weakness of the League of Nations must be attributed to an inner contradiction between the Peace of Versailles and the principles of the League. The final peace settlement after this war should wait until an international organization has come into existence, and it should be drawn up under the auspices of that organization in the sole interest of world community and world peace.

3. Institutions of World Order

BY JOHN B. WHITTON

IN THE preceding chapter Professor Niemeyer, while giving primacy to the necessity of maintaining harmony among the Great Powers, does not deny the utility of international organization as a means toward an ordered world, and in fact offers a sketch of such an organization. In line with this order of ideas, the present chapter offers a more detailed discussion of a new world organization—its basic principles, organs and activities, with special emphasis upon preventive or corrective measures to meet trouble before it becomes critical, but without neglecting provision for the use of force, if necessary, to forestall or overcome aggression.

The basic assumption underlying this chapter is that only through a "rule of law" may responsibility, power and the control of power be properly and safely combined. In other words, admitting that peace in the last analysis must necessarily depend on the effective cooperation of the Great Powers, I submit that not only in the interest of the peace of the entire world, but *in their own interest*, the great nations must agree to exert their power under the aegis of a world organization and in accordance with regular procedures defined and limited by accepted rules of law; and furthermore that, in the operation of such machinery, the active collaboration of all states, both great and small, must be ensured. For, as the great Dutch jurist Hugo Grotius expressed it, without law, all is uncertainty.

The present chapter is mainly concerned with security, discussing methods of attaining it through international principles, institutions, and procedures. But in stressing the problem of security we should not underestimate the importance of the other major tasks of world organization. In fact, should we devote all our efforts merely to the search for security, we

INSTITUTIONS OF WORLD ORDER

might fall far short even of this goal. We must also make adequate provision for needed change and for peaceful evolution and progress. Security, peaceful change, evolutionary progress—these, we believe, may be realized if the United States will help to create a new world organization and will take an active part in its work. Only thus can the American people hope to free themselves and the world from the threat of war.

BASIC PRINCIPLES FOR THE NEW ORDER

Before proceeding to describe this new world organization and to analyze its functions, let us consider the basic principles upon which the new order should be founded. There are six such principles, namely:

1. Joint and several responsibility.
2. Executive leadership.
3. Power.
4. Control of power.
5. Limitation of external sovereignty.
6. Monopoly of force in the collectivity.

1. *Principle of Joint and Several Responsibility.* Foremost among the fundamental principles underlying the new world order is the indivisibility of peace. According to this principle, any threat of force, wherever it may occur, is the immediate concern of each and every member of the community. Thus interpreted, it may be called the principle of joint and several responsibility for the maintenance of peace.

This revolutionary principle constituted the very heart of the Covenant of the League of Nations. In Article 11 we read: "Any war or threat of war, whether immediately affecting any of the Members of the League or not, is hereby declared a matter of concern to the whole League, and the League shall take any action that may be deemed wise and effectual to safeguard the peace of nations." And in the *International Law of the Future*, the work of a number of North American international lawyers, it is declared that "Any use of force or any threat to use force by a State in its relations with another State is a matter of concern to the Community of States."[1]

The responsibility for peace is not only joint; it is also several. In other words, while peace is undoubtedly the concern of the entire community of states, it is just as much the concern of each individual member of that community. This was recognized recently by a former Under-Secretary of the United States who said that all states should admit that a "threat of war anywhere throughout the globe threatens their own security."[2] Similarly, the "Draft Pact for the Future International Authority," recently issued in Britain under the sponsorship of Lord Cecil, declares that "The welfare of the whole community of nations is the concern of every one of them."[3]

Article 11 of the Covenant would be improved by the recognition that it is not only war that constitutes a danger to peace, but likewise any use of force. For armed reprisals, or other "acts of force short of war," may be as dangerous to peace as an out-and-out "legal" war, and in many cases have been merely the prelude to actual war.

The importance of the principle of joint and several responsibility can hardly be exaggerated. It is the very negation of isolation and neutrality. If respected, it would mean that never again could Americans claim that the Rhine frontier is of no concern to the United States, nor could British newspapers again contend that the fate of a "distant" Balkan state whose name

[1] *International Conciliation*, April 1944, p. 267. Note also the Final Act and Convention of Habana, signed by the Twenty-One American Republics, July 21-30, 1940, declaring "That any attempt on the part of a non-American State against the integrity or inviolability of the territory, the sovereignty or the political independence of an American State shall be considered as an act of aggression against the States which sign this declaration." *American Journal of International Law*, Vol. 35, January 1941, Supplement, p. 15.

[2] Sumner Welles, *The World of the Four Freedoms* (New York: Columbia University Press, 1943), p. 101.

[3] *International Conciliation*, February 1944, p. 131.

few can pronounce was of no concern to Britain. We have learned by our mistakes that such an ostrich-like attitude may have fatal consequences. We now know that no country can be insulated or isolated from a great war; that even a small war spreads like contagion across the mountains and beyond the seas. So far as the peace of the nations is concerned, we are indeed but "one world."

2. *Principle of Executive Leadership.* The principle of joint and several responsibility is indispensable, but it is not enough. Even if it were adopted as a basic tenet of the new world organization it would be inadequate, and in fact even dangerous, unless linked up with the principle of *leadership*. For if world peace is everybody's business it is likely to be nobody's business. Consequently careful provision must be made for executive leadership in the society of nations. The Concert of Europe, with all its defects, nevertheless provided executive leadership for the peace of Europe, and was able to deal effectively with a number of grave international situations. The new world will need some small body capable of acting with as much efficiency, but of course only within a proper system of checks and balances. Many plans provide for executive responsibility of this kind. The British "Draft Pact," already referred to, proposes to meet the situation by the appointment of a "Defense Committee," composed of the four Great Powers, plus certain elected members, aided if necessary by special regional committees, and acting under a mandate to "use their whole strength to prevent or stop any act of aggression." In my opinion, as I explain further on, this responsibility should be centered in the Executive Council of the world organization. The principle behind these plans is clear: when a crisis comes no state can feel safe unless assured that some continuing body, specially created for the purpose, stands ready to assume the responsibility for prompt, energetic and wise measures for the maintenance of peace.

JOHN B. WHITTON

3. *The Principle of Power.* The problem of leadership involves the all-important problem of power, a matter so vital that the planners for the new world can disregard it only at their peril. As Field Marshal Smuts wrote recently, "The question of power remains fundamental and it is, I think, the great lesson of this war. Peace not backed by power remains a dream."[4] The new peace structure will succeed in its struggle against aggression only if it can find a way to put behind its institutions, procedures and rules some power sufficiently strong to overcome the potential aggressor, and sufficiently resilient to act resolutely as soon as the need arises. This, as we have urged already, should occur at the time the trouble starts, before it has reached the critical stage.

If we are to avoid further illusions and errors, we must understand that all international politics are a function of actual and potential state power.[5] The failure to recognize this truth has vitiated all efforts so far made to set up an international organization; in fact this explains why the League of Nations never became a real force for peace. And the very persons who, as high-minded advocates of peace, often enjoying wide popular support, could have been a powerful aid to the League were led astray through a misconception of the whole question of power. We refer here to those who worked so valiantly for disarmament as the main road to peace, and those who placed such reliance on the Pact of Paris.

Power being essential to the success of the new world organization, where can it be found? Both leadership and power will be provided if the United States, Russia, Britain, China, and France,[6] plus certain smaller states elected for the purpose, collaborate closely within the framework of an international system in accordance with carefully formulated principles and

[4] *New York Times Magazine,* December 12, 1943, p. 9.
[5] Walter Lippmann, *New York Herald Tribune,* December 18, 1943.
[6] The inclusion of France is indispensable, otherwise continental Europe would be deprived of a permanent representative.

rules. The central agency for such power and responsibility should be an Executive Council.

4. *Principle of Control of Power.* This leads us to another fundamental tenet of the new world order, namely, the necessity for the control of power. The presence of immense power, among individuals or among states, can be a terrible menace. As Niebuhr puts it, "Whenever an individual or a group or a nation possesses undue power, and whenever this power is not checked by the possibility of criticising and resisting it, it grows inordinate."[7] Napoleon, when his power was at its zenith, might have established a peace on the Continent lasting for generations, had he followed the advice of his friend and adviser, Caulaincourt, who opposed the plan to attack Russia. But the possession of great power, instead of bringing peace in its wake, only led Napoleon to seek more power; hence his fatal march into Russia. The story of Hitler has a similar moral. If the power is in the hands not of a single monarch but of a group of three or four Great Powers acting in concert, the problem will remain, and its solution is beset with so many obstacles that the regulation of power may be considered the very crux of the entire struggle for peace. The big states may abuse their power if they stick together, or fight among themselves if they do not. Despite all possible precautions, the formidable task will be to prevent war among the great states themselves. Involved here, too, is the delicate matter of the proper relationship between the great and the small powers. The latter are torn between their desire for a world strongly armed against aggressions from which they would be the first to suffer, and the fear of a Great Power dictatorship. To blind ourselves to these difficulties would not only be unrealistic but might even lead to disaster.

The problem of maintaining harmony and teamwork among the Great Powers is crucial, and it will have to be faced no

[7] Reinhold Niebuhr, *Christianity and Power Politics* (New York: Scribner's, 1940), p. 26.

matter what international system emerges from the present war. It must be admitted that if we, Russia or Britain refused to live up to the rules of the new world organization, or should withdraw, any plan for international collaboration would crumble. If New York or Massachusetts, during the early days of our republic, had refused to respect the Constitution, or if they had seceded, the "more perfect union" would have quickly disintegrated. This peril, however, did not deter the Founding Fathers from proceeding with their plans. And as it turned out, New York and Massachusetts discovered that by remaining in the new union they gained substantial advantages which outweighed the burden of respecting laws which they found at times embarrassing or costly. Similarly, Great Britain, Russia, and the United States may find that the advantages of membership in the new world organization far outweigh its burdens.

As a matter of fact, there is good prospect for close and friendly collaboration among the Great Powers after the war. Those great dynamic states, the so-called "Have-Not Powers," which looked to war in 1939 for the achievement of their "destiny," will be disarmed and impotent at the end of this war. Moreover, all of the "Big Four"—and the same will hold true for France, which may soon resume its place among the Great Powers—will be "satisfied" states, possessing immense territories, great natural resources, a large measure of self-sufficiency and considerable stability. Each wants and needs nothing so much as a long period of peace in order to continue its present development. Another world war would be disastrous to all of them. Their leaders know this. The terrible experiences of the past must have taught them that the much-desired period of peace can be achieved only through mutual collaboration in political, social and economic fields, and that such collaboration can be maintained only within a world organization under a rule of law.

5. *The Limitation of External Sovereignty.* The foregoing discussion of the need for limitations on power brings us to a

consideration of that time-honored and much debated topic, the sovereignty of the state. It is clear from what has already been said that an effective international organization cannot be created without some limitation of the freedom of action of its members. This truth has been reiterated again and again by authors of plans for a world order from Pierre Dubois to Clarence Streit.

There is really nothing startling or unprecedented in the movement to limit the sovereignty of the state. The concept is by no means unchanging or eternal; on the contrary, being designed to serve the national interest, it is subject to modification whenever the national interest itself demands it. Necessary concessions will be forthcoming when state leaders are convinced that such a step will serve the vital interest of the nation. This explains why one nation will agree to make tariff concessions, or why it will bind itself to come to the aid of an ally. Both such decisions involve inroads on the liberty of action of the state.

Because the national interest demands it, it now seems probable that many states will be ready after this war to accept some curtailment of their previously well-guarded liberty of action. This is particularly true in the field of international security. At the beginning of this century Great Britain, in spite of its traditional policy of "splendid isolation" (a form of sovereignty), sought alliances with Russia and France when its security was menaced. Now, for similar reasons, the United States, in response to the imperative demands of security, can be expected to favor certain exceptions to the exercise of its sovereign independence, simply because there is no other way to free the world from the threat of war. Mr. Willkie has expressed this thought admirably: "I think that our use of our sovereignty to create an effective instrument of peace is the best way of protecting our sovereignty."[8] Nor is this attitude

[8] Wendell L. Willkie, "Our Sovereignty: Shall We Use It?" *Foreign Affairs*, Vol. 22, April 1944, p. 360.

confined to a few leaders; as reported in Chapter VI, our traditional fear of entangling alliances is giving way to a realization that self-interest compels us to join with others in a world-wide cooperative effort.

Of course, as past experience warns us, this remarkable change in American sentiment may not be permanent.[9] But the reasons for this change seem sound. The catastrophic lessons of this century have shown us that the threat of war cannot be obliterated so long as we or other states insist on maintaining complete liberty of action.

Security requires that states abandon a right hitherto considered an attribute of sovereignty—the right to choose isolation, neutrality or even complete indifference in the presence of a foreign war, particularly a war of flagrant aggression and conquest.[10] But security requires also that all states, great and small, agree to give up the "right" of armed intervention in the affairs of other states, and with it other uses of armed force except when authorized by the world authority. This brings us to a discussion of the sixth and final principle offered as a basis for the new world organization.

6. *Principle of the Monopoly of Force in the Collectivity.* Among individuals a most notable achievement in the development of law and order is the prohibition of "private war" (the resort to force among individuals except in extraordinary circumstances, as in self-defense) and the definite grant to the community of a monopoly of its use. Among nations, too, the collective control of the use of force will constitute a forward step of inestimable benefit to world peace. We may actually be on the threshold of realizing this goal.

Grotius showed the way in the seventeenth century when he emphasized the distinction between the "just" and the "unjust" war, a famous proposal whose first practical application came

---

[9] See Chapter 1, pp. 8-9, and Chapter 6, p. 194.
[10] See address to the nation on American foreign policy, by Secretary of State Hull, *New York Times*, April 10, 1944, *passim.*

only with the foundation of the League of Nations. Under the Covenant, a distinction was made between "licit" and "illicit" wars. In case of an illicit war (for instance, a resort to war in violation of the promise to submit certain disputes to the League), collective sanctions were to be brought to bear against the "aggressor."

The weakness and failures of the League are well known. They have not, however, been a complete loss, for they have served as useful laboratory experiments, demonstrating how, with appropriate reforms, force can eventually be more effectively controlled. Profiting by past mistakes, the architects of the new peace are in a position to design a better structure for this purpose. It will be necessary to "fill in the gaps in the Covenant" by eliminating any chance for a "licit" war, and to place behind promises of nonaggression some solid and reliable measures of enforcement. The basic principle to guide these efforts is this: the collectivity must be given a *monopoly of the use of force*. Individual force must be prohibited, with certain exceptions subject to the most severe restrictions.[11]

Under this principle, each state renounces not only the use of force but also something equally objectionable and dangerous, the threat to use force. This is a distinct improvement over anything found in the Covenant of the League of Nations. Another excellent innovation is the prohibition not only of war but of *any* use of force by one nation against another. For the definition of "war" is a matter of fine distinctions and legal technicalities which provide a convenient loophole for an aggressive state. Italy and Japan sought to evade their League obligations—the former after the bombardment of Corfu, the latter when it invaded Manchuria—by claiming in both instances

[11] Thus, the authors of the *International Law of the Future* provide that "Each State has a legal duty to refrain from any use of force and from any threat to use force in its relations with another State, except as authorized by the competent agency of the Community of States." *International Conciliation*, April 1944, pp. 268-269.

that such action in the circumstances was not war but only an "act of force short of war." Japan also contended that its use of force against the Chinese was justified under the doctrine of self-defense. This loophole, too, would be eliminated by the adoption of the principle just referred to. For while under this provision a state is permitted to repel by forceful measures an unauthorized use of force made against it by another state, the state claiming to act in self-defense must be ready at any time to submit the legality of its action to the world authority for ratification or approval, since it can be called to account if it has overstepped the limits prescribed by law for the exercise of this exceptional right.[12]

These limitations on the use of force among nations, the aim of which is to give the collectivity a monopoly of power, are similar to those in force in advanced systems of law everywhere, but thus far their application to relations among states has been beset with great difficulties. One of these is the absence among states of institutions corresponding to those existing within each state, notably courts and the obligation to submit disputes for adjudication. But the greatest obstacle of all has been the fear of attack. As nations lose their fear of being attacked they will the more readily accept such salutary restrictions on the use of force. Small states will accept such a "rule of law" because they have everything to gain thereby, and the Great Powers should likewise make such a "sacrifice" because there is no other way to end the threat of war, which brings disaster to all.

[12] See Whitton and Gonsiorowski, in *Boycotts and Peace* (New York: Harper, 1932), p. 72: "In general terms, the right of self-defense may be defined as the right of a state to resort to force in order to repel an actual or immediately threatening violent attack. The measures employed to meet the danger must be proportionate to the latter; they are limited to what is reasonably necessary to throw off the attack. A state which does not respect these principles and resorts to war does not exercise the right of self-defense."

INSTITUTIONS OF WORLD ORDER
NATURE OF THE NEW WORLD ORGANIZATION

There is little support, either in the United States or elsewhere, for a post-war organization resembling a super-state. Clarence Streit's proposal for a union of the democracies finds little favor today, and the present trend is in the direction of a general international organization of *sovereign* states. This is shown by the phraseology of both the Moscow Declaration and the Connally Resolution.[12a] Perhaps the day may come when the concept of an organized community, which gradually took form in the clan, the city-state, the loose feudal union, the weak confederation and finally the strong national state (in either the federal or unitary form), will cross the "one more river" and give rise to a great universal federation encompassing the entire planet. Perhaps this final step will be preceded by the formation of a number of regional federations, and even today there are some movements in this direction. But for the present few look with favor on any *civitas universalis*, except for some thinkers in small states so exposed that a superstate appears as the only means of preventing them from being again overrun by a powerful neighbor. Thus, only recently, a Belgian statesman proposed that his country be made a part of the British Commonwealth of Nations. Such views, however, are not very numerous, and it would seem that for the present we must content ourselves with some kind of world *confederation*, despite its weaknesses and dangers, which must never be underestimated. To expect something more ambitious now would be to court bitter disappointment.[13]

[12a] At the Dumbarton Oaks Conference, August-September, 1944, there was unanimous accord on this point.

[13] Harold Butler is of this opinion. He writes as follows: "The world will still continue to be organized in a number of separate nations. The violence of the reaction against Nazism was due more to its attempt to stamp out national freedom and individuality than to anything else. To suppose that nations which have made unprecedented sacrifices in order to preserve their national identity are going to surrender it once they

JOHN B. WHITTON

While proposals for world federation have been losing ground, the general contours of the future universal organization have been gradually emerging and gaining support. The advancement of the interests of the community of nations, and the protection of the rights of its members, require the establishment of a permanent body. Otherwise it would be impossible to assure continuity of effort and progress.[14] Hence it is indispensable to plan for a universal organization with competence to deal with any matter of interest to the common welfare. All states should enjoy the right to join this organization on a basis of legal equality, but only if they are able and willing to live up to the obligations of membership. This includes victors, vanquished and neutrals in the present war, provided that their form of government is compatible with international collaboration. Membership should be granted on a basis of legal equality but, as I shall point out further on, not necessarily on a basis of equal political responsibility.

The new world organization must be endowed with a certain number of organs for the exercise of legislative, executive and judicial functions. These organs would be six in number, namely:

1. General Assembly.
2. Executive Council.
3. "Third Chamber."
4. Secretariat.
5. World Court.
6. International Peace Center.

have regained it is surely contrary to common sense. . . . The national ideal is still the source from which the culture, and the rich diversity of our civilization will be drawn." Harold Butler, *The Lost Peace* (London: Faber and Faber, 1941), pp. 190-191.

[14] "The pages of history tell us over and over again that whenever men are living close together they need a government to prevent anarchy and conflict, and to permit progress. . . . The nations of the world must not merely agree that they wish to live together in peace; they must establish a mechanism of government to achieve this end." Harold E. Stassen, *The Saturday Evening Post*, May 22, 1943.

INSTITUTIONS OF WORLD ORDER

1. *General Assembly.* First, there must be a general representative and deliberative body, to which every government will be entitled to send at least one delegate. The provision for official representation from governments, rather than from peoples, seems necessary in order that the assembly may act with authority. Otherwise its decisions would not be accepted by the states represented. Any plan for an international legislature elected by popular vote is entirely impracticable today. This General Assembly will deliberate over the various problems of international relations and organization. It will have general supervision of all the activities of the world body and of its various committees, sections and organs. It will also provide a check on the powers of the Executive Council.

2. *Executive Council.* The larger body just described would act in accord with the principle of universal responsibility, referred to earlier, for it would give every state the opportunity to take an active interest in everything affecting the peace of the world. But such a large assembly is poorly designed to give effect to the principle of leadership. In order to ensure prompt and effective action in case of emergency, a smaller body must be created. This body, which could be called the Executive Council, should include all of the Great Powers so that responsibility would be placed directly on those with the power to implement it.[15] But in order to check abuses of this power, a certain number of the smaller states, chosen by election in the Assembly, should likewise be members. Furthermore, the exact powers of this Executive Council should be carefully defined, and its position as trustee for the common welfare definitely established. In case of any dispute over the extent of the Coun-

[15] With the United States and Russia as permanent members of the Executive Council, this body should be able to exercise a leadership in world affairs which the Council of the League of Nations, at all times deprived of the membership of one or both of these states, was never able to maintain. See *The International Law of the Future, op. cit.*, pp. 336ff.

cil's powers, the Permanent Court of International Justice should be empowered to decide the matter.

This Council, as a quasi-cabinet, would act as an executive committee. Upon it would lie the main responsibility for dealing promptly and resolutely with all matters of crucial interest to the peace of the world. Meeting more readily and more frequently than the larger chamber, this committee would have power to act on matters requiring, in the general interest, decisions of immediate application. Above all, in case of war or threat of war, the Executive Council would set into operation the machinery for the settlement of disputes and for the prevention of war. Other special matters might be assigned to this Council for deliberation and action.

3. *"Third Chamber."* In addition to the two organs just described, there is also a need in the new world order for a third chamber, more representative of public opinion throughout the world. Unlike the General Assembly, it would represent not governments but various parties, classes or interests within each state. A detailed plan for such representation would have to be devised. The International Labor Organization has employed a somewhat similar system of representation with considerable success, delegates being appointed to speak for employers, employees and governments. This third chamber, although endowed with little or no legal authority, might in practice exert considerable influence as an expression of world opinion. As such, it could affect the decisions of the General Assembly and Executive Council. And while its main task would be to reflect the opinions of peoples throughout the world, its deliberations, especially if broadcast generally by short and long wave, might have a beneficial influence on public opinion itself. However, totalitarian states would not be in a position of equality with democracies, first because delegates from the former, whether sitting in the official or the unofficial assembly, would merely voice the opinions of the government, and second, because the totali-

INSTITUTIONS OF WORLD ORDER

tarian state might prevent its nationals from listening freely to the radio reporting the discussions of the third chamber, and could otherwise interfere materially with the formation of public opinion within its borders.

4. *International Secretariat.* The work of the three institutions just described could not be carried on successfully without provision for an international civil service, on the model of the Secretariat of the League of Nations. Otherwise there would be no practicable way to handle the many international activities requiring expert advice and careful preparation. The sections of the League Secretariat, manned for the most part by very capable experts, were constantly studying vital problems of international relations—legal, economic, political and the like. It was here that projects for reform and progress were laboriously prepared for submission to appropriate League organs or special international conferences for necessary action. In times of crisis a number of these sections were called upon to work together. Moreover, certain important tasks will have to be assigned for permanent administration to this international civil service. Such activities include the control of traffic in dangerous drugs, the administration of mandated areas, and an international arms-inspection system implementing the permanent control of national armaments.

The success of such a Secretariat will depend, of course, on the ability, character and objectivity of its members. In recruiting for this service, stress should be laid not only on special competence and general intelligence but also on freedom from national bias and from undue control by the home government.

5. *World Court.* Clearly, no international order would be complete without a judicial body enjoying the confidence of all states, and with this in view the Permanent Court of International Justice, still in being despite the war, should be continued and strengthened. This tribunal, which did such splen-

did service between two wars, will be immeasurably improved and its accomplishments greatly increased if, as it is hoped, the states of the world can be induced to submit all their legal disputes to the court and permit it to decide upon its own jurisdiction. While the court is designed particularly for legal cases, it is quite capable of deciding political disputes also, provided that the interested parties can be persuaded to submit them to the court.

The World Court could exercise a very useful role in another direction. The division of authority between the General Assembly, the Executive Council and the "Third Chamber" will have to be defined, and the respective prerogatives of each body delimited. In case of dispute over the respective power of these various bodies, an appeal to the court would be appropriate. This is one method of providing checks and balances against an abuse of power, either by the Executive Council, where responsibility and leadership are centered, or by the Great Powers as members of this body.

Some plans include provision for an Equity Tribunal to deal with nonjusticiable disputes, particularly for the purpose of modifying treaties or "situations" which constitute a menace to peace. This problem—peaceful change—is of vital importance. Peaceful change must be effected mainly by means other than an imposed settlement, but a plan to set up an Equity Tribunal to which the parties, of their own free will, could submit a dispute for final decision, deserves the most serious consideration.

6. *International Peace Center*.[16] The sinister activities of Dr. Goebbels, especially his remarkable utilization of the radio

[16] Professor Joseph R. Strayer of the Princeton Group has remarked with respect to this proposal: "Would anyone pay attention to propaganda coming from a foreign source, easily discredited by extreme nationalists? It would be much safer to let each section of the World Organization publicize its own activities. Once they were successful in establishing a reputation for accuracy and honesty, it might be possible to combine their work."

as a lethal weapon of mass persuasion, have shown us the dangers of propaganda for war. Even more important, they have underlined the necessity for and have demonstrated the possibility of propaganda for peace. After this war, all peace-loving governments should give major attention to the problem of preparing their peoples for active membership in the new world order. An all-out effort must be made to break down nationalism and race hatred, and to promote international understanding. The delusions which favor war should be pointed out and exploded. But it would be most shortsighted to limit such education to "good-will propaganda." The individual citizen must be enlightened as to the realities of power politics. He must be warned of the dangers of apathy, overconfidence, and a false sentiment of security. Furthermore, he should realize the dangers of national egotism, the folly of isolation, the necessity for international collaboration. Such a campaign of education should also stress the structure and the aims of the new world organization, and should explain the role expected and required of each state if the effort to free the world from fear is to succeed.

Now while each state should undertake such educational activities, this is peculiarly a task for the new world organization itself. The latter should set up a great international peace center, disseminating throughout the world effective information and education for better international relations, in an effort to bring peoples closer together and to prepare them for the common task of international collaboration. Such a center would constitute a reliable source of information about world affairs. Furthermore, it could present the human side of the world organization, and at the same time offer to the common man in every land a chance to participate in its discussions and thus feel closer to its activities. Thus could be laid the foundation for that mutual understanding and social solidarity which are the prerequisites to a strongly integrated world organization.

JOHN B. WHITTON

The invention of radio has greatly facilitated the accomplishment of this task. The future world Secretariat, one of whose sections should be set aside for international peace education, should have at its disposal a powerful radio transmitter, capable of circling the globe, by long and short wave, with educational messages in every language. For the preparation of such programs, a highly competent staff made up of experts from many countries would be needed. The entire undertaking would require a sizable budget, but the possibilities for progress here are so great that any reasonable expense would be justified. For no effort, financial or otherwise, should be spared to establish a world peace center of widespread and lasting benefit to humanity.[17]

This, then, is a brief sketch of the world organization which, to judge by past experience, is indispensable if the nations are at last to collaborate effectively.[18] It is to be hoped that such an organization may result from an adaptation of the present organization of the United Nations, or a gradual proliferation of various *ad hoc* bodies such as UNRRA and the Combined Boards. The proposals now to be discussed for a system of security are based on the assumption that some such organization as that just outlined will eventually emerge.

[17] See Max Beer, "Peace Through Truth," *New Europe*, March 1944, p. 19: "Would the new League, even if it was composed only of democratic nations, not be a failure from its very inception if, together with the international organs set up in order to promote international cooperation, there was not a special, international system dedicated to the basic task of disseminating honest information, creating throughout the world an intelligent understanding of international problems and a strong spirit of resistance to peace-disturbing tendencies? . . . Peace through truth: there is no other way."

[18] Because of lack of space I have not considered the matter of regional international organization, stressed by Professor Niemeyer in his discussion of "regional conferences" (*supra*, pp. 47, 63), but I believe that much of the authority of the central world organization could be delegated with profit to various regional institutions, both permanent and *ad hoc*. There should be, however, a right of appeal to the larger body, and the latter should always retain the right to intervene in regional matters in case the general peace is at stake.

INSTITUTIONS OF WORLD ORDER

The new world order must not limit itself to any single road to the final goal—a just and lasting peace. There are many such roads; while some are more important than others, all must be utilized. Even those apparently of slight significance must not be neglected, for if the entire range of available procedures, measures and activities is employed with promptness, understanding and conviction, their cumulative effect should be great.

These various efforts may be divided into three main categories, as follows:

1. Corrective Measures (to avoid trouble and friction).
2. Restrictive Measures (to prevent trouble from leading to a resort to force).
3. Suppressive Measures (to suppress the use of force).

1. CORRECTIVE MEASURES

The doctor who takes no interest in his patient until the latter develops an acute case of tuberculosis is neglecting the most important part of his job. Modern medicine puts its main emphasis on keeping the disease from getting a start. Among nations, too, prevention is much to be preferred to heroic measures taken as a last resort, for the latter are much more costly, and, what is more important, often come too late to prevent the catastrophe. For instance, it is much better for outside states to come to the aid of a nation menaced by economic crisis than to sit idly by as the ravages of inflation or unemployment engender civil disturbances tempting some foreign government to intervene. A more intelligent method is to root out the trouble before it grows into a serious disturbance.[19] Here is a golden opportunity for methods of "peaceful change."

[19] Prompt preventive action is of particular importance in cases such as the following: (a) a colonial power is governing its colonies so badly that the health and welfare of neighboring states is threatened; (b) a state refuses citizenship to a growing alien group.

JOHN B. WHITTON

The importance of such preventive or corrective action is clear if one matter rarely emphasized is fully understood. This is the danger of concentrating attention upon the settling of "disputes" among nations. International lawyers, particularly, have often laid too much stress on such legal procedures. Not that this movement has been futile—on the contrary, grave disputes have been satisfactorily settled by arbitration, and such procedures must of course be made an important part of the new peace structure. But when we consider that neither World War I nor World War II arose out of any clear-cut "dispute," it is clear that post-war planners must make provision, not only for legal procedures for the adjudication of disputes, but also for other measures, some of them more radical, some of them less so. The more radical measures will be considered in a later section where I discuss collective means to suppress the use of force. As for the less radical measures, the following might prove effective:

Corrective Measures of an Economic Nature. In the economic field there is an exceptional opportunity to eliminate trouble spots before they become chronic or dangerous. Appropriate measures taken *in time* to prevent the disastrous inflation in Germany in the 'twenties, with widespread unemployment and the destruction of the middle class, might well have avoided the conditions out of which Hitler rose to power. Here is a case in which prophylactic measures of an economic nature might have served to avoid war. At other times economic troubles, if left untended, might not actually lead to war, but the result could be so to poison the atmosphere as between two or more states as to prevent them from settling some more important political controversy. Thus our tariffs on imports from the Argentine have seriously hampered the settlement of our political disputes with that country.

Most plans for the post-war order give recognition to the need for international procedures to deal with economic problems. They usually recommend the establishment of a world economic council or committee to cope with problems of world trade, currency, unemployment, the distribution of raw materials, and other economic questions of vital concern both to individual states and to the international community as a whole. Some plans call for an international planning authority endowed with very extensive authority, somewhat in the nature of a world inter-state commerce commission, with power to compel states to reduce tariff barriers, avoid unfair discrimination in their foreign trade policies, etc. Given the realities of power politics, notably the reluctance of states to accept dictation from some superior authority, it is more likely that we must be content with international economic organs endowed with more modest powers. Probably at best such organ will be given power to study the questions just mentioned, draw up reports and recommendations addressed to the General Assembly and Executive Council, and otherwise facilitate and promote appropriate action which will be finally brought about, as usual, by agreement among the states concerned. Some progress is possible, too, by adopting new rules of international law covering economic relations now outside the realm of law. Such procedures are indeed a far cry from present practices within the state, by which monopolies can be outlawed by statute, or unemployment attacked by prompt executive action, but in the international field it would not be realistic to expect rapid progress at the present time. Nevertheless, despite the necessary limitations on its powers, the world authority should be able to meet and overcome many of the gravest economic problems. Its ultimate success in this endeavor, however, must in the last analysis depend today, as in the past, on the foresight, intelligence, and spirit of cooperation of statesmen and parliaments throughout the world.

In some cases the world authority will be in a position to go somewhat beyond mere study and persuasion. Let us suppose that State A complains that plans announced by State B to increase its tariffs threaten so to reduce A's exports as to cause widespread unemployment. In this situation, the international economic authority should attempt to find an acceptable and effective solution. Upon discovering that the real reason behind B's plan to raise its tariffs is the weak condition of its currency, which the government hopes to bolster up by protecting its international position, a loan from the world bank or a currency agreement prepared and sponsored by the economic authority might provide an effective remedy, ending the trouble before it reaches the danger point. There are numerous precedents for such beneficial corrective action undertaken by international institutions, both within the League of Nations and elsewhere.

Corrective Measures of a Legal Nature. In its effort to eradicate the causes of war, the world organization should not neglect the task of creating a better system of international law. All will admit that the law of nations is at present weak and unsatisfactory. Representing the least common denominator of agreement among sovereign, independent states, international law permits many of the relations between states to remain outside its orbit. Other relations are subject to law, but the rules have become obsolete. It must be evident that so long as the law is weak, the control of power among states cannot be effective. So it is a matter of real urgency for the world organization to set up procedures and undertake activities designed to modernize international law and extend its scope and, in addition, to devise some regular means whereby in the future this law may be kept in step with a rapidly evolving world.

At present there are two ways whereby the nations can make new laws—custom and treaty. Custom has proved to be an unsatisfactory method of creating or changing law, both within the state and in the international community, for it is slow and uncertain. More progress can be expected by extending the method of making new law by treaty. A third method has been proposed by some post-war planners, namely, a scheme for veritable international legislation, whereby the General Assembly, acting together with the Executive Council, would be empowered to pass laws which automatically become binding on the members without the necessity of ratification by each state. This suggestion has much merit; international legislation is of course greatly needed. But this particular proposal has little chance of being accepted today. It is too early to expect member states, except within certain limited fields, to forego the right to discuss proposed treaties in their national parliaments as a prelude to ratification. It seems certain that in our search for procedures suitable for creating or modifying legislation we must still depend mainly on the treaty method, despite its obvious weaknesses. When the law needs to be changed or extended, the world authority will undoubtedly call a conference of interested states to consider the matter. After careful study and preparation, a law-making treaty will be drawn up and submitted to the interested states, becoming binding on the parties when ratified. This is very different from veritable international legislation. It takes too much time. Moreover, its results often prove disappointing, for sometimes representatives of states, in order not to appear obstructive, are inclined to sign a draft treaty at the conference, although well aware that the treaty-making authorities at home may long delay ratification or even withhold it altogether.

These are serious obstacles, but they can be overcome by an alert international organization equipped with appropriate procedures. Here again much could be done if the Great Powers would take the lead. One way for them to carry out their responsibility would be to grant greater authority and wider jurisdiction to the Permanent Court of International Justice. No better step toward this goal could be found than to generalize the practice of submitting all international justiciable disputes to the Court, for the Court, thus strengthened, could do much to extend the field of international law and to keep it in harmony with the times.

Another promising proposal for the strengthening of international law is to give the world authority the right, and even the duty, to deal with violations of international law, as suggested in the *International Law of the Future*.[20] Such procedures, taken in connection with the obligatory arbitration of justiciable disputes, may do much to overcome one of the greatest enemies of law among nations, namely, the temptation for states, especially powerful states, to use international law merely as a weapon of power politics. As the power of a court is substituted for the discretion of the foreign office, the range of law will tend to broaden.

Supposing that appropriate procedures have been set up, how could the world authority, by improving and strengthening international law, aid in preventing trouble and friction? I can suggest by an example or two how it could be done. One notable branch of international law now rendered obsolete by events is that of neutrality. The very backbone of neutrality is now broken, namely, the principle that if war breaks out between two states all others must adopt an attitude of impartiality and non-intervention. No world order can hope effectually to stop war so long as such a principle remains on the books.[21] It should be replaced by the principle of universal responsibility, already referred to, implemented by rules requiring action to be taken by the proper authority against the aggressor. The clear establishment of such duties on the part of each state is essential if the concept of the indivisibility of

[20] "Proposal 8. (1) Acting upon its own initiative or at the request of any State, the Executive Council should have power to take cognizance of any alleged failure by a State to carry out its obligations under international law, and if the failure is established to take such action as it may deem to be necessary for the protection of the interests of the Community of States." *International Conciliation*, April 1944, pp. 267, 271-272, 334ff.

[21] Lord Halifax, in his address to the American Society of International Law, April 29, 1944, said, "We have found that no neutrality will avail by itself to protect the interests of a neutral or even to secure its national existence." *New York Times*, April 30, 1944.

peace is not to remain a pious aspiration. Precise rules are needed, too, to implement the principle that force must remain a monopoly of the community, and to deal with freedom of the air, economic discrimination, the government of backward peoples, and many other problems, some of them old, some new. A world organization alive to the need for rules to govern these and other matters now inadequately covered by international law or even totally outside its scope could do much toward building a better world.

Corrective Measures Concerning Disarmament. There is ample opportunity in other fields for such corrective or prophylactic action. For example, a particular state may be greatly disturbed when its neighbor embarks on a vast arms policy, as by starting to build a great navy. So frightened may an exposed state become that it will immediately seek new allies or itself decide to acquire new weapons. This is a well-known feature of balance-of-power politics. It may well precipitate a general arms race and a frantic search for allies by both sides, opening the precipitous road to war. This is substantially what happened toward the close of the nineteenth century following the Kaiser's fatal decision to construct the great German battle-fleet.

At this point there is still no "dispute," only trouble, grave trouble. What can the international authority do to meet it? Although the situation is delicate, it is not yet beyond repair, provided that the states of the world remain faithful to the principle of joint and several responsibility. Perhaps the matter can be settled through a general arms convention. If the government planning an increase in its arms establishment has acted because it is itself afraid of some future aggression, menacing its frontiers or other vital interests, it may be satisfied if it is given a treaty of guarantee. If the United States and Great Britain had given to France, after 1918, the guarantee against renewed German aggression which Mr. Wilson had promised, the French government might not have felt impelled to maintain a great conscript army, build the Maginot Line, and seek new allies. As the world organization gains in authority and prestige, so that confidence in its ability to prevent war becomes general, it could the more easily persuade a state about to give way to the "great fear" that it is not in any real danger. Seen in this light, arms reduction must be regarded as more a consequence than a cause of security.

We see, then, that the intervention of the world authority may prove successful if the government planning vast arms increases is motivated merely by the fear of attack. But if its real aim is aggression, expansion or conquest, such merely corrective efforts will probably prove futile. For such a government, the world authority must keep in its arsenal more persuasive weapons, which are discussed in Section 3 under the heading "Suppressive Measures."

Other Corrective Measures. There are many other opportunities for corrective intervention by the world authority. With respect to some of these, successful international action may have little *direct* effect, but the cumulative contribution of all these measures should be great. In this way a much better atmosphere for peaceful relations among states should be created. The common fight on famine and epidemics and the effort to control dangerous drugs and to end inhuman conditions, can make a real contribution toward the attainment of this goal. Similarly, the attempt to eliminate poisonous propaganda, the fight on nationalism and race hatred, or, to put it in positive terms, the effort to promote mutual understanding and better feeling among peoples by every available means, should all have an important part in the general drive for an ordered world.

2. RESTRICTIVE MEASURES

There is always the possibility that the world authority, despite all its efforts, may not prevent an actual dispute from breaking out between states. If the leaders of a given state consider that "sacred rights" have been violated by another state and if they enjoy the support of an aroused public opinion, the critical point will have been reached. At this juncture, since the dispute has actually come, the crucial responsibility now devolving on the world authority—above all on the Executive Council—is to see that the matter does not end in a resort to force. Here is the great test for the basic principle of the new organization, the one already referred to—that any use of force is of immediate concern to the entire community of nations. One way to discharge this responsibility is to take certain measures, now to be described, which may be called *restrictive measures*. Success here depends mainly on those with leadership and power.

Peaceful settlement. The first of these restrictive measures, designed to prevent the conflict from becoming dangerous to world peace, is to induce the parties to submit it for settlement by some respected commission or tribunal. This kind of solution is especially adapted to the so-called "justiciable" dispute. This refers to controversy between states over questions involving their legal rights, for instance if it turns on the interpretation of a treaty or on an issue of international law. Such justiciable controversies should go almost automatically for final adjudication to an arbitral court or judicial tribunal, preferably the Permanent Court of International Justice. It is proposed, therefore, that each state, upon joining the new world organization, should agree to submit all its legal controversies to obligatory settlement in this way. This would be an effective step toward the collective control of power.

At one time over forty states, including most of the Great Powers, had accepted the obligatory jurisdiction of the World Court for some or all categories of their legal disputes. The United States, on the other hand, not only refused to join the World Court, but insisted on inserting so many reservations in its arbitration treaties as to make the treaties almost illusory. The United States now has another opportunity to resume its nineteenth century role as the champion of international arbitration, and to take the lead in a movement which has enormous possibilities for the advancement of peace. If successful, this movement would assure the peaceful disposition of a great number of disputes, and at the same time, by extending the competence and prestige of the World Court, would enable that body to develop and extend the present inadequate system of international law, much as the common law courts did for the advancement of the British common law.

For a state to say, in advance, that it will permit some superior court to adjudicate its legal rights as against another state, may be a difficult decision. In the long run, however, such a state will gain immensely from this step. All other states will also be making the same "sacrifice." The advantage to all will be the chance to live in a community thereby greatly stabilized and strengthened. Nor will the "sacrifice" be as great as one might imagine. Looking back on our own history, it is doubtful whether we would have suffered any measurable loss by submitting all our legal controversies to arbitration, and we would have gained great long-range benefits by helping construct a more peaceful world.

The greatest danger to peace ordinarily arises, it is true, not from the justiciable, but rather from the non-justiciable dispute. In such a case the complaining state bases its case not on an alleged violation of its legal rights, but rather on what it considers an injury to its *interests*. In other words, the dispute concerns a matter left by international law to the independent judgment of the sovereign state; it arises out of a "domestic question." For instance, State A may object to a decision taken by its neighbor, State B, greatly to increase the size of its air force. Or, to raise a question of great delicacy but one which cannot be lightly brushed aside, State A may be protesting against State B's immigration policy, specifically a law excluding from its frontiers all persons of a certain race, the citizens of State A belonging to this race. In this situation there is clearly no dispute over legal rights, for State B is entirely within its rights (unless a treaty is involved) in increasing its arms establishment or changing its immigration laws, and thus has committed no breach of a legal duty toward State A. Here is indeed a difficult situation. How is the world authority to deal with it?

Here, again, restrictive measures may be able to end the dispute. No difficulty will arise if the parties are willing to submit the matter to some superior body for final settlement. There are many instances of such action. Even before the League of Nations was founded, states occasionally gave arbitral tribunals authority to settle a controversy *ex aequo et bono*, i.e., according to equitable rather than legal principles. Under the League system, many non-justiciable disputes were disposed of successfully by the Council which, as a political body, was better equipped than a court to deal with certain "political" questions.

The situation becomes more dangerous if the parties cannot be induced to accept the advice or decision of a third party. To meet this eventuality, two quite different restrictive procedures have been suggested. Under the first plan, the international authority would have power to take full jurisdiction of the dispute and to hand down an obligatory decision. Thus, according to a proposal made in *The International Law of the Future*, the Executive Council, if unanimous (the interested parties not being entitled to vote), could give a decision having binding force.[22] Under the League procedure, too, the Council could consider a non-justiciable dispute, but the proposal just mentioned would go beyond the procedures of the Covenant in two respects. First, this new proposal gives the Council jurisdiction over *any* dispute, and not merely one held to be "liable to lead to a rupture." This is an excellent innovation, for the proper definition of the term, "liable to lead to a rupture," was the

[22] *International Conciliation*, April 1944, pp. 275, 361ff.

cause of much quibbling, and opened the way to cavil and evasion. Second, the decision is stated to be absolutely *binding* on all parties, while under the League system the report and recommendation of the Council, if unanimous, was not binding, although no member of the League could legally go to war against any state (including a party to the dispute) which accepted the Council's recommendation. Under the new proposal, in contrast, the Executive Council, under its general power to deal with a state's failure to carry out its obligations under international law, could take the necessary measures to ensure the execution of its award in case any member refused to comply.

Much as the international community would profit from some effective method of disposing of political disputes, this proposal would appear to attempt too much. Judging by past experience, it is going to be difficult enough to induce states—especially great states—to submit even their legal disputes, without reservations, to obligatory adjudication. To expect them to go further and agree in advance, in ignorance of unforeseen and unforeseeable circumstances, to allow some political body to hand down an edict which, on threat of international action, must be obeyed, would seem to be quixotic. If the new world order is to become a real force for peace, the states must undoubtedly forego some of their traditional independence of action, but to ask of them such an unprecedented "sacrifice" at the present time would be risking too much.

The alternative procedure, known technically as "conciliation," would seem to be a more realistic method of handling the non-justiciable dispute, although it cannot guarantee a satisfactory solution in all cases. According to this method, the world authority would be directed to intervene with all the prestige and influence at its command, but without authority to hand down a binding decision. If it believes the peace of the world to be threatened, the international authority, acting either at the instance of an individual state or on its own responsibility, would take cognizance of the dispute, appoint a committee to study the situation, and make an advisory report as to the best solution of the matter. The world authority would then try to induce the parties to accept this carefully prepared solution, which should consider the legitimate demands of all interested parties and also the cause of world peace.

In this attempt to bring the disputing states together, the world authority could enlist the friendly mediation of certain states, especially those of the same region, and at the same time bring to bear the influence of world public opinion. It must be admitted, however, if we are to judge by past experience, that it would be unwise to expect too much from the attempt to enlist public opinion, for dynamic leaders bent on attaining some end considered of vital importance may pay little heed to what other peoples think of their policies. States are in fact much more responsive to their own public opinion than to world opinion, a fact which the world authority should take into account.

Such authoritative interposition on the part of an alert, well-informed and experienced international authority, conscious of its responsibility and responsive to the needs of world peace, may be sufficient to meet the crisis, and there are numerous recorded cases of successful international efforts of this character. It may turn out, however, that all the foregoing efforts—both corrective and restrictive measures—will prove unavailing. The state whose arms policy has caused apprehension to its neighbor may insist on its "sovereign" right to complete its plans. The government whose immigration policy has offended a proud and sensitive race may remain intransigent. What is to be done now? Shall the world authority remain with folded arms as recriminations continue and public opinion becomes exacerbated?

If, at this crucial stage, the international authority should cease all further attempts to keep the peace, the result might be disastrous. It was one of the signal weaknesses of the League of

JOHN B. WHITTON

Nations Covenant, that in case of a dispute found by the Council to arise out of a matter solely within the domestic jurisdiction of one of the parties, the latter were in principle left to their own resources, in fact with the right to go to war within three months after such a finding by the Council. The new covenant should close this gap. The Executive Council must maintain its jurisdiction of the dispute, never halting in its search for a solution. Here is a real test for responsible leadership. Perhaps, in spite of all efforts, a definitive remedy for the trouble may not be found. The failure to solve the difficulty at once need not, however, lead to a war. Some of our most acrimonious disputes with Britain lasted for years without ending in forceful measures. This was true of Cleveland's sharp dispute with Lord Salisbury over the Venezuelan boundary, the controversy over the Northwest Frontier popularized in the aggressive slogan, "54-40 or fight," and the long drawn-out diplomatic battle over the trans-isthmian canal. But in order further to safeguard the world against a breakdown in its new peace structure, the principle of monopoly of force in the international community must be implemented. Thus each member, upon its adherence to the world organization, must promise to abstain from the use of force for the settlement of any international controversy. Another necessary obligation is the promise to refrain from intervention in the internal and external affairs of other states. We have found it feasible and desirable to accept such a self-denying ordinance as part of our Pan-American policy, and there is no good reason why this tenet of the Good Neighbor policy should not be universalized. If respected, such rules would operate to prevent war; if violated, such obligations would at least facilitate the task of the world authority in determining the aggressor, especially if accompanied in time of crisis by the imposition on the parties of appropriate interim measures. These matters are discussed in Section 3.

The net result of these comprehensive and graduated measures, some corrective, some restrictive, may be this: that while there is no immediate solution for the trouble or the controversy, at least *there will be no war*. This is of the utmost importance. True, the persistence of trouble spots is to be deplored, but if war can be prevented, the resulting benefit to the world will be immeasurable. This is elementary. Moreover, if the world authority continues its efforts to discover an acceptable compromise, it may still succeed. An atmosphere favorable to such a result will be created by the general knowledge that force for the settlement of the controversy will not be tolerated. But if, despite all efforts, the peace cannot be preserved because some state decides to resort to arms, the world authority must then be prepared to use *forceful* measures to suppress unlawful violence. It is at this point that all the basic principles outlined above must come into play: the world authority must be alive to its general responsibility for peace; each state must recognize that the matter is its own immediate concern; the Executive Council must provide the leadership and power, which it must exercise in accordance with rules of law. Finally, every effort must be made, by effective action against the aggressor, to reestablish the principle that force is an absolute monopoly of the world authority. In short, the world authority must at this point resort to "suppressive measures."

3. SUPPRESSIVE MEASURES

One outstanding lesson left us by the bitter experiences following the last war is that while force alone is an inadequate guarantee of peace, nevertheless, as a last resort, we must be ready to repel force with force. For despite the most strenuous efforts of the world authority, some recalcitrant state may try the test of arms. Thus it is not enough to provide an international judge and legislator; we must also have an international policeman. "No rational man or woman today can question the fact," said Sumner Welles in 1943 at Toronto, "that had the nations of the world been able to create some effective form of international organization in the years that followed the close of the last World War, and had they been able to bulwark that organization with judicial and police powers, the devastating tragedy which humanity today is undergoing would have been avoided."[23]

The creation and maintenance of a collective force for repressive purposes is beset with many difficulties, as will appear from the pages which follow. In general, the fundamental difficulty is that while a police force is usually an integral part of a well-organized system of government with legislative, executive, and judicial departments endowed with authority, in the international field these institutions exist only imperfectly or in embryo, and cannot be created overnight by the wave of a postwar planner's wand. This weakness in the international structure merely reflects the lack among the nations of any real social cohesion or community spirit, although this is an effect as well as a cause of the embryonic state of its governmental institutions.

There are other difficulties which involve two of the fundamental principles already referred to, namely, the necessity for power and the necessity for the control of power. The international force must be sufficiently powerful to overcome the aggressor, but at the same time so checked and limited that it will not constitute a temptation to the ambitious or a menace to the weak. An overwhelming force would be feared; a mere token force would be futile.

If the following suggestions for an enforcing agency appear to some as too cautious, it should be remembered that they are framed in the light of the realities of international politics. For the present, I do not believe in the feasibility of an "international police force," if the term is taken to mean a separate world force distinct from national forces. More workable would be a system of collective enforcement based either on economic sanctions or, when needed, on temporarily mobilized

[23] *New York Times*, February 27, 1943.

forces contributed by the individual states, or on economic and military sanctions combined. Such military forces would be used in a crisis in accordance with definite rules, under the command of a centralized general staff, and so far as possible in line with plans drawn up in advance. Such economic and military sanctions will now be considered in more detail.

Economic Sanctions. If the dreaded crisis comes, prompt measures must be taken to meet force with force. And the quicker the mobilization of the collective measures, the easier will be the task. This is a time for resolution and firmness, for, as Professor Rappard has said, "Is not the greatest danger to peace an excessive love of peace and the consequent softness and unpreparedness against aggression?"[24] This brings us to the major problem—the nature and function of the international force to be used in such an emergency.

This force need not in every case take the form of military power.[25] At times mere political pressure from powerful states may be adequate. At other times financial and economic measures would be sufficient to end a threat of aggression. The failure of economic sanctions in the one *cause célèbre* of League experience—the effort to halt Italy's aggressive attack on Abys-

[24] William E. Rappard, "Switzerland," *Transactions of the Grotius Society*, Vol. 28 (London, 1943), p. 85.

[25] The variety of measures at the disposal of the sanctions-enforcing states is shown by the following quotation from *The International Law of the Future*: "A State might be asked to sever diplomatic relations with a State using or threatening to use force; or it might be asked to discontinue exchanges of goods; or it might be asked to withhold any kind of assistance; or it might be asked to supply military forces, or to permit the passage of such forces across its territory; or it might be asked to take other measures. Nor is it to be assumed that all States would be in the same position with respect to an actual or threatened use of force; measures might be prescribed for a certain State which other States would not be in a position to take.... Yet the duty would rest upon all States, and no State would be free to frustrate the efforts of the Community of States by relying upon the nineteenth-century law of neutrality." *Op. cit.*, April 1944, p. 309.

sinia—has relegated to the background a discussion of such measures as part of the proposed post-war machinery of peace enforcement. But it is important to note that in certain conditions the economic weapon has formidable potentialities and may be sufficiently effective to restore peace. Long before the creation of the League of Nations, certain powers, acting singly or in concert, used economic weapons to gain their objectives. And, in light of the League experience, there is every reason to believe that if strong economic sanctions had been resolutely and promptly applied against Italy, Mussolini would have been forced to abandon his African adventure.

Thus, in certain conditions, depending on the economic and geographical position of the aggressor state, the length of the war, and other factors, the economic arm may be effective; in other conditions it may prove futile. It is therefore essential to provide for the possible application of stronger measures.[26] This means that all members—and this applies particularly to the United States, without whose support the system will surely fail—should squarely face the possibility that, in case of need, they must be ready and willing to use actual military force to repel unlawful force. This is a corollary of the third basic principle mentioned at the beginning of this chapter, namely, that an effective world organization cannot be created without provision for power. By frankly accepting this obligation without equivocation, the states of the world would take an immense step toward preventing the rise of some new Hitler. And the more effectively they meet this responsibility, the less chance will there be that their collective force will ever have to be used.

---

[26] See E. H. Carr, *The Twenty Years Crisis* (London: Macmillan, 1940), p. 152: "The bitter lesson of 1935-36 was needed to drive home the truth that in sanctions, as in war, the only motto is 'all or nothing,' and that economic power is impotent if the military weapon is not held in readiness to support it. Power is indivisible; and the military and economic weapons are merely different instruments of power."

INSTITUTIONS OF WORLD ORDER
MILITARY SANCTIONS

Assuming that collective military action may ultimately be required to repress an illegal resort to force, what should be its nature and organization? There are in general four alternative proposals for such an international authority; namely:

1. A veritable "international police force."
2. A quota plan.
3. A separate air force.
4. A temporarily mobilized force.

1. *A Veritable "International Police Force."* The most radical, and, I believe, the least practicable scheme, calls for an integral collective force, divorced from the control of individual states and placed at the disposal of the world authority. The collectivity would have a monopoly of all heavy armaments, including every facility for modern war. National states would be required to relinquish the possession and use of these facilities, transferring them to the world authority so as to form an overwhelming collective force, and accepting for themselves total disarmament with the exception of local militia with light equipment. These would be retained for domestic policing purposes.

This integral police force does not appear to be feasible. True, over 70 per cent of the American people, according to public opinion polls, favor the establishment of an "international police force," but apparently those who so voted had only a vague idea of the nature of such a force, and probably were merely expressing their approval of some kind of collective action to maintain peace. From all indications, the centralization of such enormous power would be feared by most states. Furthermore, disarmament would hardly be acceptable to those living in the cruel memory of past aggressions. Nor would many states entrust their future security to such untried and uncertain international machinery. Finally, there are almost insuperable obstacles to the success of the scheme which concern the command, recruitment, disposition and supply of such a force.

2. *The Quota Plan.* A second scheme is the "Quota Plan," an example of which was the system proposed by the French Government at the Disarmament Conference in 1932, and approved by nine other governments. Each state would be permitted to maintain its own military establishment, though considerably reduced, and, in addition, would be required to furnish special contingents, the size of which would be determined on the basis of relative wealth and strength, to form a separate international force to be held at the disposal of the world authority.

The Culbertson Plan offers an interesting variation from this quota plan, for it would permit each state to retain a sizable military establishment, definitely limited to a certain proportion of the world's total forces, but would also set up, as a separate international police, a mobile corps recruited solely from the small states. This force, operating under the direct control of the world authority, would be concentrated at strategic points so as to command areas of possible trouble. Neither this plan nor the French plan has much chance of adoption, for few powers would be willing to reduce their national forces in reliance on such radical, untried schemes.

3. *A Separate Air Force.* According to a third plan, the world authority would be granted a monopoly of a type of force found by experience to be particularly effective, namely, the air arm. Each state would keep its forces, other than the air forces, considerably reduced in size and to be used only against domestic disorder or international aggression. The enforcement of peace would thus depend mainly on an overwhelming international air force, recruited from the individual states, and operating from some 50 air bases at strategic points throughout the world. This force would be ready to act in any emergency, attempting to end any aggression promptly, but at least holding

the fort until the arrival of the land and sea forces of the peace-enforcing nations.

The plan for a separate air force for use by the world authority is probably little more acceptable than the plan first mentioned above—a veritable international police force. Military and civil aviation are so closely integrated, and the value and potentialities of both are so vital to the national interest, as is shown by current discussions of air rivalry after this war, that most states, for these reasons alone, would insist on retaining full control of aviation production and operation. Nevertheless Soviet Russia is reported to have proposed an international air force at the Dumbarton Oaks Conference.

4. *A Temporarily Mobilized Force.* It is possible, of course, that some day the international community may set up an international sheriff backed by a separate force, created through quotas contributed by individual states, or even a special air arm such as has just been described—but certainly not in the near future. For the present, the repression of illegal force will probably be left to a temporarily mobilized force made up of contingents contributed *ad hoc* by individual states and acting under the direction of a combined general staff. Each state would thus retain its national forces, land, sea and air, but considerably reduced by agreement, for the sake of both economy and security. Judging by past experience, however, the task of finding acceptable quota reductions will not be easy.

In case of a threat to peace—which may be not only an out-and-out attack on a given state but a mere violation of an arms agreement, if sufficiently serious—individual states would contribute such armed force as may be required by the particular circumstances of the case. While the contribution of small powers should not be underestimated, the main burden would ordinarily fall upon the Great Powers. This underscores once again the need for their continued cooperation and the necessity for assuring the use of their power only in accordance with

JOHN B. WHITTON

rules of law.[27] In some cases, an all-out effort by many or all peace-enforcing states might be necessary; in other cases—for example, an outbreak between two small maritime states—action by a single fleet in the name of the world authority should be sufficient to restore order.

Plans for the use of such a temporarily mobilized force must be worked out in advance by a general staff responsible to the world authority. Mr. Churchill, in his speech at Harvard University on September 6, 1943, stated that the Combined Chiefs of Staff Committee directing Anglo-American strategy in this war might well be continued after the war, "probably for many years."[28] A better plan would be the immediate creation of a Supreme War Council of the United Nations as the nucleus of a post-war security committee, drawing up even now definite plans for policing the world in the future. An important task of such a Council would be to supervise the continued disarmament of proved aggressors. The task of this post-war Supreme War Council should be greatly facilitated by the present close collaboration among the forces of the several nations. These are fighting today in close cooperation, often as a single force under a single command. And as the war in Europe will probably end some time before final victory in the Far East, United Nations forces can gain invaluable experience for the permanent task of maintaining peace as they police together the ex-enemy or reconquered lands for longer or shorter periods,

[27] Professor Jessup envisages a solution of this kind. "It would not be surprising if the Big Four were accepted as the law-enforcing group. They might be unwilling to surrender their power but nevertheless be *willing to harness it to the needs of an organized international community.* They might agree not to use it except in accordance with the decision of the international organization. When they did act, they might do so through a Combined General Staff which would delegate authority to task forces of the state most strategically located" (italics supplied). Philip C. Jessup, "UNRRA, Sample of World Organization," *Foreign Affairs*, Vol. 22, April 1944, p. 373.

[28] *New York Times*, September 7, 1943.

to supervise demobilization, keep order, and prevent rearmament and renewed aggression.

ARE SANCTIONS WORKABLE? (QUIS CUSTODIET?)

The application of sanctions, whether economic or military, involves a number of difficult problems, one of the gravest of which is expressed in the Latin maxim, *Quis custodiet ipsos custodes?* In other words, by what method may the sanctions-enforcing states be induced to live up to their obligations? This question involves two problems: (1) How may we ensure that the international organization will itself authorize the use of military force, actually calling on individual states for their contribution? (2) If such a call comes, how ensure that the member states will live up to their previous agreement, and will use their economic and military power to support the world authority in its effort to prevent or repress aggression?

These questions are fundamental. In its crucial tests, the League of Nations failed to uphold the peace largely because the Council did not even order the imposition of really effective sanctions. This failure was due mainly to obstructionist tactics employed by British and French leaders who, for various reasons, were not disposed to use strong economic, not to mention military, measures.

There is no simple solution for these problems. We are perhaps justified in hoping that world leaders have actually learned a lesson from the failures of the past 25 years and their cruel, almost fatal consequences (see above, pages 69-70, 75). This lesson demonstrates clearly and eloquently that the new world authority must promptly order out the guard when aggression threatens. It also proves that, unless the peace machinery is to fail, national leaders must heed the call when the world authority enlists their cooperation. This is particularly important because sanctions will deter a potential aggressor only if it is clear in advance that the machinery for enforcing peace

JOHN B. WHITTON

can be expected to work and that the proposed aggression is therefore too hazardous to be risked.

The danger that the world authority may not act in a crisis is due in part to its peculiar composition. The Executive Council will be necessarily composed of politicians and diplomats, their personnel constantly changing and subject to the control of more or less temporary governments. The latter may be more interested in local politics, domestic problems, or selfish national aims than in the specific aggression. This was proved to be the case more than once between 1920 and 1939.

The solution may be found in some method designed to give the right of decision on the application of sanctions not to a political body, but to a *judicial* body acting under rules of law. Dr. Arthur O. Lovejoy, in an address given before the American Political Science Association on January 23, 1944, suggests a plan of this nature which is worthy of serious consideration. He believes that the decision to apply sanctions should be divorced from the field of politics and diplomacy, so that once the aggression has been determined the application of repressive measures would be as nearly as possible automatic. This would be accomplished by leaving the crucial decision as to whether a state is guilty of an unlawful use of force to a permanent, non-political and judicial commission or court, empowered to impose interim measures (described in the next section). Upon the declaration of that body that a state has resorted to force illegally, every state would be under a "legal obligation to provide forthwith such forces as may be necessary to compel obedience to the judicial commission's injunction and to impose such economic or other penalties upon the offender as that commission may decree." If the member states could be thus assured in advance that the international repressive action is not to be a mere matter of political expediency, "there should be less reluctance to bind themselves to cooperate in the equal and uniform enforcement of a brief and simple code of fundamental laws of international

INSTITUTIONS OF WORLD ORDER

conduct, agreed upon in advance and requiring for their application in specific cases only a clear-cut and impartial determination by a judicial body of the fact that a state is violating one of those laws."[29]

DETERMINATION OF AGGRESSOR

Whether the crucial decision as to the illegal use of force is made by an impartial, non-political body such as we have just described, or is left, as we have proposed, to the Executive Council of the world authority, it will be necessary to lay down in advance certain rules for the determination of the aggressor. To judge by past experience, it would be unwise to make such rules too rigid, or to attempt to cover in detailed terms every possible contingency. In place of such rigid formulas as were found in the Geneva Protocol or the famous "Russian Definition of Aggression," it would seem preferable to agree upon a few rather simple principles, leaving it to the world authority to apply them to each particular case.

In actual practice, the problem of determining the aggressor did not prove to be nearly as difficult as had been feared. Confounding its critics, the League of Nations promptly declared Italy to be an aggressor after it had attacked Abyssinia in violation of its commitments. Nevertheless the adoption of certain general rules would considerably facilitate the task of the world authority in this matter. In accordance with the general principle that the collectivity must be given a monopoly of the use of force, no state may use force for the purpose of settling its disputes. Each state must renounce the so-called right of intervention in the affairs of other states, as the United States has done vis-à-vis its Latin American neighbors. This would not prevent *collective* intervention in case conditions within a particular state became so intolerable as to constitute a menace to world peace. At Moscow the four Great Powers took a step in this direction, agreeing "that after the termination of hostilities

[29] Memorandum, privately circulated, by Professor Arthur O. Lovejoy.

they will not employ their military forces within the territories of other states except for the purposes envisaged in this declaration and after joint consultation."[30]

It is impossible to draw up in advance any definition to cover all possible future aggressions and it is more practicable to approach the matter from the point of view of procedures, even irrespective of the merits of the particular dispute. Pending a consideration of the matter by the appropriate world authority, the latter might impose interim or provisional measures of a conservative nature on the parties involved. Thus, if two states have ordered their troops to march against each other, the commission could declare an armistice and direct both sides to withdraw their troops behind a given line. Such action was taken with complete success when the League Council, in 1925, halted an incipient war between Greece and Bulgaria. Any state violating the terms of such conservative measures could be deemed the aggressor.

DO SANCTIONS MEAN WAR?

Before leaving this discussion of international sanctions, we must consider a fundamental objection sometimes urged against such measures. It is said that while the expressed object of military sanctions is to do away with war, in actual practice their result is to legalize war. For, in the attempt to suppress private wars, collective or police wars are legalized. This argument cannot stand up under closer scrutiny. In the first place, provision for a strong collective force should actually lead not to more war but to less, for if the potential aggressor is convinced in advance that he is sure to be met by a greatly superior force, he will think twice before resorting to arms. "What paralysed sanctions in 1935-36," says E. H. Carr, "was the common knowledge that the League Powers were not prepared to use the military weapon."[31]

[30] *American Journal of International Law*, Vol. 38, January 1944, Supplement, p. 6.
[31] E. H. Carr, *op. cit.* (*supra*, n. 25), p. 152, n. 2.

INSTITUTIONS OF WORLD ORDER

Secondly, it must be understood that a collective war undertaken as a police action is quite a different thing, both in nature and effect, from a "private" war between two states. States acting together to repress illegal force are like the policeman who fires on the burglar; they thus act as agents of the community and in the common interest. But the state illegally attacking another is like the man who shoots his neighbor in revenge; they are both acting on their own, and to the detriment of the general welfare. Even more important—with states as with individuals—individual aggression in the long run leads to more violence, collective police action to less.

These proposals for a collective force will hardly satisfy the more ambitious post-war planners. But in the light of the realities of international relations, they may be considered as a practicable middle-ground solution. To expect much more at the present time would, it must be repeated, be quixotic. The states of the world are not yet ready to grant very great powers to a central authority, and even if they were, such powers could not be exercised successfully until the international society had developed greater cohesion and a stronger spirit of solidarity. In an effort to take these realities into account, I have suggested a type of international force which, while strong enough to serve as a bulwark of peace, does not demand from individual states such sacrifices as would deter them from joining the new world organization. A veritable international police force is certainly utopian. The old League of Nations sanctions scheme is too weak. Responsibility and power must be furnished mainly by the Great Powers, acting together as trustees for the peace of the world, but their vast strength must be exerted within the Executive Council, governed by definite rules, supervised by a General Assembly representing governments, and checked by a "Third Chamber" reflecting public opinion.

On the assumption that it is both indispensable and possible to submit all states, great and small, to a "rule of law," I have enumerated certain fundamental principles for the new world organization—responsibility for peace, leadership in maintaining it, power to enforce it, controls to prevent an abuse of power, the limitation of state sovereignty and, most important, a grant to the world authority of the sole right to use force. Then, attempting to implement the principles just mentioned, I described the main agencies of the new world organization—General Assembly, Executive Council, Third Chamber, World Court, Secretariat, Peace Bureau. Finally, I have described the activities of the foregoing agencies. The world organization should be equipped to undertake preventive, corrective, and repressive measures, the first two to meet trouble before it becomes critical, the third to stop aggression in a crisis by the use of collective coercion. Here, then, is a suggested organization whereby the "rule of law" among states can become a reality. These suggestions are in accord with the advice given recently by Secretary of State Hull when he outlined an international organization to maintain peace and prevent aggression:

"Such an organization must be based upon firm and binding obligations that the member nations will not use force against each other and against any other nation except in accordance with the arrangements made. It must provide for the maintenance of adequate forces to preserve peace and it must provide the institutions and procedures for calling this force into action to preserve peace. But it must provide more than this. It must provide for an international court for the development and application of law to the settlement of international controversies which fall within the realm of law, for the development of machinery for adjusting controversies to which the field of law has not yet been extended, and for other institutions for a changing world with new problems and new interests."[32]

[32] *New York Times*, April 10, 1944.

4. Economics and Peace

BY FRANK D. GRAHAM

THE famous dictum of Clausewitz, that war is but the continuation of a national policy hitherto pursued by other means, assumes that national policy is essentially invidious and that the interest of any one nation can be served only at the expense of others. To Clausewitz the state was essentially a fighting agency, inevitably predatory toward its neighbors, and the only important question was as to the means by which the predation should be carried on. Changing conditions might make it expedient to filch rather than rob, to use guile rather than force, to supplant frank and brutal violence by chicane, but the end was eternally the same—the exploitation and eventual destruction of rival states to the aggrandizement of one's own. War, in the broad sense of the term, was the natural, the persistent, the inevitable, relationship between states. The role of the statesman, therefore, was merely to choose the most effective means for its prosecution. Such international business as was carried on, in the interval between military conflicts, was merely a milder form of war, partly a substitute and partly a preparation for imminent military conflict. All other states were regarded as alien or hostile to one's own; their gain was your loss and their loss was your gain. The national objective in international transactions was to overreach, to deceive, and to exploit.

The attitude of Clausewitz reflected the traditional, the immemorial, view of business as well as political relations. It is a matter of melancholy reflection that, until the advent of the classical economic writers in the late eighteenth and early nineteenth centuries, the notion of trade as mutually beneficial to the participants finds almost no place in man's ideas.[1] The

[1] Clausewitz was either not aware of the work of the classical economists or, more probably, viewed it with suspicious contempt as the

FRANK D. GRAHAM

ancients did not dignify trade by writing about it. Greek and Roman literature is all but completely devoid of discussions of economic topics, and what there is is largely on the administration of landed estates. Traders were despised as, at best, parasites, and their activities condemned as unworthy of anything but vituperation. With the decline of the Roman Empire trade was almost obliterated in western Europe, but it was revived, on what we would now call an international basis, in the Lombard and Hanseatic cities. There was, however, practically no theoretical discussion of commerce until, with the advent of the jealous, bellicose, and clearly articulated national states of early modern times, the lush literature of Mercantilism appeared.

THE PHILOSOPHY OF MERCANTILISM

No one can understand the international aspects of Mercantilism, in the period from the beginning of the sixteenth to near the end of the eighteenth century, unless he looks on Mercantilism as essentially a political rather than an economic phenomenon. It is true, particularly in the later phases, that Mercantilism was perversely pressed on nations in the belief that economic progress was thereby promoted. In essence, however, Mercantilism had a purely political motivation. Its rationale was the rationale of war. Militarily weak states got no shrift unless they could play on the jealousies that the strong felt for one another. Special, non-reciprocal, favors were exacted from the weak states by the various strong powers and, at the same time, the weak states were conjured to cancel such favors to others. In this embarrassing position, and in a regime of international anarchy, their survival, if possible at all, was a matter of lucky accident. The Great Powers, with some vicissitudes, grew greater, and the small powers disappeared.

Men were obsessed with the idea of *étatisme*; ruthless national aggression was the order of the day; and economic life

machinations of perfidious Albion. Cf. Carl von Clausewitz, *On War* (London: Kegan Paul, Trench, Trübner and Company, 1911).

was entirely conditioned by the real or supposed necessities of the state. The common man had no rights that the state was bound to respect and his economic well-being was, at best, a subordinate object of state endeavor. Low wages were, in fact, supposed to promote the competitive and the military power of the state. The function of the laborer was to work, obey, and fight; but never to enjoy. Sumptuary laws confined the spending of the niggardly wages of the worker to lines prescribed by the state. Coercion, inequality, and status were at once the means and the inevitable result of regimentation of the several populations for the perpetual conflict between the nations. The state was everything; the duty of the individual was to die for its aggrandizement; the chief end of man was to glorify the Prince and extend his regime.

It is no accident that it was in Britain that the political reaction against such slavery first strongly appeared and that men there dared to assert that the state was made for man and not the contrary. For Britain, behind its moat and fleet, was relatively safe, and could thus afford to indulge the luxury of domestic freedom. The leaven of Locke's political ideas presently seeped into economics, and Smith's *Wealth of Nations* is not only a polemic against the restraints of the Mercantilists, as ineffective to their own ends, but, much more important, is a repudiation of the whole *Weltanschauung* on which they were built.

For the first time in history the true philosophy of trade, the mutual benefit of the parties, was set forth in unmistakable terms. Condemning restraints on trade as a senseless frustration of the real interest of individuals, and of harm to the state, Smith called for a return to the "obvious and simple system of natural liberty." In this philosophy, the individual was exalted and the state played down; men were to choose their own ends and, apart from coercive action, realize them as best they could. Personal freedom, equality of opportunity, free contract, and fair competition, were held to be the means by which economic progress and the prosperity not only of citizens but of the state might best be advanced, and statesmen could regard without envy an increase in the wealth of other states as not inconsistent with the prosperity of their own.

Despite his castigation of Mercantilism, Smith was wary of dropping such restrictions on freedom as seemed to him necessary to the defense of England and, in the well-known passage in defense of the restrictive Navigation Laws, insisted that defense was of more importance than opulence. His attitude, no doubt, was that restraints on some forms of freedom were indispensable to the preservation of any freedom at all. It was, nevertheless, ominous, for it meant that circumstances might at any time require the maintenance of much of the panoply of Mercantilism.

Smith's triumph over the Mercantilists (which ran counter to his own expectations)[2] is almost entirely attributable to the relatively irenic conditions which developed after the fall of Napoleon, and the reversion, in the late nineteenth and in the twentieth centuries, to the international anarchy of earlier times more or less justified the restoration in international trading relations of all of the restrictive, discriminatory, and exploitative practices of Mercantilism.

The closing decades of the eighteenth century were marked by the break-up of hitherto aggressive empires. They were replaced by a congeries of smaller states eager to avoid war.[3] The spirit of nationalism, far from consolidating states, was then disruptive of them, and the small states into which the great em-

[2] "To expect . . . that the freedom of trade should ever be entirely restored in Great Britain is as absurd as to expect that an Oceana or Utopia should ever be established in it." Adam Smith, *Wealth of Nations*, Book IV, ch. 2.

[3] The French lost India and Canada to the British, who in turn lost their American colonies; the Spanish and Portuguese Empires disintegrated in the early decades of the nineteenth century; Turkey was losing most of its European possessions; and possessions of Austria, Holland, and Sweden had been lopped off. The Napoleonic episode reversed the process temporarily, but, after the fall of Napoleon, it was resumed.

pires were split were, as a matter of survival, disposed toward neutrality in any disputes that might arise between the remaining "Great Powers." Their attitude is expressed both in the "Farewell Address" of Washington, where he asserted that "the great rule of conduct for us in regard to foreign nations, is, *in extending our commercial relations*, to have with them as little political connection as possible," and in Jefferson's declaration for *"peace, commerce, and honest friendship with all nations*—entangling alliances with none." (Italics supplied.)

To both Washington and Jefferson it seemed quite possible to divorce trade from politics, to have close trading relationships and, therefore, interdependence with other nations, and yet to stay free of any political associations. They were associationists in economics and isolationists in politics. Their attitude was not irrational, *if* they could count upon a balance of power in Europe so nice as to nullify any threat to peace. But we should not forget that it was the pacifist Jefferson who made war in the interest of commerce, the free-trading Jefferson who established embargoes on trade, and the isolationist Jefferson who was ready, on occasion, to have the United States marry itself to the British fleet and nation.

The essence of trade is arm's length dealing, cool and dispassionate. If loyalty, friendship, fear, or hate enter into an exchange of goods, if it takes place on any basis other than that of strict neutrality, it is already political rather than economic. Neither of the parties to true trade can have any power to affect the decision of the other, whether by fear, force, or favor.[4] True trade therefore requires peace, but not love. Trade is possible, and desirable, between men and nations of the most diverse ideology and institutions, so long as neither party is able, or seeks, to coerce the other. Coercion is, on the other hand, the

[4] To paraphrase Smith, it may be said that one does not rely, for one's supply of meat, bread, and candlesticks, on the good-will of the butcher, baker, or candlestick maker, but solely on their self-interest. No merchant, on the other hand, who relies heavily upon the good-will of his customers, will long retain it.

core of *realpolitik* and, whenever it enters the economic scene, war in its incipient stages is already present.

That the aspirations of Washington and Jefferson were largely vindicated after the fall of Napoleon is attributable to the evolution of the environment in which such aspirations could alone be valid. Since favors cannot be shown by any nation to any other without provoking the resentment of the latter's rivals, the United States had early declared for a policy of equal treatment of foreigners. The new South American states, similarly motivated, followed our example, and a wholly new spirit was thus brought into international economic relations. Peaceful attitudes in commerce were expressed in the growth of a web of commercial treaties in which the contracting parties declared their readiness to renounce invidious policies. It is true that a conditional interpretation of the most-favored-nation clause was given to these treaties by many countries, ourselves included, but, even so, the treaties represented a great advance over the forthright discrimination that had hitherto prevailed. In 1846, Great Britain took the next and final step, and, in a wholehearted adoption of the principles of liberty, opened its ports to all the world in free and equal competition. In so doing, the British not only refused to discriminate among foreigners but went over to complete cosmopolitanism, and abandoned any intention, or desire, to distinguish in favor of their own citizens against the outside world. So liberal a policy did not fail to find a response and, though no country went as far as Britain in entirely removing protective tariff barriers, tariff walls were greatly lowered in a number of countries among which the United States was prominent.

All this was possible, however, only because the spirit of aggressive nationalism was, for the time being, inert. Men believed in the ultimate and, indeed, the early triumph of freedom. For half a century, following the defeat of Napoleon, such wars as occurred were almost exclusively internal conflicts fought to establish or maintain civil or sectional rights, or to

ECONOMICS AND PEACE

obtain freedom from domination by imperial governments, in areas which, rightly or wrongly, felt a sense of oppression. In the revolts in South America and in Greece, Belgium, Poland, Spain; in the widespread revolutions of 1848; in the uprisings in the various parts of what is now Italy; in the revolt of the Southern States of the American union—in all of these, this was the character of the conflict. There was little tendency for such wars to spread beyond the original area, since they offered no threat to any power but those initially engaged, and they were therefore regarded with complacence, or positive satisfaction, by any states which felt themselves to be actual or potential rivals of the challenged authority.

The lust after imperial power was not, of course, completely lacking. The British had lost the American colonies only to begin a new process of territorial accumulation. But they had been chastened by their American experience and, for the most part, built up their later empire in a spirit quite alien to, and infinitely better than, that which had prevailed before 1783.

The later British Empire is, in fact, the first in history that ever broke up without breaking down, no doubt because it was the first that ever essayed to prove that the bonds of freedom are stronger than any fetters. With some more or less conspicuous exceptions, Britain has been no menace to freedom. On the contrary, it has been as consistent a champion of freedom as any country in the world.[5]

The only worthwhile peace is a peace of freedom and justice, and not the least of British efforts toward such a peace was the maintenance of free trade in the home country for the better

---

[5] The most striking example of the salutary tone of British "imperialism" is the unchurlish acceptance at Westminister of the refusal of Eire either to take part in the present war or even to go as far as Portugal in giving the use of its ports to the United Nations. It could be maintained that the British attitude is attributable to prudence rather than magnanimity but the point is that a fire-eating imperialistic country would not be "prudent." If the case of Eire could become a generally accepted precedent, both within and without the British Empire, international armed conflict would be at an end.

part of a century. The great virtue of free trade is that it puts at the disposal of all nations, on equal terms, the natural resources with which they have been so unequally endowed by Nature. With trade free there is, therefore, no economic occasion for national envy or aggression. The cotton fields of Mississippi, the oil of Venezuela, the copper of Katanga, Canadian nickel, and Chinese tungsten are then the resources of other nations as well as of those in which they happen to lie. Confined to its own natural resources a Denmark, a Switzerland, a Sweden, or a Germany, would inevitably be poor. But, even with a none too flourishing international trade, they have been among the most prosperous countries in the world, and German economic health was impaired chiefly by self-inflicted wounds. Even with all that has been done to restrict international trade in recent decades, the so-called "Have" nations, against which the greatest complaints have been laid by those who intended aggression, did not retain their resources for their own exclusive use but put them on equal terms at the disposal of all the world. Irrational envy was practically the sole basis of the complaints brought against them.[6] The complaining powers them-

---

[6] Germany, for instance, always received much better treatment than, in power, she has ever accorded even to "favorites." The alleged lack of external markets for German goods was certainly no greater than for any other country, and the cry of lack of foreign exchange was a case of the wolf charging the lamb, down-current, with muddying the stream. Any shortage of foreign exchange in Germany arose because foreigners did not desire German exchange. But they were reluctant to acquire German exchange solely because the Germans refused to let them use it for any purpose but that which the Germans prescribed, and because the Germans indulged in continued confiscations of foreign holdings of marks. The Germans were short of foreign exchange because foreigners were intractable enough to resent, and avoid, robbery.

Whatever, on moral grounds, one may think of the German practices, they were not wholly stupid. This is more than can be said of many of our own. The Germans, albeit with evil intent, exorcised that fear of production and of imports under which all of their opponents, aside from Soviet Russia, so gravely suffered. They were, therefore, always short of foreign exchange in the sense in which any of us is denied much that we should like to have. This is a quite normal "shortage." Unless we can

ECONOMICS AND PEACE

selves were the instigators of the neo-Mercantilism which has recently run riot and, if their complaints are to be accepted at face value, must be held to have been hoist with their own petard.

The leaders in the free trade movement in England had been ardent proponents of peace, and they thought that free trade would bring peace in its train. They mistook symptoms for causes and put the cart before the horse. Restraints on trade are rather the reflection than the cause of a warlike attitude, and their elimination is much more a result of a peaceful disposition than a prerequisite thereof. Though protection was nowhere, except in Britain, completely discarded, there had been no disposition to resort to discrimination between foreigners so long as the world remained free of the prospect of imminent international violence. But when, in the 'sixties and 'seventies of the last century, a new era of aggressive and illiberal empire-building was inaugurated, the results were as immediately apparent in the commercial as in the more purely political world. It is the great tragedy of our times that, after a peaceful spirit had been brought into international relations and the noncoercive ideals of economics had begun to sway the minds of men, the world did not proceed from strength to strength, in the conquest of war, but was overwhelmed in a resurgence of the wave of the past and not only reverted to, but exaggerated, all the invidious practices of Mercantilism in the apparent belief that theft rather than thrift is the road to wealth. The free traders in England had expected, and welcomed, the full independence of the various sectors of the British Empire. The parvenu empires were, therefore, not the result of any menace, but solely of national egotism.

The leader in the reversion to the bad old ways was Germany. In reviving the whole array of Mercantilistic practices, in-

so improve our institutions as to banish our fear of goods, war is probably inevitable as a highly effective means of getting rid of all that we can produce.

cluding unprovoked assaults on other nations, the Germans have argued that they were doing nothing that other states had not done before them. This is true but irrelevant. To accept the argument as a valid excuse for predatory conduct would be to put an end to all progress toward a better world.

The policy of discriminations between one foreign country and another, whatever its immediate motivation, is seldom other than a prelude to war. Counter-discrimination is then the only policy that makes sense. In a peaceful, freely trading, world the sovereignty over territory rich in natural resources would, apart from envy, be a matter of complete indifference. In a warlike world, however, the sovereignty over natural resources is a matter of life and death. It is quixotic for any nation possessing raw materials useful in war to put them at the disposal of those who would use them to encompass its destruction. Nothing could better demonstrate the good will, and poor sense, of Britain and the United States than their continuance to the last in their practice of supplying the nations that intended to attack them with the materials necessary to make the attack effective. This was no doubt magnificent but it was not war. Our folly lay in the failure to recognize that the present war began long before the shooting. No sensible person, looking backward to the 1930's, can think of a non-discriminatory commercial policy as other than a dangerous benevolence at that date. Rather than serving to promote peace it went far to bring on war and to put in frightful danger the nations that practiced it. Had the Germans and the Japanese, with the initial impetus of preparation facilitated by their victims, been able to seize just a bit more of the world's resources they would, sooner or later, have made good in their attempt to enslave the world.

PEACE MUST COME FIRST

The lesson of the last century clearly is that we cannot get peace through liberal economic policies but that we may get liberal economic policies through peace. Given international peace, there is every reason to believe that the mutual advantage to be obtained from commerce will progressively level existing barriers to trade. *But peace must come first.* If there is no peace or prospect of peace the only sane policy for any nation richly endowed with natural resources indispensable to war is to deprive potential enemies of access to them. This being so, we must make the approach to world peace in the political rather than in the economic sphere.[7] As the political prospect improves, the possibility of liberal economic measures will increase, and we may then go on from peace to prosperity. A temporarily more prosperous world would not necessarily be peaceful but a peaceful world would surely promote prosperity.

One of the major difficulties in establishing peace will be the lack of assurance of its permanence, and liberally-inclined countries must be careful that they do not kill themselves with kindness to their enemies. It would seem wise, therefore, that all countries ready to enter, with obligations, an organization to suppress international aggression should extend to one another most-favored-nation commercial treatment and that they should deny it to those who insist on remaining outside. This would greatly strengthen the disposition toward peace by rewarding those who were committed to it and by punishing those who were not.

The ideal should, of course, be free trade, but its early realization, even within the group cooperating to maintain peace, is beyond the range of reasonable expectation. The opposing

[7] It would be foolish to deny that, in the vicious circle of resentment and retaliation, invidious national practices in the field of predatory business foster the hostility of which they are a frequent expression, or that, in a virtuous circle of good-will and beneficent reciprocity, a primary disposition toward peace would not be furthered by liberal economic attitudes. But the point is that we do not get surcease from conflict by crying "Peace, Peace" when there is no peace; on the contrary, we strengthen those who are preparing for war.

forces of vested interest, of nationalism, and of ignorance, are immensely strong and it would be quixotic to expect all trade barriers to be levelled in the near future. No such action, fortunately, is indispensable. It is, as already noted, not necessary to peace that we love our neighbors as ourselves, but merely that we accept the rule of live and let live. To attain the minimum requirements of peace will not be easy and, if our reach should very far exceed our grasp, we are likely to fail, miserably, in the chief task. We should, therefore, concentrate on the problem of scotching international aggression and not now be diverted by a whole range of objectives, desirable in themselves, but incapable of realization if the primary objective be not attained.

Nationalism is the most potent force in the modern world. It will be necessary in some degree to overcome it in order to secure peace, but we would err in attempting to impose any but the most essential limitations upon national sovereignty. Economic theory is cosmopolitan but political fact is nationalistic. Economic theory assumes peace but our current task is to get it. To do so, we must concentrate on essentials in the knowledge that, if we attain them, all other things may in time be added unto us, but that if we snatch at shadows we shall certainly lose our bone. Nations are not yet ready to love each other as themselves and cosmopolitanism is not yet feasible. But international crime can be prevented. What, then, are the economic minima for a peaceful world?

THE MINIMAL ECONOMIC CONDITIONS OF PEACE

1. *Full Employment.* The economic method of attaining the material means to happiness is to work for them; the method of *realpolitik* is to take them from someone else. If the economic method is barred, to men or nations, a resort to the predatory method is inevitable. Beggar-my-neighbor policies will then flourish and, with them, international ill-will. Full employment is, in consequence, of first importance in the preservation of peace, and it must be attained within the framework of free-

dom. The maintenance of full employment in any nation is, however, a domestic, not an international, responsibility. Full employment in the United States (which produces and consumes between 40 and 50 per cent of the world's output of goods) would go far to promote full employment elsewhere.[8] But full employment in the United States could neither be granted nor taken away by the presence or absence of salutary international action. There is a widespread notion that an expanding international trade is a condition of full employment in this country. The notion is unfounded. International trade, per se, has no bearing on the volume of employment but only on its composition. So far as employment in the industries supplying foreign markets is expanded, a compensatory reduction in employment takes place in industries more or less directly competitive with the imports which, if we are to have trade rather than gifts, must correlate with exports.[9] This does not mean that total employment may not increase with an expansion of international trade. But it is also true that it may expand without it. The function of international trade is not to increase the total of employment but to make it more effective. There is not the slightest reason to believe that, after the pains of adjustment were over, total employment would be diminished by a thoroughgoing isolationism in this country. We should simply be poorer, not less busy. Freedom of trade, on the other hand, would give us as many adjustment difficulties as complete isolation and would not solve the problem of unemployment though it would increase the productivity of such employment as we had. Full employment everywhere would probably promote international trade, to the mutual benefit of the trading

[8] This is true even though foreign trade has played a very small proportionate role in the economy of this country in recent decades.

[9] The correlation may be postponed when foreign lending is in excess of interest payments currently received, but this will sooner or later occasion an excess of imports over exports and thus ultimately confute the "lack-of-consuming-power" reasoning in which capital exports are imagined to be a remedy for unemployment.

parties, but this is by no means a foregone conclusion. In any event, international trade is neither a *sine qua non* nor a guarantee of full employment. There is no reason, therefore, to despair if economic internationalism does not, at a stroke, replace the nationalistic policies now long prevailing and no reason to believe that full employment, anywhere, will be precluded by such restrictions on international trade as it may prove impossible to remove.

2. *Access to Raw Materials.* The world's raw materials, however, must be at the disposal of all nations, on equal terms, if a scramble for sovereignty over the territory in which they occur is to be prevented. There must, therefore, be trade enough to take care of the requisite movement of raw materials. The nations that could best get along without international trade in raw materials are not necessarily those with the richest resources, but rather those whose resources, whether good or bad, are so diversified as to parallel the resources of the world at large. Nations with almost no natural resources are, of course, supremely dependent on international trade in raw materials. But nations with very rich resources, in some lines only, are equally interested in international trade, especially on the export side. Unless they have such trade their rich endowment in certain materials may be of small use to them. The Japanese, for instance, are at the present writing highly endowed with resources for the production of rubber which, with international trade, would be of great value to them. But the power of the Japanese to command goods in exchange for rubber cannot now be very great. It is only the world's demand for unequally distributed natural resources that enriches their possessors. It is, therefore, quite as much to the interest of the possessors of rich raw material resources to put them at the disposal of other nations as it is to the interest of those other nations to have free access to them. There is, therefore, not much reason to expect any denial of natural resources to any country of pacific intent. If, on the other hand, any country is, for other reasons, deter-

mined to challenge existing sovereignty, it would be well to deny it the means.

3. *Control of Monopolies.* The interest of the parties to trade in raw materials, while mutual, is not identical. The interest of the purchaser is in free competition since this would ensure the maximum supply at the lowest price compatible with the maintenance of volume. The immediate interest of the producing area, on the other hand, is in the restriction of the supply, on foreign markets, to the amount which will yield it the maximum net return. Though mutual prosperity is readily feasible, it is not strictly true that the prosperity of one country is irrevocably bound up with the prosperity of all. In the short run, of course, prosperity and depressions tend to be world-wide and the interest of all countries in avoiding depressions is a common interest. But, quite aside from the fact that productivity in any one country may, in the long view, rise indefinitely while other countries are stagnant or retrogressive, it is also possible for one country to prosper by milking others. Recourse to monopoly is the principal means of attaining this end. Under ideally free competition—that is, with numerous competitors on both sides of the market—no one has the power appreciably to affect either the price, the volume of output, or the volume of demand. Productive power is then the sole means of emolument, and the greater the power exerted by any producer the more is the social interest advanced. But monopoly is a means of exerting power over the market, and of obtaining emolument, not by expanding output but by restricting it, or, on the buying side, by restricting demand. By thus raising the price of what he sells, or reducing that of what he buys, the monopolist may secure so much larger a share of the community's restricted production as greatly to improve his status. Any such privileged position, of course, requires the buyers of the monopolist's goods, and the sellers of other goods, to be in competition. As soon as monopolies become widespread, with each seeking to exploit its position by restricting production, they all begin to suffer,

along with mankind as a whole, from the general restriction of output. The more or less equal power of the monopolies precludes the triumph of any of them, though it ensures the ruin of the community at large.

The reversion to predatory politics in the later decades of the nineteenth century had, as noted, been attended by a recourse to the predatory business tactics of Mercantilism, but monopolies, which had formerly been attained by governmental favor, were now for the most part established by private action. Technological developments greatly facilitated the process until free competition (in the economists' sense of the word) was very gravely impaired. Free competition was still typical of agriculture, and agriculture all over the world was, in consequence, exploited. Eventually, governments came to the aid of agriculture, but they did so not by breaking down industrial monopolies but by assisting agriculturalists to establish their own. With all branches of production in a position to restrict output, it is small wonder that business depressions, unemployment, and poverty became chronic. The totalitarian states cut the Gordian knot of mutually restrictive monopolies by merging them into a single all-powerful unit. This permitted an expansion of production but on a servile basis. To believers in freedom the only real solution of the problem is the abolition, not the consolidation, of monopolies.

Monopolies have not been as prominent in the international as in the domestic sphere, partly because nationalistic jealousies have prevented the easy collusion of producers of different nationalities. There have, however, been numerous efforts at collusion; some of them have succeeded; and even war has not fully disrupted such relations. Peace, however, provides much more promising soil for international monopolies than does war, and one of the urgent problems of peace will be to prevent their growth. This type of "international cooperation" is at the expense of exploited populations, who will view their exploitation in nationalistic terms and place the blame for it upon the foreign, rather than the domestic, element in the combination. Such combinations, therefore, carry within them the seeds of future wars no matter how amiably disposed to one another the various national groups in the exploiting combination may prove to be. Free access to resources is a matter of individual, as well as of national, concern and monopolies are the denial of such access. "Resources," in any meaningful sense, moreover, cover much more than the primary products of land or sea. Free access to occupations is, for many, the only means to free access to resources. Both are essential to peace, and both will require the eternal vigilance of all governments committed to the abolition of special privilege and predatory power.

The elimination of monopolies seems destined to be one of the hardest nuts to crack in the attempt to meet the needs of peace. Not only does technology, to some extent, favor their formation, but almost the sole means of meeting a monopoly is to counter with another. If, however, we really believe in free competition as the only system which, to paraphrase Jefferson, does not fly in the face of the rights of man, we must establish it whenever we can, and must resort to monopolies only as a fighting instrument against those who will not forego their use.

It is true, of course, that a monopolist might, for one reason or another, refrain from exerting his power and, where this is the case, no difficulty arises. It might thus happen that, where foreign trade is carried on as a monopoly by the state, the state's interest in peace might be sufficient to prevent any effort to use the monopoly to gouge foreign buyers. It is also true that states might cooperate to "regulate" international monopolies with an eye to expansion rather than restriction of output. But the history of "regulation" of domestic monopolies, to say nothing of this type of international cooperation, is not encouraging. A careful study of the alleged social advantages of monopolistic cooperation will show that they are almost exclusively based upon the assumption of recurrent depressions. Here again, then, the only promising solution of the problem is the maintenance of full employment, for, with full employment, much of the incentive to monopoly would disappear.

If we, in the United States, would keep the peace, it is to our strong interest 1) to put some teeth into our traditional policy of suppressing monopolies; 2) to make it a criminal offense for any American company to enter into any international cartel, "gentleman's agreement," community of interest, or the like, except under governmental auspices, and 3) to discriminate in our own markets against the products of international trusts. Since freely competing groups, both on the buying and selling side, will, however, be subject to exploitation in their dealings with a nation which monopolizes its foreign trade, it will probably be necessary, in countries desiring so far as possible to preserve free individual enterprise, to set up governmental corporations to handle that part of their foreign trade which issues to, or from, any such nation.

Before we leave this topic it should be recognized that competition has its failings and that quasi-monopolistic international action may be essential to their elimination. The principal instances arise in connection with agricultural commodities. For most agricultural commodities it is impossible to predict the yield, in any year, of a given employment of productive resources and, for some, the diversion of resources cannot greatly alter the prospective yield within a quinquennium. In such cases the use of a reservoir, to stabilize flow, is clearly requisite to prevent ruinous price fluctuations with consequent adjustments which are not only without any tendency to promote equilibrium but are of actively perverse effect. No single country, unless it be virtually the sole producer of a commodity, should be required to set up a "reservoir" since it will then carry an expense from which its expense-free competitors in other countries will benefit. There can, however, be no objection to international cooperation in this field provided the international machinery is used for the purpose of stabilization only, and not as a means of raising the price of the product above the competitive "norm." To this end consumers must be at least as strongly represented as producers in the management of the "reservoir."

PROTECTIVE TARIFFS

The maintenance of full employment, the provision to all peoples peaceably inclined of free access to resources, and the suppression of monopoly except as a countervailing measure, would seem to be the conditions in the economic sphere of real importance to peace. There has been some disposition among economists to fix upon protective tariffs the responsibility for the evil state into which the world economy has recurrently fallen, and, by transference, the responsibility for the deterioration of political amity. But, however much protection is to be deplored as a factor in reducing the world's potential prosperity, a cogent case could be made for the contention that the greater the tariff-fostered self-sufficiency of national states, the less widespread the repercussions of depression in any one of them, with a consequent decline in international ill-will. Despite a widespread opinion to the contrary, it is doubtful whether import duties have done great long-run harm to any other than the levying countries. The tendency of any protective tariff is, of course, to force self-sufficiency on other states as well as on that which levies it and, if protection were carried to its logical conclusion in every state but one, that one would perforce be as economically self-sufficient as all the rest. The benefits of international division of labor would then be lost even to the state that wished to secure them and, for any small state, this would be disastrous. Protection, however, has never been carried to any such extreme; there is no prospect that it will be; and there is no evidence that it has gravely injured those that repudiated it. Even in the growingly protectionist world of the late nineteenth and twentieth centuries, free-trade Britain was so fully specialized as to secure most, if not quite all, of those advantages arising from the territorial division of labor that would have accrued to it under world-wide free trade. So long as most countries wish to push their exports (and this is the neo-Mercantilistic counterpart of the ban on imports) they will, in spite of themselves, provide a market for imports (which will permit of almost unlimited specialization in any country that wishes it) or they will give their goods away. The latter procedure, per se, could never ruin the recipient countries once adjustments were made to the situation.

Most states are dissatisfied with that composition of their economic structure that would evolve under free trade, and there is little prospect of a general removal of protective duties. Though, on a cosmopolitan view, this is regrettable, it is, as already noted, not in itself a substantial bar to peace or to the prosperity of any country that does not share the general enthusiasm for protection.

The disturbances in international commercial relations, associated with protection, largely issue not out of tariffs as such but from sudden changes in them. Once an export industry has been built up in any country, in the supply of another's markets, the levy of a prohibitive duty on the import of the products of such an industry is a serious blow to producers. Its repercussions on other industries in the exporting country may be so great as to produce a general collapse. The more or less inevitable retaliations cumulate the disruptive effects, and worldwide depression may follow. The United States has been the world's chief sinner in its reckless disregard of the consequences of sharp and widespread changes in its tariff schedules, and the general direction of changes has been so frequently shifted that the readjustment to a given change that would have rendered it innocuous could never be made before the situation was disturbed anew by another shift. These changes gave quite unnecessary shocks to established trading relations and were as harmful to our own country as they were to others.

There is every reason to expect the success of an international effort to reduce the violence of any changes that any country may wish to make in its tariff schedules. This requires no more than horse sense and should occasion no opposition from any vested interest. If we can attain to the international political cooperation necessary to peace, there should be little difficulty in eliminating this wholly gratuitous disturbance of stability.

There is ordinarily a military reason for any tendency toward discrimination between different foreign nations in the tariff schedules of any state. In a peaceful world most of such discriminations could be expected to disappear and their only justification in the interest of peace would be as sanctions directed against predatory policies. It must, however, be admitted that there are occasions when two countries with contiguous and more or less complementary economies desire to establish preferential trading relations with one another with no military purpose. In some cases, moreover, a mutually preferential market involving a large and a small country is, in a protectionist world, all but indispensable to the small country. The truth about discriminations is that the intent is of more significance than the fact and that no general rule will cover all of the discriminations that may arise. If the intent is peaceful they might best be ignored: if it is aggressive they should be met by retaliations.

INTERNATIONAL MONETARY MECHANISM

The national control of monetary policy is jealously and properly guarded as a sovereign right of the state and it is not necessarily true that what would be good policy for one state would be good for another. Identity of monetary policies in the various countries is, therefore, not likely to be attained. This means that we must give up the attempt to secure universal fixity of exchange rates, since fixed exchange rates are a highly disruptive factor in international trade between countries of diverging monetary policies and price levels. The attempt to maintain fixed rates between the currencies of countries with price levels not moving in unison was a large factor in the financial collapse of 1931 and would again fail in the absence of universal agreement or a monetary policy established for all by some supernational authority. Stability in international trading relations does not require fixed exchange rates (the contrary is the case if price levels in the various countries are not unchanging and do not move in unison). It requires, rather, stability in the relationships between the internal purchasing powers of the several currencies and their exchange values.

If it is possible, after the war, to obtain universal agreement on a given monetary policy for any group of countries, fixed exchange rates between them would be feasible. But in the absence of a common monetary policy for all countries the only course consistent with freedom and the prompt elimination of maladjustments is a frank recognition of the necessity for flexible exchange rates between countries of different monetary policies, with provisions for the elimination of wild (i.e., wholly non-functional) movements. Perhaps the most promising procedure to this end is the establishment of a not too narrow zone of fluctuation about a moving norm based, at any moment, on the current relationship between national price levels or, what will usually be the same thing, on the requirements for long-term equilibrium. This may be far from ideal but, in a regime of diverging monetary policies, it is definitely superior either to the system of fixed exchange rates (which, with "international cooperation," piled up dislocations in the latter half of the 1920's and resulted in the international financial collapse of the early 1930's), or to the system, under the Tripartite Agreement of 1936, which simply failed of its purpose more or less indefinitely to "stabilize" the rates of exchange of the currencies of the parties to the agreement.

An international monetary authority could best promote its purposes by offering to buy or sell freely, at fixed prices in international monetary units, what might be described as "representative bales" of the principal raw materials of world commerce.[10] This would not only stabilize in international currency the world raw material price level (leaving the price of individual commodities to fluctuate freely in accommodation of supply to demand) but, in obverse, would fix, in real terms, the value of the international monetary unit. International investment, in terms of this unit, would thereby be greatly facilitated and individual countries could fix, or otherwise determine, the value of their own currencies, in terms of the international unit, along the lines suggested in the semi-official proposals now current.

If, in the post-war world, we are to reduce the use of foreign exchange controls and help eliminate bilateral exchange clearing arrangements, multiple currency devices, and other discriminatory foreign exchange practices, we face the choice of:

a. Fixation of exchange rates, with unison in the otherwise uncontrolled movement of price levels. The best means to this end would be a general reversion to the unmanaged gold standard. But the consequent instability in price-level movements precludes the recommendation of this procedure.

b. National independence in monetary management (whether or not this involves in any given country the stabilization of price levels) along with functional movements of exchange rates. The appropriate means to this end is an extension of the practices of the British Exchange Equalization Account which, in its best days, sought neither to unload unemployment on its neighbors through a depression of the exchange value of ster-

[10] The authority would deal only in warehouse receipts (giving title to the goods in bonded warehouses in the principal market for each commodity), covering units of fixed physical composition.

ling below the level warranted by its domestic purchasing power nor to change the freely competitive terms of trade, in favor of Britain, through an undue elevation of the exchange value of the British currency. The chief difficulty here is in international long-term contracts.

c. Laissez-faire both in domestic monetary matters and in exchange rates. This is libertinism rather than ordered freedom and will prevail, if at all, only by default. The stickiness in entrepreneurial costs, characteristic of modern production, would make it highly unsatisfactory.

d. Enforced stabilization of price levels and fixation of exchange rates through the imposition, on all countries, of the requisite monetary policy, with some central bank or central banks as the ultimate governing authority. The struggle for control of such a bank would be fierce and would be resolved, if at all, only by giving the lion's share to the lion or, not improbably, to the eagle. The chances are strong that the system would be sabotaged by the action of countries reluctant to follow the general policy of the controlling authority or in disagreement with the methods by which it sought to make its policy effective. This is not, perhaps, a matter for regret, since Freedom must always look with a skeptical eye on an international organization which would bind all to a single monetary scheme laid down by some omnipotent, but fallible, authority.

e. Progressive voluntary stabilization of price levels and exchange rates (with exchange rates, in any case, always in correspondence with the relative national purchasing powers of the various currencies) through the free selection by the various countries of their monetary standards in an international regime in which money is *somewhere* linked to goods on a stable basis. This is the most promising of the alternatives, and the United States could make no greater contribution to international monetary stability than through the stabilization of the purchasing power of the dollar.

ECONOMICS AND PEACE

INTERNATIONAL INVESTMENT

The entry of governments into the fields of foreign investment has almost always been associated with war, and there are few reasons for governmental entry to any other end. There is no evidence that any part of the earth, offering good possibilities of return, is not cultivated by the private investor. If war is banished, or remains only a remote prospect, private foreign investment will flourish; otherwise most foreign investment, except such as will promote the military strength of the lending country, is folly. Foreign investment is sometimes embraced as a means of stimulating employment in the lending country but, in this respect, it has special virtues over domestic investment only so far as no return is received from abroad—and, if goods are to be given away, it would be quixotic to forget that charity begins at home.

There will, of course, be some need, on the conclusion of the war, to put devastated countries on their feet. Private lenders might then be in a position to exploit the distress of the borrowers and would, in any case, be niggardly in a situation that calls for generosity and boldness. Governmental action will, therefore, be required. But there is little to be said for prolonging, beyond the stage of rehabilitation, the governmental intervention which will here be necessary, except, perhaps, in an effort to reduce inequalities of flow and counterflow.

CONCLUSION

To an objective observer there is no convincing evidence that the failure to obtain full international economic or financial cooperation has been a *cause* of modern war. The wonder is that there was so much of this type of cooperation in a warlike world. In spite of the restrictions on international trade, imposed by all states in our time, a large measure of economic interdependence remained. The fact is that the effort to restrict trade is self-defeating inasmuch as it cheapens goods where they are already cheap and enhances their price where they are already dear. The *impulse* to trade is therefore strengthened with every restriction that is imposed upon it. No country, therefore, is ready to carry economic isolation to its logical conclusion. The trouble is that countries that isolate themselves by restrictive measures in international trade are thereupon moved to acquire sovereignty over constantly expanded areas so that the trade for which they hunger may be domestic rather than international.

The choice before the world, then, is either international economic cooperation—the more the better—or a series of wars out of which some great power will eventually establish worldwide dominion. To the economist the existing economic interdependence of nations calls for peace as a means of realizing the former alternative, but to the ardent nationalist in a strong state it calls for war as a means of realizing the latter. A large part of our international economic difficulties arise from the fact that states in pursuit of a belligerent policy create the adverse conditions from which war then seems to them the only feasible means of escape. If it were made hopeless to get control of coveted resources by war there is every reason to believe that the mutual interest of buyers and sellers in their distribution would result in reasonably satisfactory arrangements for their purchase and sale.

Except in the monetary field, we could in international trade do no better, in the interest of peace and prosperity, than revert to, and extend, the institutions of the mid-nineteenth century. There is, however, good ground for believing that economic depressions are largely the result of defective monetary systems, among which must be included the international gold standard of the traditional type. Efforts are already under way to improve the international monetary mechanism. Without taking a position for or against any one of the semi-official proposals in this field it may be doubted whether much can be accomplished until the domestic monetary systems are put upon a sounder footing. If, by monetary reform or otherwise, large-scale unemployment, along with fluctuating price-levels, is banished within the various nations, we should find that many of the restrictions on, and discriminations in, international trade would presently be relaxed. It is futile, on the other hand, to hope for liberality in international trade if unemployment, within the several nations, remains to plague us.

It is nowadays fashionable to advocate a wide variety of "controls." We ought not to forget, however, that the problem of freedom, and of any worthwhile prosperity, is the attainment of the happy mean between the conditions of the jungle and those of the jail. If the purpose and operation of any control is to enlarge the general freedom it will contribute to peace. Any control, however, is subject to capture by a resolute minority motivated by narrow self-interest. The tendency of all controls is to prevent change. In the political field this issues more or less directly in war. In the economic field it results in such a divergence of stabilized supply from an inevitably volatile demand as to ensure eventual collapse. Such collapses are provocative of conflict. The mobility that characterized the nineteenth century economy has so far disappeared that a country that supplies the world with low-priced goods is now likely to be regarded as a disturber of world peace. If this situation continues the only peace we could get would be that of a house of detention. We need such controls as will secure the conditions of equal opportunity; but all else is suspect. It should be clearly recognized that controls (which mean coercion) are necessary to prevent international, or any other, aggression, but their multiplication beyond the necessary minimum would provoke the very aggression we seek to avert.

There is, however, broad scope for volitional measures in amelioration of international economic and social conditions. The work of the League of Nations in this field should be greatly enlarged. It might be well, however, to separate this work from the purely political task of maintaining peace and to put it under an independent organization. A certain odium is bound to attach to the policing necessary to peace and this could be nothing but a handicap to an organization working on the basis of free will. Having no concrete power the functions of such an organization would be that of inquiry, information, consultation, convention, and leadership.[11] To obviate exclusive national spheres of interest it might organize international investment consortia in backward areas and, in general, take over and develop the non-political work of the League and the early activities of the Bank for International Settlements.

Modern wars are essentially wars for the control of territory and, if we see to it that there is no economic ground for coveting one's neighbor's territory, we shall have done most of what is possible in the economic field to prevent war. This can be accomplished by providing free access to resources, by suppressing monopolies, and by reducing economic chaos without any real invasion of national independence. This might not give us all of the economic advantages that a cosmopolite might wish, but it would serve the purpose. We should greatly injure our chances of abolishing international conflict by imagining that success in this field depends on the full attainment of the cosmopolitan ideal of the Manchester school. The writer is of the opinion that the latter goal will be more difficult of attainment than will be the banishment of armed conflict between states and is disposed to believe that, unsatisfactory as have been the conditions in international economic affairs, they were not primarily responsible for war. Their improvement will be a *sequitur* rather than a *sine qua non* of political peace.

[11] Cf. Chapter 3, pp. 88ff.

5. The Senate and the Peace[1]

(With a Note on Sovereignty)

BY EDWARD S. CORWIN

JUSTICE HOLMES said in a celebrated case, "When we are dealing with words that also are a constituent act, like the Constitution of the United States, we must realize that they have called into life a being the development of which could not have been foreseen completely by the most gifted of its begetters. . . . The case before us must be considered in the light of our whole experience and not merely in that of what was said a hundred years ago."[2]

These words are strikingly applicable to the subject of this chapter. At the very outset of its history the Senate's role in the business of treaty-making was committed to a line of development which culminated one hundred and thirty years later in the defeat by the Senate of American participation in the League of Nations. But meantime other developments had occurred, some of which have today attained such scope that they afford an efficient corrective to the earlier one, and so lead us to believe that nothing comparable to the fiasco of 1919-1920 can take place at the close of the present war. To show all this is the purpose of the following pages.

THE TREATY-MAKING AUTHORITY SPLITS INTO TWO AUTHORITIES

The Constitution, Article II, Section 2, paragraph 2, reads: "He [the President] shall have power, by and with the advice and consent of the Senate, to make treaties, provided two-

[1] This chapter is a revision of Chapter III of my *The Constitution and World Organization* (Princeton: Princeton University Press, 1944).
[2] Missouri v. Holland, 252 U.S. 416 (1920), at p. 433, where the extent of the treaty-making power was the constitutional question.

thirds of the Senators present concur." The great thing to notice about this phraseology is that it associates the President with the Senate *throughout the entire process of treaty-making*. Commenting on this fact in *The Federalist* 64, Jay notes but one exception to the rule. Occasions may arise, he explains, when the *initiation* of a negotiation may require great secrecy and dispatch, and at such times the President must undoubtedly start the ball rolling; but otherwise all negotiations of treaties will be the joint concern of President and Senate. "Thus we see," he concludes, "that the Constitution provides that our negotiations for treaties shall have every advantage which can be derived from talents, information, integrity, and deliberate investigation on the one hand, and from secrecy and dispatch on the other."[3]

Some thirty years later Rufus King, who had been a member of the Philadelphia Convention, advanced in the Senate itself closely similar views concerning the relations of that body and the President so far as treaty-making was concerned. I quote:

"In these concerns the Senate are the Constitutional and the only responsible counsellors of the President. And in this capacity the Senate may, and ought to, look into and watch over every branch of the foreign affairs of the nation; they may, therefore, at any time call for full and exact information respecting the foreign affairs, and express their opinion and advice to the President respecting the same, when, and under whatever other circumstances, they may think such advice expedient. . . .

"To make a treaty includes all the proceedings by which it is made; and the advice and consent of the Senate being necessary in the making of treaties, must necessarily be so, touching the measures employed in making the same. The Constitution does not say that treaties shall be concluded, but that they shall be

[3] *The Federalist*, Earle, ed. (New York: The Modern Library, 1937), pp. 416-423.

made, by and with the advice and consent of the Senate; none therefore can be made without such advice and consent; and the objections against the agency of the Senate in making treaties, or in advising the President to make the same, cannot be sustained, but by giving to the Constitution an interpretation different from its obvious and most salutary meaning."[4]

Indeed, even as late as 1908 Woodrow Wilson, having noted in his *Constitutional Government* that there could be little doubt that the Convention of 1787 intended that the Senate should advise the President as to appointments and treaties "in the spirit of an executive council associated with him upon terms of confidential cooperation," declared that on this premise it was still not only the President's privilege, but his best policy and plain duty to deal with the upper chamber on that footing. He thereupon added: "If he have character, modesty, devotion, and insight as well as force, he can bring the contending elements of the system together into a great and efficient body of common counsel." How far Mr. Wilson came himself from realizing this ideal eleven years later is a matter of recorded history.[5]

The somber truth is that the conception of the Senate as a presidential council in the diplomatic field broke down the first time it was put to the test. The episode, the importance of which for American institutions and for the development of American foreign policy has rarely if ever been sufficiently appreciated, is narrated from the point of view of the Senate by Senator William Maclay of Pennsylvania in his *Journal*, from which I take the following pertinent extracts:[6]

"August 22d, Saturday [1789].—Senate met, and went on the Coasting bill. The doorkeeper soon told us of the arrival of the President. The President was introduced, and took our Vice-

[4] *Records of the Federal Convention*, Farrand, ed. (New Haven: Yale University Press, 1921), Vol. III, pp. 424-425.
[5] *Constitutional Government in the United States* (New York: Columbia University Press, 1908), pp. 138 and 141.
[6] *Journal of William Maclay* (New York: 1890), pp. 128-132, *passim*.

President's chair. He rose and told us bluntly that he had called on us for our advice and consent to some propositions respecting the treaty to be held with the Southern Indians. . . . Seven heads . . . were stated at the end of the paper which the Senate were to give their advice and consent to. They were so framed that this could be done by aye or no."

It speedily transpired, however, that the Senate was not inclined to stand and deliver forthwith, and presently Robert Morris, also of Pennsylvania, rose and moved that the papers communicated by the President be referred to a committee of five, a motion which was promptly seconded by another member. To continue Maclay's narrative:

"Several members grumbled some objections. Mr. Butler rose; made a lengthy speech against commitment; said we were acting as a council. No council ever committed anything. Committees were an improper mode of doing business; it threw business out of the hands of the many into the hands of the few, etc."

Maclay himself now spoke at length in favor of commitment "in a low tone of voice." "Peevishness itself," he asserts, "could not have taken offense at anything I said." Yet, he continues:

". . . the President of the United States started up in a violent fret. *'This defeats every purpose of my coming here,'* were the first words that he said. He then went on that he had brought his Secretary of War with him to give every necessary information; that the Secretary knew all about the business, and yet he was delayed and could not go on with the matter. He cooled, however, by degrees. Said he had no objection to putting off this matter until Monday, but declared he did not understand the matter of commitment. He might be delayed; he could not tell how long. He rose a second time, and said he had no objection to postponement until Monday at ten o'clock. By the looks of the Senate this seemed agreed to. A pause for some time ensued. We waited for him to withdraw. He did so with a discontented air. Had it been any other man than the man whom I wish to regard as the first character in the world, I would have said, with sullen dignity."

Maclay then adds his own interpretation of the event in these words:

"I can not now be mistaken. The President wishes to tread on the necks of the Senate. Commitment will bring the matter to discussion, at least in the committee, where he is not present. He wishes us to see with the eyes and hear with the ears of his Secretary only. The Secretary to advance the premises, the President to draw the conclusions, and to bear down our deliberations with his personal authority and presence. Form only will be left to us. This will not do with Americans. But let the matter work; it will soon cure itself."

The prophecy of these last five words has been amply verified by history. Washington went back to the Senate the following Monday for its answers to his questions, and while the ensuing colloquy seems to have moved along without any of the earlier jars, no President of the United States has since that day ever darkened the doors of the Senate for the purpose of personal consultation with it concerning the advisability of a desired negotiation.

From that time forth, in fact, the relations of President and Senate in the realm of diplomacy came rapidly to assume a close approach to their present form. The history of the making of the famous Jay Treaty five years later is a prime illustration. The treaty was negotiated in London under instructions in the framing of which the Senate had no hand, and when it was laid before that body the latter, instead of rejecting or accepting it outright, as it would have done in dealing with a nomination to office, proceeded in effect to amend it as if it had been a legislative project; nor did the Administration challenge the Senate's right to pursue this course, although the British government was at first disposed to do so.[7] In a

[7] Hayden, Ralston, *The Senate and Treaties* (New York: Macmillan, 1920), pp. 149-153.

word, the Senate's *character as an executive council was from the very beginning put, and largely by its own election, on the way to absorption into its more usual character as a legislative chamber*, and subsequent developments soon placed its decision in this respect beyond all possibility of recall.

One such development was the creation by Washington, early in 1793, of what soon came to be called "the Cabinet" out of the heads of the chief executive departments, to advise him as to the diplomatic crisis occasioned by the outbreak of war between France and Great Britain. Another was the formulation by Hamilton, under the same stimulation, of a sweeping theory of presidential prerogative in the realm of foreign relations which came in time to embrace the doctrine that negotiation is exclusively a presidential function. Still another was the increase in the membership of the Senate between 1789 and 1795 from twenty-two to thirty-two members, thus foreshadowing a body too numerous to trust safely with some kinds of state secrets and too unwieldy for intimate consultation. Yet not until 1816 did the Senate, by setting up the standing Committee on Foreign Relations, formally recognize the realities of the situation which both its increasing size and its predominantly legislative role created;[8] and even then it still clung to the "executive session" in the consideration of treaties until the fight over the Treaty of Versailles, when this last vestige of its character as a council was ruthlessly sacrificed to its character as a chamber of unlimited debate.

And it is the latter character which Senator Connally invoked recently in an effort to justify the evident purpose of the Committee on Foreign Relations to administer to the Fulbright Resolution the treatment it had already dealt out to the Ball-Burton-Hatch-Hill Resolution, the so-called, "B_2H_2."[9] Among other things Mr. Connally said:

[8] *ibid.*, Chapter VIII.
[9] S.R. 114 (78th Congress, 1st session), *New York Times*, March 14, 1943.

THE SENATE AND THE PEACE

"The Committee on Foreign Relations does not desire at this particular moment to afford opportunity for intemperate and trouble-making debate on the floor of the Senate. It is known to all well-informed men that the utmost freedom of debate is permitted under the Senate rules.

"It is further known that Senators do not hesitate to avail themselves of that unlimited freedom. International relations are delicate and sensitive. Unity and harmony require consultation and cooperation. We cannot perform the task alone."[10]

The Senator appears to be casting a nostalgic glance back to a past which was never a present, a time when the Senate felt itself to be an executive council and behaved like one. At the same time he contrives to admit that the role which the Senate has today come to occupy in the field of foreign relations is, in view of that body's habitual method of doing business, a standing menace to the peaceful conduct of such relations and hence to the country as a whole.

The failure of the United States to enter the League of Nations in 1919-1920 was due, therefore, only in part to the two-thirds rule which the Constitution lays down for Senate approval of treaties. Much more largely it was due to the operation of that rule in a situation which the framers of the Constitution had not anticipated and for which the two-thirds rule was not designed. To repeat, *the wording of the Constitution itself visualizes treaty-making as one continuous process to be performed by a single authority, the President acting throughout in consultation with the Senate. From the first, however, the Senate insisted upon asserting its independence of identity in the treaty-making business, thereby splitting the constitutional authority into two authorities, performing separate differentiated functions, a presidential function of formulation and negotiation followed by a senatorial function—completely legislative in character and motivation—of criticism and approval, with or without amendment, or of criticism and re-*

[10] *ibid.*, September 25, 1943.

jection. And subsequent events have only confirmed this divorcement—unattended by any obligation of support on either side—into two often politically antagonistic, and always more or less rival, organs. In short, the two-thirds rule was an anomaly before it was ever put into operation, and everything that has happened since 1789 both within the constitutional system and outside of it has contributed to aggravate its anomalousness.

SELF-CORRECTIVE POWERS OF THE CONSTITUTION

The question arises, consequently, whether there is any way of constitutionally obviating the potential difficulty which the two-thirds rule today opposes to entrance by the United States into an international organization. That the difficulty might be validly removed by constitutional amendment is of course evident. In 1943 the *New York Times* urged editorially that if an amendment empowering the President to conclude treaties subject to the approval of a legislative majority in the two houses were to be presently submitted to conventions in the states, its ratification by the required three-fourths of the states would in all probability be forthcoming before the end of the war.[11] Not only does the "if" in this suggestion brush aside entirely too casually the supreme difficulty, that of obtaining the consent of two-thirds of the Senate to the submission of such a proposal, but it also ignores the ominous circumstance that whereas the states have ratified twenty-one of the twenty-six amendments thus far submitted to them, and one is still pending, this small number comprises the sole survivors from the legislative gauntlet of more than four thousand proposals. Fortunately, a constitutional amendment is not in this instance necessary.

The fact that the constitutional document has not been greatly altered by formal amendment so far as the make-up

[11] *ibid.*, August 29, 1943.

THE SENATE AND THE PEACE

and powers of the national government are concerned ought not be permitted to obscure the further fact that the *working* constitution to which the document lends legal and moral sanction has from the first undergone constant changes. The stock illustration of the latter kind of constitutional change is furnished by the declension as early as 1796 of the "College of Electors" (which is pictured by Hamilton in *The Federalist*[12] as acting with almost superhuman aloofness from vulgar partisan prejudices and interests) into a political sideshow of party marionettes. Another example is the emergence of the President's Cabinet, referred to a moment ago, and still another is the one we have just been considering, the rejection by the Senate at the outset of the role of collaborator with the President in the formulation of foreign policies for that of an independent organ vested with unrestricted power to criticize, amend, and reject such policies as reach it from the hands of the President in the shape of treaties.

What, however, interests us in the present connection is the extent to which even this largely *negative* role of the Senate has been affected by developments down the years. It is no exaggeration to say that a President who enjoys the support of reliable *legislative* majorities in the two houses is today in a constitutional position to elaborate his diplomatic policies with very little thought for the predilections of what the late John Hay baptized "the recalcitrant one-third plus one man of the Senate." Conversely *no* President, whatever support he is able to command in the Senate in getting its imprimatur affixed to his treaties, can pursue very long a foreign policy which lacks the legislative backing of *both* houses, for without this backing or an outright *coup d'état*, taxes cannot be laid, funds paid out of the Treasury, the credit of the United States pledged, armies raised and supported, navies provided and maintained, or many other things done that the prosecution of a foreign policy is sure sooner or later to require.

[12] No. 68; Earle ed., *op. cit.*, at pp. 441-445.

EDWARD S. CORWIN

An examination of our constitutional history discloses that the President's powers in the international field came early to approximate, except for treaty-making, the prerogative of the British Crown;[13] that Congress's powers in the same field are today the legislative powers of a centralized government;[14] that both these vast reservoirs of "cognate powers" may be united in the hands of the President at any time at the option of Congress.[15] In these doctrines alone basis exists for a powerful direct assault upon "the recalcitrant one-third plus one man of the Senate."

More than that, however, a wealth of precedents also exists which, even without the support lent them by the above principles of our constitutional law, bodes no good for the Senate's prerogative, and which with that support bodes considerably less. Such precedents fall into three main groups: (1) those which have rootage in the President's powers as organ of foreign relations and as commander-in-chief, whereof the "executive agreement" properly so-called is the outstanding illustration; (2) those which stem for the most part from Congress's enumerated powers, although they, too, frequently assume the shape of "executive agreements" in a looser sense of the term, in consequence of a delegation of power by Congress to the President; (3) a group in which congressional action takes on all the characteristics of sovereign action.

THE EXECUTIVE AGREEMENT[16]

An early instance of "treaty-making" by the President without the aid or consent of either Congress or the Senate was the

[13] See my *President, Office and Powers* (New York: New York University Press, 2nd ed., 1941), Chapter VI, *passim*.
[14] See my *The Constitution and World Organization* (Princeton: Princeton University Press, 1944), pp. 16-20, and citations.
[15] *ibid.*, pp. 23-24, and citations.
[16] Much of the illustrative data in the following paragraphs of the text are from my *President, Office and Powers*, pp. 236-238 and 413-415. For a wealth of similar material, see Wallace McClure's *International Execu-*

THE SENATE AND THE PEACE

exchange of notes in 1817 between the British Minister Bagot and Acting Secretary of State Rush for the limitation of naval forces on the Great Lakes. Not till a year afterward was it submitted to the Senate, by which it was promptly approved. Nearly ninety years later occurred the parallel case, with appropriate deviations from the original model, of the first Roosevelt's treaty with Santo Domingo for putting the customs houses of that bankrupt nation under American control in order to forestall an attempt by its European creditors to seize them. When the Senate failed to ratify the treaty with reasonable promptitude the President proceeded to put it into force as an "executive agreement," whereupon the Senate, following one or two face-saving gestures, capitulated. And some years earlier, in 1900, President McKinley had on his own sole authority as commander-in-chief, contributed a land force of 5,000 men and a naval force to cooperate with similar contingents from other powers to rescue the legations in Peking from the Boxers; and a year later had, again without consulting either Congress or the Senate, accepted for the United States the Boxer Indemnity Protocol between China and the intervening powers.

Outstanding among recent executive agreements is the Hull-Lothian agreement, whereby the President in the late summer of 1940, some sixteen months before we entered the war, handed over fifty units of the United States Navy to Great Britain in return for leases of certain sites for naval bases in the

tive Agreements, Democratic Procedure under the Constitution of the United States (New York: Columbia University Press, 1941). About nine hundred treaties were proclaimed by Presidents between 1789 and 1929, while another two hundred or more never became effective on account of adverse action—or inaction—of the Senate. In the same period over 1,200 agreements were consummated with foreign countries, without the consent of the Senate. Kenneth Colegrove, *The American Senate and World Peace* (New York: Vanguard Press, 1944), p. 96.

The State Department inaugurated the separate *Executive Agreement Series*, October 1929. In the decade following more than one hundred executive agreements were made simply by an exchange of notes between our own and the other contracting government or governments; David M. Levitan, 35 *Ill. L.R.* 365 (December 1940).

British West Indies and elsewhere. The transaction represented an invasion by the President of a field of power heretofore regarded as reserved by the Constitution (Article IV, Section 3) to Congress exclusively, and overrode definite statutory provisions governing the disposal of over-age naval craft. It was nevertheless justified by the Attorney General as within the President's powers as commander-in-chief and as organ of foreign relations, and was to all intents and purposes ratified by Congress itself when this body appropriated funds for the construction of the bases.[17]

And recently there issued from the Moscow Conference several quite definite pledges to one another by the governments which were parties to it respecting future action, and the maturing of several of these is predicated for the period following the strictly military phase of the war. The recognition, however, in the fourth paragraph of the joint Four-Nation Declaration of "the necessity of establishing at the earliest practicable date a general international organization . . . for the maintenance of international peace and security," must undoubtedly be set down as of the nature of a proclamation of intentions rather than, accurately speaking, an international act.[18]

Writers on the subject sometimes assume that "executive agreements" are sufficiently differentiated from "treaties," in the making of which the Senate participates, whenever the former can be explained as issuing from the President's prerogative as commander-in-chief or his power as organ of foreign relations. But obviously this mode of reasoning ignores the essential question, which is not whether the President can constitutionally enter into executive agreements with other governments—a point universally conceded—but what *scope* these may today validly take.

It is submitted that if an executive agreement is a convenient

[17] *New York Times*, September 4, 1940; McClure, *op. cit.*, pp. 394-403.
[18] *New York Times*, November 2, 1943.

instrument for carrying out a conceded executive power—or if an executive agreement, in the broader sense of the term, is a convenient instrument for effectuating a power of Congress, or merged powers of President and Congress—then the employment of this method of reaching an understanding with another government cannot be warrantably characterized as an "evasion" of the treaty-making power in which the Senate participates. It is true that executive agreements of both sorts are resorted to nowadays much more freely than formerly, but ordinarily this is simply from the plain necessities of the case. Even the most convinced critic of the executive-agreement device would scarcely contend that the President ought to go to the Senate every time he finds it desirable to arrive at a common understanding with one of our allies regarding matters of military policy. Yet if the President is not required by the Constitution to do this it is only because the subject-matter of the agreement, being within his power as commander-in-chief, was not removed therefrom by the circumstance that he was called upon, in order to exercise it most effectively, to covenant with the representatives of another government or other governments. Nor does anybody seem to have argued to date that the Senate ought to have been consulted regarding the alliance or alliances which these minor agreements implement, although if there was anything that suggested "treaty" to the men of 1787 it was "a confederation or alliance." And whereas in World War I we spoke of our "associates," we nowadays use the term "allies" quite unabashedly.

The truth seems to be that the critics of the executive agreement who raise the cry of "evasion" rest their case in the last analysis on the idea, never clearly expressed, that all constitutional development—by which they generally mean any departure from their own conception of what the Constitution means—ought to be by formal amendment, and that there is something essentially dishonest about constitutional changes which are brought about by practice and usage, at least as soon as such changes have reached the stage where people become generally conscious of them. I should be disposed to contend, to the very contrary, that *the most beneficial type of constitutional change is that which issues gradually from, and so has been thoroughly tested by, successful practice.* To be sure, there are often limits to the possibilities of this type of constitutional change under a written constitution like our own, and there are occasions when the amending process ought to be resorted to in order to round out and perfect some change which long practice has shown to be desirable. Thus, although popular choice of Senators had been practically established throughout a great part of the union prior to the adoption of the Seventeenth Amendment, yet that amendment was quite properly felt to be essential in order to make available the full possibilities of the reform.

From another angle it has been argued at times that executive agreements, in contradistinction to treaties, are not, unless they were initially authorized or have been subsequently approved by Congress, "law of the land," and hence are not noticeable by the courts. But if this was ever sound doctrine, it is no longer so in view of the explicit holding of the Court in 1937 in *United States v. Belmont.*[19] The point at issue in the Belmont Case was whether a district court of the United States was free to dismiss an action by the United States, as assignee of the Soviet government, for certain moneys which were once the property of a Russian corporation whose assets had been appropriated by the Soviet government. The court, speaking by Justice Sutherland, held not. The President's act in recognizing the Soviet government, and the accompanying agreements, constituted, said the Justice, an international compact which the President, "as the sole organ" of international relations for the United States, was authorized to enter upon without consulting the Senate. Nor did State laws and policies make any difference in such a situation; for while the supremacy of

[19] 301 U.S. 324 (1937).

treaties is established by the Constitution in express terms, yet the same rule holds "in the case of all international compacts and agreements from the very fact that complete power over international affairs is in the National Government and is not and cannot be subject to any curtailment or interference on the part of the several States."[20]

Nor can it be admitted on the basis of either principle or practice that, as some have contended, the *international* obligation of the United States under an executive agreement resting on Presidential power alone terminates with the Administration which entered into it. Conceding that the agreement was within the power of the President as the recognized constitutional organ of foreign relations, there is no reason why the nation should not be regarded as bound by it according to its plain terms just as truly as it would be by a treaty. And as for the precedents—it took the Washington Conference and at least two solemn treaties to rid us of the incubus of the Lansing-Ishii agreement of 1917; while the "Gentlemen's Agreement," first drawn in 1907, by which Japanese immigration to this country was regulated for some seventeen years, was finally put to an end only by an act of Congress. Moreover, the actual effect of an executive agreement on the foreign policy of the country, and thereby on its future welfare, may be quite as extensive as if the agreement had been a full-panoplied treaty. Thus the "Fifty Destroyer Deal," although its immediate and inducing purpose will have been accomplished with the end of the fighting phase of the present war, creates nonetheless a relationship between the United States and Great Britain of the nature of a regional defensive alliance which will considerably outlive the war, even if one accepts the most gloomy prognostications as to the date of the termination of the latter, inasmuch as our leases of the British bases are for ninety-nine years.

[20] *ibid.*, 330-332.

EDWARD S. CORWIN

PRESIDENT AND CONGRESS VERSUS "THE RECALCITRANT ONE-THIRD PLUS ONE"

We turn now to those precedents which stem primarily from Congress's powers. Some of these, as was noted above, spring immediately from a delegation of power by Congress to the President and so take the form of "executive agreements" in the broader sense of the term, the outstanding illustrations being the so-called "foreign trade pacts," of which Secretary Hull has latterly been such an exponent. The McKinley Tariff Act of 1890 furnished an ambiguous authorization for the earliest of these, the constitutionality of which was attacked on the ground both that they represented a delegation of legislative power to the President and that they invaded the field of jurisdiction of the treaty-making power; but in the leading case of *Field v. Clark*[21] both contentions were overruled, the latter without further comment by the court than its general observation that the challenged provision was a "necessary and proper" law for carrying Congress's power to regulate foreign commerce into effect. The precedent and supporting doctrine thus established have since been gradually expanded until by the Act of 1934, which was renewed in 1937, 1940, and again in 1943, the President is authorized to lower customs rates as much as 50 per cent on imports from other countries in order to obtain equivalent concessions from them. Nor is the validity of the agreements by which such legislation is implemented longer open to serious question in view of the decisions.

Yet that the same results could be obtained by treaty is certain. Indeed, in 1787 and for long afterward, that is exactly the way in which comparable results were obtained. So what this line of precedents establishes is that *if the subject matter to be regulated falls within the powers of Congress, the latter may constitutionally authorize the President to deal with it by*

[21] 143 U.S. 649 (1892). See also Hampton v. U.S., 276 U.S. 394 (1928).

negotiation and agreement with other governments, the treaty-making power to the contrary notwithstanding.

A further illustration of the same principle is afforded by the Act of February 9, 1922, by which a commission was created to effect agreements covering the debts owed this country by certain other governments. Since these agreements were to be laid before Congress, not before the Senate in its treaty-making capacity, Senator Walsh of Montana protested the measure as unconstitutional, a contention which Senator McCumber of North Dakota answered with the sweeping assertion that "anything done by treaty could be done by statute."[22] And unquestionably what was done by statute on that occasion, by warrant presumably of Congress's power to dispose of property of the United States, could have been done by treaty by virtue of the fact that the subject was one the settlement of which unavoidably involved international negotiation and agreement.

Similarly the Lend-Lease Act of March 11, 1941, is the fountainhead of the numerous Mutual Aid Agreements under which our government has to date furnished our allies in the present war nearly thirty billions worth of munitions of war and other supplies. In the case, on the other hand, of the United Nations Relief and Rehabilitation Convention, which was drawn up by a conference of United Nations representatives at Hot Springs, Virginia, in 1943, a different course has been adopted, but one which seems likely to lead to the same general result. It was originally the intention of the State Department to treat the convention as an executive agreement, but protests from certain Senators against this procedure led to a series of conferences between representatives of the Department and a subcommittee of the Foreign Relations Committee. These conferences, in turn, led to a revision of the convention in certain particulars and a pledge by the subcommittee to recommend its validation by an act of Congress authorizing appropriations

[22] *op. cit.*, in note 13, at p. 413.

EDWARD S. CORWIN

to carry it out, and apparently this plan is being followed.[23] It is interesting to note in passing that Senator Vandenberg, who was a member of the Senate subcommittee and approved the compromise plan just mentioned, took the position earlier that the convention was in every respect a treaty, and that the representatives of several of the signatory states signed *ad referendum* on the same assumption.[24]

But the most striking cases wherein the treaty-making process is superseded by legislative process are those which have occurred in direct consequence of a breakdown of the former, either actual or prospective. Thus it was by simple congressional resolution that Texas was annexed in 1845 after the upper chamber had defeated a treaty for the same purpose. It was thus that Hawaii was annexed in 1898 after a treaty for the purpose had been blocked by a group of Cleveland Democrats; and it is altogether probable that the Philippines would have been acquired in the same manner the following year had the Senate eliminated, as it seemed likely for a time to do, the applicable provision of the Treaty of Paris. Likewise, it was by a joint resolution that war with the Central Powers was finally terminated July 2, 1921, following the defeat of the Treaty of Versailles. Also, it was by a joint resolution, passed June 19, 1934, that Congress authorized the President to accede to Part XIII of the Treaty of Versailles, establishing the International Labor Office.[25]

[23] *New York Times*, July 9, August 18 and 19, 1943, and January 13, 1944; also Kenneth Colegrove, *op. cit.*, pp. 28-31 and 92-95. Legislation to authorize the transfer of certain lands in Panama to the Panama government and to carry out other provisions of an agreement negotiated by the Department of State was attacked in the Senate on December 3, 1942, as an effort to "by-pass the Senate," but was passed by the Senate the following day. *New York Times*, December 2, 4 and 5, 1942.

[24] See Lucile Cardin Cram's letter, published in the *New York Times* of May 25, 1944. A volume of special interest in connection with recent executive agreements is *United Nations Agreements*, edited by M. B. Schnepper, with Foreword by Arthur Sweetser (American Council on Public Affairs, Washington, D.C., 1944).

[25] U.S. Code, tit. 22, §271. A vigorous attack was later made on the

THE SENATE AND THE PEACE

But now, let it be noted as to this third group of precedents that, except possibly the one first mentioned, in support of which the historically unallowable argument was concocted at the time that Congress was merely exercising its power to admit "new States into this Union," *all of them exemplify Congress's indefinite power in the field of foreign relations, its power, in other words, as the legislative organ of a nation which is sovereign at international law.* But while they exemplify this power, they do not demark its scope or extent. This, in principle, must be as great as the external requirements of the nation itself, provided only that the power does not in its exercise run counter to some specific limitation of the Constitution; and the prerogative of the Senate in the making of treaties does not, as the precedents which have just been reviewed attest, comprise such a limitation.

LEGISLATIVE APPROVAL PREFERABLE TODAY TO SENATORIAL APPROVAL

Suppose, then, that the dominant sentiment of the country should find itself frustrated by a "recalcitrant one-third plus one man of the Senate" in its efforts to put our government into an international organization for the maintenance of peace, would the country have to reconcile itself to such an obvious breakdown of constitutional machinery? I see no reason why it should do so any more than it did do so on the occasions just reviewed; and I see several reasons why it should not.

The Senate, composed as it is of two members from each state regardless of size of population, is peculiarly unfitted by the very principle of its make-up to be the custodian of a power requiring an extraordinary majority for its exercise. The criti-

resolution's constitutionality by Representative Tinkham. *Cong. Record*, February 5, 1935. Mr. David J. Lewis of Maryland introduced in the House on March 19, 1934, a similar measure to end, as he declared, "the impasse which has for years enabled thirty-three Senators to delay final action upon American membership in the World Court." *New York Times*, March 19, 1934.

cism which Hamilton levels in *The Federalist* 22 against the Articles of Confederation in their entirety applies almost to the dotting of its "i's" and the crossing of its "t's" to the participation of the Senate in the treaty-making function. This is what he says: "The right of equal suffrage among the states is another exceptionable part of the Confederation. Every idea of proportion and every rule of fair representation conspire to condemn a principle, which gives to Rhode Island an equal weight in the scale of power with Massachusetts, or Connecticut, or New York; and to Delaware an equal voice in the national deliberations with Pennsylvania, or Virginia, or North Carolina. Its operation contradicts the fundamental maxim of republican government, which requires that the sense of the majority should prevail."[26]

But, it may be contended, Hamilton goes on to recite, that the departure which the principle of "equal suffrage among the States" marks from the principle of majority rule is harmless because all important decisions of the Confederation have to be made by a vote of nine states, "and it may be thence inferred, that nine States would always comprehend a majority of the Union." This argument he counters as follows:

"What at first sight may seem a remedy, is, in reality, a poison. To give a minority a negative upon the majority (which is always the case where more than a majority is requisite to a decision), is, in its tendency, to subject the sense of the greater number to that of the lesser.... The necessity of unanimity in public bodies, or of something approaching towards it, has been founded upon a supposition that it would contribute to security. But its real operation is to embarrass the administration, to destroy the energy of the government, and to substitute the pleasure, caprice, or artifices of an insignificant, turbulent, or corrupt junto, to the regular deliberations and decisions of a respectable majority.... The public business must, in some

[26] Earle edition, at p. 134.

THE SENATE AND THE PEACE

way or other, go forward. If a pertinacious minority can control the opinion of a majority, respecting the best mode of conducting it, the majority, in order that something may be done, must conform to the views of the minority; and thus the sense of the smaller number will overrule that of the greater, and give a tone to the national proceedings. Hence, tedious delays; continual negotiation and intrigue; contemptible compromises of the public good. . . . When the concurrence of a large number is required by the Constitution to the doing of any national act, we are apt to rest satisfied that all is safe, because nothing improper will be likely *to be done*; but we forget how much good may be prevented, and how much ill may be produced, by the power of hindering the doing what may be necessary, and of keeping affairs in the same unfavorable posture in which they may happen to stand at particular periods."[27]

In short, to apply Hamilton's argument to the present issue, *the anomaly presented by the two-thirds rule is vastly aggravated by the principle of equal representation of the States in the Senate*; and if this was true in 1788, it is doubly true today. Thus, whereas in 1788 a "recalcitrant one-third plus one man" of the full Senate could not have been recruited from states containing less than one-seventh of the population, an equally lethal combination can today be compounded out of Senators *representing less than one-thirteenth thereof*. Nor, in fact, is this the extreme possibility. For a quorum of the Senate comprises only forty-nine members, of whom eighteen would be rather more than "one-third plus one man"; and these eighteen might come from the nine states which lie most immediately to the east of the Rockies. That is to say, a coherent bloc of states which have many traditions and interests in common, but which *contain less than one-thirtieth of the population of the country*, could, with a bare quorum of the Senate present, defeat a treaty.

And that the staid world of 1788 produced far fewer situa-

[27] *ibid.*, pp. 135-137.

tions requiring positive and prompt action by government than does our own split-second world is too obvious a consideration to require more than mention. "Tedious delays," says Hamilton —one recalls that it took the Senate twenty-one years to get around to approving the re-cession of the Isle of Pines to Cuba! "Contemptible compromises of the public good," he adds—one recalls the ridiculous pettifoggery of a few Senators by which we were kept out of the World Court.

Furthermore, we of today are not free, as Hamilton was, to ignore the theoretical demands of democracy, we who stand at the receiving end, as it were, of that whole course of development whereby the national government and its procedures have been progressively democratized from the beginning. I must say, therefore, that I find very persuasive the views expressed in 1943 by the author of the Fulbright Resolution regarding the relative validity of Senate and Congressional approval of treaties. I quote again:

"I submit [says Mr. Fulbright] that an undertaking approved by a majority of the House of Representatives and of the Senate is just as solemn as action by two-thirds of the Senate . . . such action by both houses is more binding, has greater validity, greater permanency and consistency for the future than has a policy imposed by the power of obstruction, possessed by thirty-four [sic] Senators who, in any given instance, probably will represent a very small fraction of our total population. It seems to me that to be consistent and positive over the years our foreign policy must be supported by the majority of our people. I do not think that one can deny that the House of Representatives is, on the whole, more responsive to, and more truly reflective of, the will of the people than any other body in our government. The fact that they must be elected every two years by relatively small constituencies induces in them a genuine humility and a profound respect for the will of the people. It prevents the growth of that detached arrogance which sometimes accompanies a long and secure tenure of power.

THE SENATE AND THE PEACE

"If this is true of the Representatives, then it seems to me that ... the most 'binding sanction' would be that procedure which more accurately than any other translates into definite action the will of the greatest number of our citizens. This procedure is, I submit, a joint resolution approved by not less than a majority of both houses of the Congress."[28]

Permit me in emphasis of Mr. Fulbright's words to repeat something I said earlier: The Senate's imprimatur, however unanimously or enthusiastically given, is not going to guarantee that the United States will continue a helpful member of an international organization. That can be assured, so far as the government can assure it, only by the President and Congress, the national executive power and the national legislative power. Once the Senate has acted in its treaty-making capacity it is *functus officio*—a god remote, unconcerned for the results of its single generative act.

Lastly, this point is perhaps worth considering even though not strictly relevant to the immediate purpose of this inquiry. The anxious question, What will the Senate do? is prompted by what happened to the League of Nations Covenant twenty-five years ago, and that may turn out to have very little bearing on the way in which peace will come about after the present war. In December 1943 General Smuts, observing that after the war America, Britain, and Russia would hold world power, made the prediction that peace "would come very slowly, perhaps so slowly as never to make possible a peace conference at all, but only a comprehensive armistice that would permit a long process of working out solutions."[29] Are such solutions to be referred when and as they occur for the approval of the Senate? The Republican Platform of June 27, 1944, promises that they will be so referred if that party is victorious in the elections this year. Of that imbecility more later. As a matter of fact, such solutions are at this moment in course of being worked out

[28] *New York Herald-Tribune*, November 3, 1943.
[29] *New York Times*, December 3, 1943.

without any account being taken of the Senate, and not merely at places like Cairo and Teheran, but in less conspicuous theaters of action. Only a few days after General Smuts's statement and as if to point it up, the late Secretary of the Navy Knox informed the country, via the English Speaking Union of Chicago, that the existing collaboration at sea of the American and British navies would be continued after the war as a "peace patrol."[30] Yet nobody has arisen to question the competence of the President to enter into such an arrangement.

The matter need not be elaborated; what it boils down to is this: that the final instrument for setting up an international organization for the maintenance of peace is likely to embody already established institutions and practices from which the United States could not withdraw without serious loss, both moral and material. And the durability of such arrangements is going to depend far more upon favoring action by the President and favoring legislation by Congress than on a vote of consent of the Senate which, from the necessities of the case, must be largely perfunctory.

THE SENATE'S DILEMMA

One of the authors of that much parented, albeit abortive, prodigy of statesmanship, the "B_2H_2 Resolution" (S.R. 114), is quoted as saying: "The whole world knows and our Allies know that it is this United States Senate which will finally decide what will be the foreign policy of our country when the war ends."[31] When confronted with the resolution itself and its unimpressive outcome, this very confident pronouncement sounds somewhat inflated. The resolution urged American leadership (step A), "in calling meetings of representatives of the United Nations" (step B), "for the purpose of forming an organization of the United Nations" (step C), "with specific and limited authority" to do five different things (steps $D^i, D^{ii}, D^{iii}, D^{iv}, D^v$).[32]

[30] *ibid.*, December 18, 1943.   [31] *ibid.*, March 17, 1943.
[32] *ibid.*, March 14, 1943.

THE SENATE AND THE PEACE

Although the resolution never even came to a vote in the Foreign Relations Committee, let alone in the Senate, three of the five things it listed had either been done already or have since been done by the United Nations without benefit of the advice and consent of the Senate.

The Connally Resolution (S.R. 172), which was passed by the Senate on November 5, 1943, by the overwhelming vote of 85 to 5, is a rather different affair. After declaring in favor of waging the war "until complete victory is achieved," the resolution further resolved:

"That the United States cooperate with its comrades-in-arms in securing a just and honorable peace.

"That the United States, acting through its constitutional processes, join with free and sovereign nations in the establishment and maintenance of international authority with power to prevent aggression and to preserve the peace of the world.

"That the Senate recognizes the necessity of there being established at the earliest practicable date a general international organization, based on the principle of the sovereign equality of all peace-loving States, and open to membership by all such States, large and small, for the maintenance of international peace and security.

"That pursuant to the Constitution of the United States, any treaty made to effect the purposes of this resolution, on behalf of the Government of the United States with any other nation or any association of nations, shall be made only by and with the advice and consent of the Senate of the United States, provided two-thirds of the Senators present concur."[33]

There are those who argue that this language was intended as a notification to all and sundry that, come hell and highwater, the Senate would *never, never*, on any account, recognize or lend countenance to an international organization for the preservation of peace if our entry into it is not effected by a

[33] *ibid.*, November 6, 1943.

treaty which "two-thirds of the Senators present" have approved. For myself I fail to see that the phraseology of the resolution supports any such contention. Not only is the term "constitutional processes" in the second paragraph noncommittal, but so too is the statement as to treaty-making in the fourth paragraph, which says, in effect, that *if* the United States elects to enter an international organization by the treaty route, the treaty will have to be approved by the Senate, by a two-thirds vote of the Senators present, a statement which nobody who has read the Constitution will be likely to question.

But where the Senatorial archangels feared to tread the Republican platform architects at Chicago rushed valiantly in. The portion of the Republican Platform to which reference has already been made reads as follows:

"We shall sustain the Constitution of the United States in the attainment of our international aims: and pursuant to the Constitution of the United States any treaty *or agreement* [italics mine] to attain such aims made on behalf of the United States with any other nation or any association of nations shall be made only by and with the advice and consent of the Senate of the United States, provided two-thirds of the Senators present concur."

The chief thing to be remarked about this declaration is the recognition it renders of the impossibility today of distinguishing the proper field of treaty-making from that of agreement-making, and *vice versa*. Otherwise Senator Taft and his co-workers would hardly have cared to turn their backs on a constitutional device which reaches back more than 150 years and which Republican Presidents have utilized repeatedly. This explanation of the declaration, however, only makes it the more absurd. It is, in truth, not a "plank," but a "trap" waiting to be sprung. The interesting question is, who—or what—is the expected victim?

THE SENATE AND THE PEACE
SUMMARY

Everything considered, the Senate's role in the conduct of foreign relations has been a diminishing role. First, it was to be sole legatee of the Congress of the Confederation in this respect; then it was to collaborate as a council with the President throughout the entire process of treaty-making; finally, as early as the Jay Treaty, it found itself reduced to the largely negative role of critic and censor of Presidential projects, although with a quasi-legislative power to amend them. In this last capacity, to be sure, the two-thirds rule afforded the Senate great strength, yet an unmerited strength, in that the rule was based in part at least on the early discredited assumption of conciliar collaboration, while today it is completely out of line with the democratic assumptions which have generally come to underlie the functioning Constitution, and all the more so because of the principle on which the Senate itself is constructed.

And in other ways, too, the two-thirds rule has become an anachronism. The sectional jealousies which accounted for it to some extent in 1787 have long since disappeared. Today the predominant interest in the field of our foreign relations is the interest of the country as a whole, whereof Congress in its legislative capacity is a far better representative than the Senate alone. Furthermore, in the long run the dependence of any President on Congress's legislative support of his foreign policies, something which the Convention of 1787 apparently overlooked completely, renders the Senate's special role in connection with treaty-making a fifth wheel to the governmental coach, and a fifth wheel of a very cumbrous and out-of-date model when we consider the Senate's characteristic methods of transacting business.

But the anomalous character of the Senate's prerogative is attested most of all by the devices for avoiding that prerogative which the practical conduct of our foreign relations has first and last given rise, especially when these are taken in conjunction with certain doctrines of constitutional law. As has been shown, no issue can arise in the realm of foreign relations as to which Congress cannot legislate, provided it does not invade the President's prerogative, and there is no issue in this realm as to which Congress cannot at any time merge its powers with the President's, as by authorizing him to enter into international agreements respecting it. What is more, the field which has, first and last, been covered by executive agreements is so broad as to render the distinction between such agreements and "treaties" incapable of formulation except by the statement that the latter must be submitted to the Senate.

But what does all this sum up to if not the fact that *constitutional principles supported by precedents of practice today provide the United States an alternative route into an international organization for the maintenance of peace, one which from the point of view of the requirements both of democracy and sound government is the preferable route?* Nor is it a question of calling a "treaty" an "agreement," or *vice versa*, should difficulty arise with the one method or the other. *It is simply a question of choosing between two methods which constitutional practice, supported by principles of constitutional interpretation, has developed, and which are equally available for the same purpose.*

NOTE ON SOVEREIGNTY

Probably no term known to political science has been more variously defined than "sovereignty," but whatever definition of it is adopted, it must be evident that the United States can hardly claim to be *more* "sovereign" than several other nations which a viable international organization must include—Great Britain and Russia, for example. Clearly, to take the position that the United States could not because of its *sovereignty* accept obligations which Great Britain and Russia were able to accept would lead to the paradox that the United States was actually less sovereign than they, less capable of forming international relationships. The question of sovereignty, nevertheless, may not be dismissed in quite this cavalier fashion, embodying as it does issues which have long troubled both theorists and practical men and which on that score at least demand some passing notice.

Three possible conceptions of sovereignty which have bearing on the problem here under discussion are suggested by the pertinent literature of the subject: (1) national sovereignty may be regarded as a concept of international law and hence as limited by the obligations which that law imposes upon members of the family of nations, including the obligation to observe their contractual engagements with one another.

Or (2), it may be held that "sovereignty" is an inherent characteristic of state existence as such, which is anterior to international law and membership in the family of nations, and which leaves its possessors always free in the last analysis to determine on the basis of interest alone the extent to which they shall observe the requirements of international law and of their engagements to other nations. Or, in more concrete terms, a *sovereign* nation is bound by international law and by the international conventions to which it is party only to the extent that those who determine its foreign relations think expedient at any moment.

Or (3), it may be held that "national sovereignty" so-called is merely an honorific term for such powers as the family of nations has seen fit from time to time to bestow upon its several members; in other words, that the family of nations is the only *real* sovereign, and that the so-called sovereign nations are in the contemplation of international law merely its organs and appendages.

This last is the view, for example, of the "Austrian School" of which Professors Kelsen and Verdross have been in recent times the outstanding spokesmen.[34] Inasmuch as this view logically

[34] Josef L. Kunz, "The 'Vienna School' and International Law," *New York Univ. L. Q. R.*, Vol. XI, pp. 1-52 (1934); same, "La Primauté du

interposes no difficulties in the way of even a complete mergence of existing national "sovereignties" into a world state, it may for our purposes be dismissed with a brief word. When set over against the actual record of the relations of the Great Powers during the last three hundred years, this theory is seen to be a *tour de force* of heroic rationalization directed toward a selected ideal, and little else. By the same token, it provides a ready-made rationalization for any pretensions to power which an actual organization of the states of the world may be able some day to assert in actual practice. The importance of this theory therefore, if it has any, lies in future possible developments in the international field. For our purposes it is negligible.

Theory (1), above, possesses, on the other hand, very impressive historical support. This theory asserts that international law itself imposes certain limits on the sovereignty, and hence on the freedom of action, of members of the family of nations, and that every nation upon its entrance into the family of nations consents to be bound by those limits and continues thus bound so long as it remains a member of the family of nations. Such limits are accordingly essential ingredients of each nation's sovereignty—sovereignty, in short, exists *within* international law and the international order, not outside and above them; it is *the obverse of international obligation.*

That this was the theory most generally held by the founders of our own nation is not open to question.[35] Indeed, it is by analogy to it that the idea was launched that the states of the United States, although bound by the Constitution, were still "sovereign" states. The notion has, moreover, been invoked myriads of times by our Department of State when entering protest against claims or acts of other sovereign governments

Droit des Gens," *Revue de Droit International et de Législation Comparée,* 3rd series, Vol. VI, pp. 556-598 (1925).

[35] J. B. Moore, *A Digest of International Law* (Washington: Government Printing Office, 1906), Vol. I, pp. 1-9.

which it asserted to be unwarranted at international law. Conversely, our government has at times conceded claims which were urged against it by other governments on the same ground, a notable instance being its acceptance in 1914 of Great Britain's protest, which was based on a certain interpretation of the Hay-Pauncefote Treaty of 1901, against the exemption of American coastwise shipping from paying tolls for the use of the Panama Canal.[36]

Unfortunately, modern international law also sanctions another concept which ultimately undermines and defeats the concept of a legally limited national sovereignty; I mean the concept of an unlimited right on the part of the members of the family of nations to resort to war against one another—a claim which the theory of total war expands into the right to wage war by any means which appear to promise success. So long as sovereign nations retain by the concession of international law itself the right to make war upon one another at will, the doctrine that national sovereignty is a legally limited sovereignty involves a *felo de se*; the two concepts are mutually unassimilable.

The fact is that the founder of international law perceived the destructive paradox just pointed out, and endeavored to remove it by elaborating a distinction between "just" and "unjust" wars; and American statesmen and jurists have repeatedly voiced the notion that war is merely *a mode of redress for wrongs at international law*. These theories, however, have heretofore failed of their intended effect because of the lack of an international organization capable of enforcing the limitations which they imply on the right to make war. But now suppose that the United States should consent to participate in such an organization, could it then be soundly contended that the obligations which it thereby assumed were an infringement upon its "sovereignty"? Such an argument would clearly reject

---

[36] C. G. Fenwick, *International Law* (New York: Century, 1924), pp. 276-277.

the conception of sovereignty as an attribute which members of the family of nations enjoy *under* international law; and replace it with the conception (concept (2) above) that national sovereignty is an inherent, self-bestowed, element of a nation as such, which arises coevally with it and continues unchanged and undiminished so long as the nation continues—which is, in short, the fundamental test of full nationality.

Coming back, then, to concept (2), above, of national sovereignty, we are compelled to concede at the outset its substantial harmony with nineteenth and early twentieth century juristic concepts, and especially those which are comprised in the so-called Positive, or Austinian, Theory of Law.[37] The notion of *legal* sovereignty—concept (1) above—was an outgrowth of the doctrine of natural law and natural rights, the notion, in Justice Holmes's words, of "a brooding omnipresence in the sky" which bound men in all their relations and whose precepts were addressed to and discoverable by human reason. By the Positive Theory, on the contrary, law is the speech of some definite *human* authority, and the highest human authority is the state, more especially the nation-state. By this theory all law, from whatever source it may take its *content*, receives its *legality*, its claim to obedience, exclusively from the nation-state, whence it follows that the legal competence of the nation-state is limitable only by itself, and the limits thus imposed may be with equal facility cast off.

Several criticisms are in order. To begin with, as was indicated above, so overvaulting a conception of sovereignty "o'erleaps itself and falls on t'other side," implying, as it does unavoidably, that a sovereign state is incapable, just because of its sovereignty, of entering into *legally binding* engagements;

[37] W. W. Willoughby, *The Fundamental Concepts of Public Law* (New York: Macmillan, 1924), pp. 282-308; Albert Kocourek, "The Century of Jurisprudence since John Austin," *Law, A Century of Progress* (New York: University Book Store, 1937), Vol. II, pp. 195-230; Harold Laski, *The Foundations of Sovereignty* (New York: Harcourt, 1921), p. 17.

that in this respect sovereignty, in the sense of capacity to act, is not illimitable but seriously limited. And seeking to avoid this paradox, supporters of the Positive Theory offer a distinction between "legal" and "moral" obligation, conceding the latter to international agreements while denying them the former. The concession is either ineffectual, or it is destructive of the position which it purports to bolster. If it implies that "moral" obligation is less compulsive upon those who are subject to it than "legal" obligation would be, then by so much does a state's sovereignty still impair its capacity for fullest international relationship. If, on the other hand, "moral" obligation is the more compulsive type of obligation, then all talk about "illimitable" sovereignty was meaningless phraseology from the beginning.

Moreover, when we turn from verbal abstractions to the actual history of international intercourse, we find that one of the chief instruments whereby such intercourse has always been furthered in the past has been what the governmental parties to them have undoubtedly regarded as binding engagements, engagements which limited, sometimes drastically, their own immediate freedom of decision and action in promotion of a remoter good. And what has been true in the past will probably continue to be true in the future—a probability which the idea of an international organization for the promotion of peace takes for granted. But the limitation on sovereignty which thus results will, theoretically at least, affect all states alike. It will be reciprocal, and the United States will not find itself at any peculiar disadvantage.

Briefly, then, sovereignty is primarily a logical or verbal concept, or rather it is several such concepts, although wrapped within each of these concepts is a common factual core—that of national independence. When the logical implications of the several theories of sovereignty are closely scrutinized they are found to interpose no obstacle in the way of the participation by the United States in an international organization for the maintenance of international peace. On the contrary, the view

EDWARD S. CORWIN

of national sovereignty and of its relation to international law which American statesmen have generally espoused in the past affords a positive argument for such participation, inasmuch as law always implies the existence of *institutions to support the obligations which it imposes*. And when we turn to the central value connoted by the word "sovereignty" (national independence), the force of this argument is vastly multiplied, certainly for the great majority of states. But even as regards the United States, powerful nation that it is, what greater compulsion upon the freedom of decision and action of our government and upon our own individual lives can be imagined than that imposed by our participation in the current war? It is indeed impossible to imagine an international organization being seriously proposed for our acceptance whose requirements would amount to any comparable surrender of our actual independence as a community or of our freedom as individuals—a surrender we must always be prepared to renew so long as the unlimited right of states to wage war upon one another remains. *When Total War is the price of Total Sovereignty, the price is too high!*

6. Public Opinion and the Peace[1]

BY JEROME S. BRUNER

FOREIGN policy, like all national policy, endures and is made vital by the consent of the governed. There was a time, not long ago, when foreign policy was only nominally the concern of the people. But a shrinking world is robbing the professional diplomatist of his exclusive domain. What the public thinks now and is likely to think in the future about America's relations with the world must be of the gravest concern to all.

This chapter has to do with emerging public opinion on America's foreign policy. For the purposes at hand, public opinion is here equated with the results of public opinion polling. Briefly, five topics will concern us: (1) the bases of American opinion on foreign affairs, (2) the growth of internationalism in popular thinking, (3) the public's conception of the mechanics of collective, international action, (4) the dual problem of dominance and sovereignty, and (5) the stumbling blocks on the road to internationalism.

But before we look at the facts and figures of American public opinion, an assessment of the influence of the public on policy may prove useful.

First, public opinion rarely has a *direct* influence on foreign policy. The President and the State Department have not surrendered their prerogatives. Referenda in the field of foreign affairs are rare. The influence is indirect. Even in the most effective democracy it takes time for public opinion actually to affect foreign policy.

Second, public opinion is effective to the extent that it is

[1] Parts of this chapter have already appeared in print. See J. S. Bruner, "Public Opinion and America's Foreign Policy," *American Sociological Review*, Vol. IX, February 1944. For a more complete discussion of problems treated here, see J. S. Bruner, *Mandate from the People* (New York: Duell, Sloan and Pearce, 1944).

organized. Leaders of organized groups may and often do have more to say about policy than The People. A one-man poll of Ed O'Neal of the Farm Bureau might yield more accurate insight into some future tariff schedules than would a careful sampling of the total population.

Third, public opinion frequently abates in the face of a *fait accompli*. The less personal the issue, the more likely is this to be true. Foreign policy is highly impersonal to the citizen.

But though there be reservations about the direct influence of public opinion in the short run, there should be no doubt about its importance for the long haul. There has been a tremendous advance in public thinking about international problems during the past twenty years. Improved technology during the next twenty will accelerate this trend. The result will inevitably be a world-wide growth of international-mindedness. It is no longer a question of whether the states of the world will orient themselves toward nationalism or internationalism. The question now is: How long will it take for internationalism to grow to effective strength?

THE BASES OF OPINION ON FOREIGN POLICY

There seem to be six primary facts concerning public thinking on foreign policy.

1. *Our habits of collective international action are of recent origin.* It is quite unnecessary to point out that this country has rarely participated in joint international councils. Our past has been notable for a nationalism marked by a tendency to confine formal commitments to bilateral international agreements. "Entangling alliance" has been the bogeyman both to the schoolboy acquiring his first wisdom about America's role in the world and to the average citizen. Let me go back to 1935 for a reminder of our old habits. In that year, this question was asked of a sample of the population by interviewers of the American Institute of Public Opinion (AIPO):[2]

[2] Abbreviations will be used to indicate the organization responsible for

PUBLIC OPINION AND THE PEACE

If one foreign nation insists upon attacking another, should the U.S. join with other nations to compel it to stop?
28% felt that we should join with others, *but*
67% were opposed to collective action, and
5% were undecided.

Because our habits of collective action are recent, we are still subject to backslidings and, more important, still relatively uninformed about the necessary details of effective collective measures.

2. *The basic American point of view is not isolationism. It is, rather, the belief that we can be isolationist or internationalist, depending upon the advantages of each position.* We shall see presently that in 1944 the overwhelming majority of the American people believes that the most profitable course of action is internationalism. But conditions may change. A recent visitor from England, a keen observer, remarked that to the American people foreign policy is like a necktie. When you get tired of one, you put on another. The coming task as far as this country is concerned is not so much the stamping out of isolationism. That philosophy is dying a slow death in any event. What Americans must learn is that a nation cannot trim the sails of foreign policy to the winds of expediency alone. We are not free agents in the field of international affairs. To that fact we have yet to awaken.

3. *Apparent self-interest is the primary fulcrum upon which opinion on foreign policy turns.* Given a situation involving America's relations with other countries, it is our habit to look first and longest at what *we* get out of it. Apparent self-interest changes with time and is subject to fashions. The extent to which apparent *national* self-interest becomes identified with

poll results cited in these pages. AIPO is the American Institute of Public Opinion, FOR is the Fortune Poll, NORC is the National Opinion Research Center, OPOR is the Office of Public Opinion Research of Princeton University.

collective international self-interest will determine, of course, the degree to which we shall become world citizens.

An example of self-interest at work: Consider the sharp difference in the constellation of attitudes held by those who, in March 1941, favored sending aid to England even if it meant war, and those who were opposed to such aid (OPOR).

Do you think that:

	THOSE WHO FAVORED RISKING WAR BY SENDING AID	THOSE WHO OPPOSED RISKING WAR BY SENDING AID
Germany will attack America in ten years?	75%	33%
Germany will control trade if she wins?	73%	32%
Axis victory will restrict U.S. freedom?	72%	30%

4. *Our desire for action in foreign affairs is influenced only secondarily by abstract ideological doctrines.* Barring the operation of self-interested motives, ideological factors *do* prevail. They prevail to the extent of enlisting our sympathies. But action and sympathy are not the same thing. Public opinion will reach fever pitch for action on any particular issue in proportion to the dramatic coincidence of apparent self-interest and morality. Where moral scruple and apparent self-interest conflict, the latter and not the former tends to govern.

The gap between ideological sympathy and direct action is nicely illustrated by American opinion in the immediate prewar years. Between May 1940 and November 1941, the proportion of Americans holding the view that we should send aid to England even if it meant risking war rose from 35% to 70%. However the rise be interpreted, it is an appreciable growth of sentiment even for a year and a half. To find out whether our opinion of Britain's war aims was changing correspondingly, the country was asked periodically whether Britain was fighting primarily for democracy or for the maintenance of her power and wealth. Between March 1940 and November 1941, the percentage holding the former view of Britain's war aims rose from 38% to 39% (OPR).

The consequences of our "apolitical" world view are both healthy and unhealthy. We are not easily thrown off the track by fine words. But occasionally our memories of them are short. A few weeks after the meeting at sea between the President and Prime Minister in August 1941, some three-quarters of the public knew that a meeting had occurred and that the Atlantic Charter had emerged. Five months later, only a quarter answered "yes" to the question, "Have you heard or read of the Atlantic Charter?" (AIPO).

5. *The primary international peace aim of the American people is the prevention of future war.* As an aim, the prevention of war is negative. A negative aim is not of itself deplorable; only when there is a hopeless gulf between a negative aim and the positive means through which it can be achieved is there cause for alarm. The American people have some rather positive ideas about how to achieve the prevention of war. Some of these will be discussed below.

Because the prevention of war is a primary aim and the adoption of specific measures to that end is secondary, the American people are still capable of making some bad blunders. They are like the countryman whose barn has recently burned —he is ready to buy every kind of lightning rod or fire insurance he can find, good, bad, and indifferent. The analogy is not a complete one, to be sure, for we are far from ready to buy isolationist war-risk insurance. But we still need plenty of tutoring on the methods of preventing war.

6. *Americans have an admirable faith in the practical kind of internationalism that has worked in wartime.* Wartime collective action is an understandable model, based on the interests of all concerned. Lacking a vivid past history of peacetime collective action, we are slowly but surely adopting the model of wartime cooperation suitable in general terms for peacetime. As yet, the feeling is uncrystallized. It goes something like this:

JEROME S. BRUNER

"We all work together when there's war. Why can't we stick together after it's over to prevent other wars?" Though still vague, the feeling of logical transition from war to peace is a potent factor in our thinking about internationalism.

But, alas, most of us realize that the common interest of wartime—a common self-interest—is not so easily maintained in peace. And there, indeed, is the rub. Yet be it noted that there are areas of common interest in peace as in war. From the sections which follow, it will clearly appear that the people want these areas expanded.

So much for the bases of American opinion on foreign policy. Let us consider now the position on foreign policy to which Americans adhere at present.

FOREIGN POLICY: THE PEOPLE'S VERSION

As this is written, the great majority of Americans believe it is in our best interest to take an active part in world affairs after the war. To say this is to say a great deal. Ever since Pearl Harbor, the American people have been strong in this conviction. Consider these figures—from Pearl Harbor to the end of 1943—in answer to the question whether America should take an active part in world affairs or stay out of world affairs (OPOR and AIPO). To prove that the issue is not one of domestic politics, the opinions of Republican and Democratic voters are also included.

U.S. SHOULD TAKE ACTIVE PART IN WORLD AFFAIRS

	Total Population (incl. non-voters)	Republicans	Democrats
January 1942	72%	74%	73%
March 1942	73	81	77
June 1942	68	73	73
October 1942	67	84	78
January 1943	76	79	80
May 1943	68	69	71
November 1943	68	73	70

The meaning of an "active part" in world affairs has changed under the impact of experience. One week after Pearl Harbor

PUBLIC OPINION AND THE PEACE

a cross-section of Americans was asked whether we should play a larger, smaller, or the same part in world affairs compared with our role before the war. Fifty-nine per cent voted for a larger part at that date. Eighteen months later, in June 1943, 77% wanted us to play a larger part than before (FOR).

Nor are these opinions merely ephemeral expressions of good will. In June 1942 exponents of interventionist and isolationist post-war sentiments were tested to see if they could be swayed from their position. Those who favored an active part for the United States in post-war world affairs were asked (OPOR):

> Have you ever considered the possibility that we might have to keep up a large army, navy, and air force at great expense to help police the world if we want to take an active part in world affairs? Do you think this expense would be justified?

Ninety-three per cent of the interventionists thought it would be. Then they were asked this purposely tendentious question:

> If our trade with other countries after the war gets us involved in entangling alliances and power politics, as Europe always has been, would you still think it would be best to take an active part in world affairs?

Only 20% of the interventionists deserted their ship. Sixty-one per cent would still want us to take an active part. The rest were not sure.

The isolationists were just as firm in their position.

> If it should happen that there is trouble and other nations get ready for war, do you think we should stay out of world affairs then?

Six in ten of the isolationists were obdurate: stay out of world affairs, regardless. Fewer than three in ten came over to internationalism. Then:

> Suppose our standard of living is reduced when we try to get along on what we grow and produce at home. Would you still think it would be best to stay out of world affairs?

Again, six out of ten stood firm. Isolationism would still be best. Scarcely two in ten were converted. The fortunate thing about all this is, perhaps, that there were better than three advocates of participation in world affairs for every isolationist.

The determination to take an active part does not mean we desire to postpone action for permanent peace until the end of the war. As far as the public is concerned, the time to begin setting up a new international order was some time back. Three-quarters of the nation indicated (AIPO), as far back as January 1943, that they thought the "Government should take steps now, before the end of the war, to set up with our allies a world organization to maintain the peace of the world." And in November 1942, in the polling booths, the voters of the Commonwealth of Massachusetts voted 75% in favor of a resolution instructing the state legislature to petition Congress and the President of the United States to "call at the earliest possible moment" a world convention to discuss the formation of an organization of nations. Why the legislature failed to do so is a problem in machine politics, not in public opinion.

We are therefore ready and willing—and the Moscow, Cairo, and Teheran conferences showed us able—to move in the direction of internationalism. But what kind of internationalism? With what sort of machinery?

THE MACHINERY OF COLLECTIVE ACTION

The average American is even less of an expert than the average Czech or the average Briton on how nations can and should work out the arrangements of collective organization. But two things the American people *do* believe about international organization. The first is that to have an adequate international order, there must be an organization; the second, that international order must be backed by the threat of force.

The growth of faith in international organization is a tremendous advance. In 1936 when a Gallup poll asked the American people whether they thought a league of nations or alliances between strong countries (i.e., a balance of power) was the better method of maintaining peace, two-thirds chose alliances

(AIPO). In October 1943, when polls asked people whether a league of nations or arrangements between individual countries was better for settling international disputes, seven people in ten chose the organizational method (NORC)—a complete reversal in seven years.

It is hardly necessary to give statistics on the number of Americans who favor our joining in a "general organization of nations after the war." The figures run in the range of 75%-85% depending on the peculiarities of the question used. All sections of the country, all economic classes, all educational levels, all religious groupings, all occupations, both sexes, and both parties deliver healthy majorities in favor of American participation in an organization of nations. They did so before the Moscow Conference, before the Connally Resolution, before the Fulbright Resolution.

Nor is our willingness to participate made conditional upon our being the dominant world power. Sixty-two per cent favor joining even if Britain has the same power in league affairs as we do. Fifty-five per cent are willing even if Russia wields equal power (NORC, January 1943).

What functions should a league have? Regulation of armament in all countries? Almost eight in ten agree. Promulgation of international law? Again "Yes," by an overwhelming majority. Regulation of international commerce? The same result (NORC, September 1943). In March 1943, moreover, the *Fortune* Poll reported these reactions of a cross-section of Americans to various proposals concerning the power of the "next" organization of nations:

	FAVOR	OPPOSE	NO OPINION
Prevent one country from starting a war against another	79%	7%	14%
Settle disputes between two nations	76	8	16
Decide taxes to be paid to international organization by members	70	9	21
Decide military strength of members	69	14	17

JEROME S. BRUNER

	FAVOR	OPPOSE	NO OPINION
Regulate international air rights	61%	14%	25%
Maintain police force stronger than army of any member state	54	23	23
Decide tariff rates of members	45	23	32
Decide guilt and take sides in civil wars	43	32	25
Set minimum international work standards	32	45	23

Are we fair-weather internationalists? Do we really mean all this or would we retreat at the first demand for sacrifice? During January 1943 Americans were asked whether they would be willing to make certain sacrifices if these were necessary to try out an organization of nations (NORC). The results are encouraging. No, we will not make all sacrifices. But there are many which we are disposed to approve. Consider these figures.

To try out an organization of nations after the war would you be willing to:

	PER CENT WILLING
Continue rationing to feed other countries?	82%
Have part of our army stay overseas?	76
Pay more taxes than other countries?	64
Consider lend-lease a gift to Allies?	42
Disarm along with other nations?	42
Admit foreign goods without tariff?	28
Forget reparations from our enemies?	28

Let us now consider the second principle of international organization—necessity for the use of force. There exists no fair way of measuring the fact, but there is, nevertheless, some reason to believe that our conviction in the necessity of force to maintain international order is stronger than our belief in the efficacy of organization.

Since our paramount international peace aim is the prevention of war, it is not surprising that peace formulae which provide explicitly for forcible measures against the outbreak of another war receive strong support from the American people. One such proposal—one, incidentally, which has captured the popular

PUBLIC OPINION AND THE PEACE

mind—is the international police. There has not been a time since July 1942 when three-quarters or more of the American people could not be enlisted in support of American participation in world policing (OPOR). No section of the country, no social or economic stratum, fails to show a huge majority in its favor.

In September 1943 an attempt was made to find out how the public conceived the *scope* of an international police force (OPOR). Was it to police only the Axis? Or everybody? The results were heartening. Respondents were faced with three alternatives:

> Policing Axis countries only
> Policing Axis countries and small countries
> Policing all countries including the United States

Nine per cent chose the first alternative—policing the Axis only. Ten per cent chose the second. But 76% cast a favorable vote for the broad conception of universal policing.

Accompanying our conviction in the utility of force for peace-maintenance is our unwillingness to see general disarmament adopted as a principle after the war. Disarmament is not a popular peace plan. Eighty-seven per cent of the population were opposed to universal disarmament in the fall of 1942 (AIPO). They are opposed even if a successful international police force is created (OPOR, September 1943). But more of that in a moment.

This, in brief, is the picture of opinion with respect to the machinery of cooperation—organization and force. We turn now to two matters which, of necessity, will temper opinion on all foreign policy questions. The first is the question of dominance. The second, closely related, is "national sovereignty."

DOMINANCE AND SOVEREIGNTY

Were it not for the fact that "apparent self-interest" is so central in our thinking about America's relations with the rest of the world, the question of dominance or "position" would not

JEROME S. BRUNER

be so urgent. But it is urgent. We can take it as axiomatic that the American people will take no interest in, will fail to support, or will resist a world order in which the United States does not play a dominant part or at least a conspicuous part. Let us consider some of the pertinent facts.

First, let us compare American and British public opinion. Which country *should* have the most to say about the peace? Eighty-two per cent of the American public blandly name the United States (FOR, April 1942). Forty-three per cent of the British public name Britain (FOR, September 1942). Which country *will* have the most to say? Six in ten Americans think we will (FOR, April 1942). But only three in ten Britons think England will (FOR, September 1942).

America's animal spirits may be difficult for other nations to understand. Our willingness to join a league on equal terms with Britain and Russia—as already demonstrated—convinces me, at least, that our animal spirits are not necessarily malignant. The problem is to find the proper outlet for those spirits, to achieve a formula of cooperation with others which provides a "moral equivalent for dominance." A vigorous and enlightened information policy, one which allows Americans to understand their country's real influence and stake in world affairs, would help greatly. We do not now have such an information policy.

The problem of protecting our sense of national sovereignty in cotton wool I would rate as less important than the problem of canalizing our will to dominate. But sovereignty, if ever it did get to be an issue, could do more to wreck our chances of effective participation. So much nonsense has been uttered about America's sense of sovereignty that I should like to state a few simple propositions concerning it.

First, the sense of sovereignty, in America at least, is normally not at all a conscious, active attitude. Properly speaking, it is a frame of reference of which we become conscious only under certain circumscribed conditions.

The conditions which arouse the sense of sovereignty, bringing into play our national prides and prejudices, are two: *threat* or *actual attack*. An activated sense of national sovereignty is a symbol of insecurity. German *Enkreisung* is an example.

Second, *any* issue of foreign policy contains two emphases: one concerns the effect on our sovereignty of the settlement of the issue; the other has to do with the *intrinsic* merits of a possible solution. A particular trade pact, for instance, may be viewed either from the point of view of limiting our freedom of action or of benefiting the machine-tool industry.

Third, the extent to which the second, intrinsic, emphasis is brought to the fore will control the degree to which sovereignty can be an issue. Intrinsic emphasis—apparent self-interest, if you like—can be brought to the fore only if the public is well-informed. The public can be well-informed only if foreign policy is the object of a vigorous and well-contrived information policy. It goes without saying that the higher the level of general information on foreign affairs, the easier it is to inform the public about the intrinsic pros and cons of a particular measure and, consequently, the easier it is to forestall a battle over sovereignty.

Finally, as Sumner Welles so ably pointed out in his address before the Foreign Policy Association in October 1943, and as Professor Corwin shows in his chapter in this book, we have willingly relinquished some degree of sovereignty every time this country has entered with another country into an agreement, pact, protocol or treaty. A policy of restricted sovereignty will at least not be suspect because of novelty.

What can be said of public opinion on this question? That America feels relatively safe about her place in the post-war sun is obvious. That type of insecurity, in the political sphere at least, is not likely to stampede us into tall talk about "sovereign and inalienable rights." Where we do not feel secure is in the military realm. We know now that getting into war is like falling off a log. It is much too easy. A majority of Americans believe that there will be other wars (NORC, September 1943). But it is almost because of this type of insecurity that the intrinsic merits, the apparent self-interest, of binding ourselves with others outweighs the dread of entangling alliances. We know the military limitations of isolationism. But, more important, we are yet to learn the strength of international coalition.

Our ardor to use force to prevent war is such that questions which might normally evoke a righteous sense of sovereignty no longer have that effect. We have seen, for example, that the majority of the public conceives of a police force in inclusive terms—we, along with others, are to be policed. How strong shall the police force be, say, in comparison with the post-war American army? Two-thirds of those with opinions believe that it should be at least as strong as our own armed forces (OPOR, September 1943). Finally, the public was asked whether a strong police force might be a threat to the United States. Only a quarter of the population agreed that it would be (OPOR, September 1943). If sovereignty does not warp materially our conception of how military power shall be allocated after the war, need it prove an obstacle in spheres where the danger to America is less apparent?

CERTAIN DANGERS

There can be no doubt about one fact: public opinion on questions of foreign policy is more vigorous and forward-looking today than it has ever been before. There is a minimum of cavil about sovereignty. We are willing to take our place in the congress of nations. The atmosphere, the climate of opinion, is venturesome and experimental. We want to give things a try.

But there are two clouds on the horizon. One of them can be dissipated by a well-conducted campaign of popular education. The other is likely to trouble us for many years to come.

We may call the first cloud capriciousness in our choice of methods for cooperation. We want a great army and navy after the war; we also want a strong police force. The two can, of course, co-exist. But eventually they may bring friction. The answer will be given in time. If and when internationally-controlled force proves effective, we as a people will reconsider our opinions about America's armed might.

Another example of caprice can be found in the conflicting opinion about America's post-war international commitments. In the fall of 1943, a strong majority of Americans went on record as favoring a mutual-aid alliance with Britain (AIPO). At the same time, a great majority favored our participation in a general organization of nations. Few people yet see any contradiction between bilateral commitments and membership in a general league. The Russo-Czech alliance, for example, went virtually unnoticed by the public. Yet the co-existence of alliances and a league can constitute a threat to international security. In time, perhaps, this fact will dawn on us. It has not yet done so.

Our confusion is to some extent reflected in the split of opinion over the control of power in a future league of nations (FOR, March 1944). Asked whether the member states should all have equal rights or whether a few of the greater states should dominate, 50% took the former alternative, 40% the latter. The split is too even for comfort. In our own minds we are not yet clear about international power. It may be that the man in the street takes the view—perhaps the most realistic one— that it makes no difference whether one decides in favor of a system of security dominated by four powers or a pure league system. The strong will dominate the show anyway. That may be the basis of our uncertainty over the allocation of international power. As yet, however, we do not know. Eventually opinion will crystallize and some of our uncertainties will be resolved. The unfortunate thing about it is that the pressure of events and not prior deliberation may well determine which way we will jump.

The second cloud on the horizon, one which gives promise

JEROME S. BRUNER

of stormy weather, concerns America's post-war economic position. On questions of international economics we are still, at heart, trading Yankees. Ours is an attitude of protectionism. We must protect ourselves from the competition of states with lower living standards. *The Economist* of London sums up the matter tartly: "In political matters, the tide [in the United States] is flowing toward Wilson; but in those questions of economic cooperation which are the lifeblood of an enduring settlement, there are signs of a return to the big stick and the ideology of McKinley."

Essentially, the confusion in our thinking can be briefly described by saying that we have not yet learned that in order to sell one must also buy. We are afraid to buy lest we be flooded with cheap goods. Yes, it is fear—fear and economic insecurity —that keep us from learning that to buy internationally is also to sell.

The role of fear in bolstering economic isolationism is not hard to demonstrate. Take this question as an example:

> After the war, should the U.S. try to develop its own industries to the point where it does not have to buy any products from foreign countries?

In April 1943, 47% said, "No," 48% said, "Yes" (OPOR). But the national figures are not so interesting as the replies of different income strata. When the figures are broken down in that way, the role of economic security becomes inescapably clear. Consider that:

> 71% of those with above-average income oppose autarky;
> 51% of those with average income oppose autarky;
> 35% of those with below-average incomes oppose autarky.

More than education is required. To the man who feels that he is barely hanging on to his job, the argument that we must trade as much as possible with other nations in order to raise our standard of living will sound hollow. If one talks about it to the shoe-worker in Lawrence, Massachusetts, the first thing that will come to his mind is the threat of cheap Czech shoes. In addition to education, there will have to be a prior guarantee that our economy is vigorous enough to provide jobs for all. A veteran Washington correspondent once remarked that every time the economic sledding gets tough, Congress starts hitting the tariff bottle. Congress thus has much in common with its constituents.

There is, of course, a paradox involved here. Can we build a strong domestic economy before we devise a decent foreign trade policy? The point is a moot one. Certain it is that paradox should not prevent us from trying to do both things at once. And while we are about it, there is still the job of teaching the public the very elementary facts of international trade. The majority of Americans, for example, still have no idea of the nature of a reciprocal trade treaty (AIPO, December 1943).

There is no ready solution to the problem of American opinion on international economic problems but there is much that can be done to improve our understanding, and we must proceed on many fronts at once and hope for the best.

SOME CONCLUSIONS

One obvious conclusion to be drawn from practically everything that has been said in these pages is that the American people are sorely in need of information about foreign affairs. If one were rash, one might say that all that has to be done is for the government to step up its information program. There is no doubt that such a move would help—given the proper safeguards against governmental usurpation of the media of communication. At the beginning of 1944 the State Department in its reorganization established an Office of Public Information which has as one of its functions the enlightening of public opinion. Eventually, the State Department may get an Assistant Secretary who will handle the job of information as his exclusive domain. All of these steps are in the right direction. Yet none of them is enough. The job of informing the people must not be postponed until the average citizen reaches the voting age of twenty-one. Present teaching in primary and secondary schools is obviously not preparing American youth to decide intelligently on questions of foreign policy. The road to an informed public is through an informed youth aware of the basic issues which underlie the making of foreign policy.

That, of course, is a long-run project. There are many things that can be done now which would facilitate the making of a more intelligent peace. One of them concerns the time of writing the peace. At the present time the people are sure about certain basic objectives. They want the establishment of an international organization and they want a system for enforcing peace. In a very real sense our leaders have a mandate from the people on these points. The time to act upon them is now. If our leaders wait, the effect on public opinion may be disastrous. To wait may be to give rise to the impression that the task of international organization is perilously difficult. Such an impression could have the effect of frightening the public into indecision. All this is not to say that our leaders must blueprint the future in detail. The public is willing to see the details put off, but it is not willing to see the basic pledges of cooperation delayed.

What of the much-talked-of "return to normalcy"? It is, to be sure, a danger; but in no sense is it either inevitable or automatic. Regression to isolationism after the last war was not of the people's fashioning. Isolation was a legislative *fait accompli* which people accepted because there was nothing else to do about it. We were disillusioned. But it was not inevitable that we should have been disillusioned.

A "return to normalcy" is not out of the question after the war. But it is wrong to assume that it *has* to take place. Regression can be accelerated by certain conditions. If these conditions are kept under control, this danger can be avoided.

Perhaps the first condition, least controllable, is fatigue. We shall be tired after the war. But fatigue is a relative thing. The businessman who is tired after a day's work suddenly finds himself fresh when faced with the pleasant prospect of a half hour of handball before dinner. In combating fatigue, the most important precaution is to see that there is a new and different and clearly defined activity to which to turn after leaving the old. If planning the peace can be made such a new, different, and clearly defined activity, the dangers of regression will be immeasurably decreased.

But peace planning cannot serve as an anti-fatigue measure unless certain psychological conditions are satisfied. First, peace planning must not awaken a sense of insecurity in the American people. We must not be made to feel that we are being threatened, for example economically, by our former allies. As soon as insecurity enters, the will to cooperate with others, to participate in joint planning, will be sapped by the desire to withdraw to safety. A recrudescence of anti-Russian and anti-British propaganda at the end of the war would amount to psychological sabotage. To be brutally realistic about the matter, we had better expect that post-war anti-allied propaganda *will*, in some measure, dampen our determination to work together and to try new solutions.

A second, extremely dangerous, stimulus to regression is confusion. If post-war negotiations get hopelessly confused by a welter of incomprehensible issues (incomprehensible from the American point of view), the inevitable reaction will be a demand for the familiar. Crystal-clear information and a well-informed public are the two most dependable foes of confusion. It is hopeless to expect that both these conditions will be fully met. To be realistic, again, we must expect an impulse to normalcy from this quarter.

The press has a grave responsibility for keeping post-war issues unmuddied. For it has in its power the means of confusion as well as the means of clarification. The lamentable journalistic practice, so often witnessed during the war, of creating "issues" and "conflicts" and "differences" for the sake of making news, can cause great harm. The task of the press, to be sure, is not to gloss over differences—nor is it, however, to amplify them. Responsible journalism has as its primary duty, with respect to controversial issues, the reporting of differences in their proper perspective and the explanation of those differences in comprehensible terms.

A return to old pre-war squabbles at the peace table can also serve as an impetus toward normalcy. To move ahead, to map out new ways of preventing war, to work jointly with others— all these things require new frames of reference. Anything that drags us back into the 'twenties and 'thirties will serve to violate the new frames of reference that have been developing during the war. A land-grab squabble, confusion over border disputes, bickering for commercial advantages—if these develop, the new will for internationalism may be quickly superseded by old ways of thinking. Since there are bound to be disputes of this type, casualties among the ranks of the internationalists are likewise inevitable.

Finally, the longer we wait before tackling the problems of the post-war world with our allies, the greater will be the fatigue to be overcome, the better the chances of confusion, the more likely a revival of old disputes, and the weaker the momentum of post-war planning. Every month of delay will weaken public support for an international order. Already the majority of the American people feel that planning should be under way. In many important respects it has indeed been started. But we have probably already waited much longer than it is safe to wait. Our delay means that the will for post-war pioneering has to some extent been jeopardized.

These are some of the dangers we face. Let no one assume that, because opinion is favorable to internationalism today, there are no worries for the future.

We need consider but one more matter. The time has come when the ratification of treaties can no longer be left safely in the hands of the Senate. Now that foreign policy is becoming a matter of immediate concern to all, it is abundantly clear that

PUBLIC OPINION AND THE PEACE

one-third plus one man of the Senate should not be allowed to block measures which represent the public will. In September 1943, the Gallup poll indicated that a majority of Americans favored a constitutional amendment providing for treaty ratification by the President and a majority of both Houses of Congress. If it is our aim to make foreign policy more democratic, such an amendment (or an adequate substitute) is imperative.

The world is shrinking. America can no longer afford to be ignorant of the issues of foreign policy. There are signs of a public awakening. Those signs are good. The best safeguard against future wars is an informed and active public opinion.

7. American Ideals and the Peace

BY GEORGE F. THOMAS

THE neglect of moral questions in recent discussions of our foreign policy is one of the most disturbing signs of the times. Some of our leading publicists treat the problem of foreign policy as if it could be solved in a moral vacuum. The only questions they consider adequately are those which have to do with the use of power for national security. They make no attempt to show that the order imposed by the Great Powers will be based on justice and will therefore be preferable to any alternative order. They seem to assume that the national interests of the Great Powers, rightly conceived, will not lead any of them into aggressive acts and that in their agreements they will respect the rights of the smaller nations. But will states rightly conceive their national interests? The general tendency of immense power to corrupt nations and tempt them to aggrandize themselves must never be forgotten. Can one really believe that dynamic powers like Russia and America—the "adolescent giants" of the twentieth century—will use their great energies for the good of humanity if in their foreign policy they are motivated by no end more inspiring than their own national security and envisage no method but that of power politics?

Because of the crucial importance of moral issues in the current debate over foreign policy, it may be well to consider some of the ideals which dominated American democratic thought in the last century and to ask what they demand of us as we face the urgent twentieth century problem of world order. Professor Ralph Gabriel's statement[1] of these dominant ideals will serve as a useful point of departure. American democratic

[1] *The Course of American Democratic Thought* (New York: Ronald, 1940), Chapter 2.

AMERICAN IDEALS AND THE PEACE

thought, he says, has been characterized not only by a passion for individual liberty but also by a profound belief in an eternal and unchanging *moral law* by reference to which all human acts and laws must be judged, and by a *sense of national mission* as a beacon light of freedom among the nations of the earth. These convictions, he recognizes, have been modified by the operation of historical forces in our national life, and in recent years each of them has been rudely challenged.[2] Individual liberty has in a measure given way to collectivism, the freedom of the individual to the authority of the state. The existence of an eternal moral law, whether divine or natural, has been called in question by moral relativism, and with many expediency has become the basis of human law and conduct. The idea of national mission has been widely discredited by the international anarchy to which nationalism has led. Despite these severe shocks to our dominant ideals, however, Gabriel thinks that the democratic faith is still vital. If so, it would be futile to frame a foreign policy which took no account of the main articles of that faith.

These dominant American ideals are deeply rooted in the Hebraic-Christian and the Greco-Roman traditions which have shaped our whole western civilization. They also bear upon them the marks of distinctively modern forces and ideas—e.g., economic individualism, nationalism, humanitarianism, and belief in progress. The belief in *individual liberty* is derived primarily from the classical, humanistic conception of the dignity of the individual as a rational being capable, with the help of education, of determining his ends and acts for himself. It has also been deeply influenced by the Christian conception of man as a spiritual being made in the image of God, ultimately responsible to God alone, and hence entitled to moral and religious liberty beyond the control of state authority. The exaggerated emphasis in America upon the individual and his unrestricted liberty, however, has been due to modern factors

[2] *ibid.*, Chapter 31.

GEORGE F. THOMAS

such as economic individualism and an interpretation of democracy which has stressed liberty at the expense of equality and fraternity. The belief in an *eternal and fixed moral law* is derived from both the Christian and the classical sides of our tradition, though in the one case it is identified with the revealed will of God and in the other with nature as understood by reason. Finally, the sense of *national destiny* as a beacon light of liberty for all humanity represents a secularization of Christian and classical ideals under the influence of democracy and nationalism. By the middle of the nineteenth century we had all but lost the Puritans' vision of Providence leading the "elect" to establish a land where they could enjoy religious liberty and where the Word of God would be the source of law. But the sense of a mission to serve higher and more universal ends survived in a secular form—the democratic dream of political liberty and economic opportunity for all mankind.

The primary purpose of this chapter, however, is not to trace these ideals to their origins, but to indicate some of the ways in which they throw light upon the question of our responsibility for world order. We shall, therefore, use them merely as signposts to point in the general direction in which answers to certain questions about our foreign policy should be sought. We will begin with that optimistic belief in progress which has run like a golden thread through the whole pattern of American democratic thought and has given us hope and courage to face the future without bondage to the past.

OUR BELIEF IN PROGRESS

One of the symptoms of the disillusionment of our time is the reaction against the optimism of the nineteenth century. In the minds of many Americans today, our earlier belief in progress was naive. The reasons for this reaction are complex. The widespread influence of naturalistic philosophy since the time of Darwin has blighted the spiritual aspirations and paralyzed the moral wills of many. If man is only a complex animal, using his

200

AMERICAN IDEALS AND THE PEACE

reason simply to satisfy his impulses and with no freedom to direct his actions by moral principles, he cannot hope to rise far above the level of the animal kingdom. The struggle for existence or the will to power tends to become the last word in social relationships. Under the influence of this way of thinking, social prophets or philosophers of history like Marx and Spengler have written as if the future is primarily determined by impersonal forces rather than by personal wills. Thus for Marx, economic forces are leading inevitably through the class struggle to a classless society, while for Spengler historical determinism spells the decline and fall of western culture. This philosophical determinism is given point by the inarticulate feeling of countless numbers of ordinary men and women that they are powerless to resist or control the vast social forces that seem to be sweeping them onward toward a new "dark age" of impersonal collectivism and increasingly destructive wars. Since this pessimism about the future makes men despair of the very possibility of enduring peace under an international organization, it needs to be carefully examined. It may be that it is as unjustified as the extreme optimism to which it is opposed, and that what is called for is a sober and realistic belief in the possibility of progress.

In the first place, the earlier uncritical belief in inevitable and unlimited progress must be abandoned. The idea of progress advanced by eighteenth century thinkers like Condorcet was based upon the triumphs of reason in natural science and the assumption that the scientific method would solve our moral and social problems. Education and technology, it was hoped, would make the benefits of new scientific discoveries available to all, and social reforms would emancipate men from outworn institutions. It was assumed that man is by nature rational and good, and that the evils from which he suffers are simply due to ignorance, error, or faulty environment. The rapid industrial expansion and political development of the nineteenth century made this idea of progress plausible, and the theory of evolution encouraged many to think that the improvement of the human species by the operation of natural laws was inevitable.

Since the First World War, however, these hopes have revealed themselves as dangerous illusions. Natural enough in a time of scientific, economic, and political advancement, they intoxicated men and blinded them to the increasing moral and social disintegration of the western world. But they vanished like a dream when the First World War, the Great Depression, and the approach of the Second World War showed us the dark abysses yawning at our feet. We have now come to see that scientific, technological, and industrial progress does not necessarily bring with it progress in moral discipline and political wisdom. We have seen reason, developed by education and using the scientific method, become a mere servant of individual selfishness or of the demonic will to power of a race or state. We have been made aware, moreover, of the irrational and subconscious impulses in ourselves and of the way they corrupt our moral and political judgments. In a word, we have come to know the depths of human egoism in greed, sensuality, and pride. This rediscovery of what Christians have called sin makes us suspicious both of the eighteenth century faith in man's rationality and goodness and the nineteenth century faith in historical and biological forces bearing him forward irresistibly toward perfection.

But, in the second place, we must also guard ourselves against the opposite extreme of pessimism. Those who do not accept the naturalistic dogma that man is only a complex animal, or the historical determinism that tends to accompany it, need not fear the future.

There is, to be sure, some evidence that economic individualism, fanatical nationalism, and moral confusion have gone too far to be easily arrested and that the western world may be entering a period of prolonged and widespread revolution. Economic and political institutions are undergoing profound changes, and the spiritual basis of our culture has been seriously weakened. No one can say with confidence that western civilization can survive these shocks without even more radical changes in our social institutions and without a revitalizing of our spiritual life.

But there are elements of strength in the western democracies which give us reason for hope. The democracies have shown more vitality during the war years than many thought possible. It had been thought by Marxists and Fascists that democracy was so closely associated with rugged individualism and exploitation that it could not achieve unity even when its existence was challenged. At the least, they were certain that in a crisis it would reveal its inefficiency and lack of heroism. Both suppositions have been proved largely false. It may well take a long time to tame the excessive individualism of our economic system and to realize even approximate equality of opportunity for all our people. But Great Britain and America have already taken long strides in the direction of social legislation for the benefit of the whole community. The willingness of the great majority of all classes, poor and underprivileged as well as rich and fortunate, to support the war effort is one of the fruits of this concern for the common welfare. It is a convincing proof that political democracy is more than a mere instrument of exploitation wielded by the prosperous middle classes, and encourages us to believe that the class struggle and the racial tensions we are facing can be dealt with in the spirit of moderation and compromise. As for the danger of world wars in the future, this book is an attempt to show that we need not fold our hands in despair; indeed, the very magnitude of the problem is stimulating great numbers of men to action. Moreover, on logical grounds, the pessimism of philosophies of history like Spengler's is superficial. It depends upon a false analogy between the history of a culture and the life cycle of an organism from birth to death, and derives much of its plausibility from the false assumption that history must repeat itself and the American republic decline and fall as Rome did.[3]

But there is a more profound pessimism which is based not upon contemporary ills and wild speculations but upon the radical evil in human nature. If we fail, many assert, it will not be because of an essential weakness in democracy or the operation of impersonal historical laws, but because of a fatal flaw in ourselves. The revelation of the appalling depths of evil in human nature has been disclosed to us by the events of the last decade. The Christian doctrine of sin and its consequences for the lives of men and nations had been impatiently dismissed as fantastic since the discovery of the natural rationality and goodness of man by the Age of Enlightenment. Even the churches had put it into the background and had virtually capitulated to the optimistic humanism of the modern world. But recently prophetic voices have been making themselves heard, denouncing the social Utopianism of much liberal thought and reminding us that the individual and collective egoism of man is a universal fact. For the individual, this means that moral perfection can never be attained; for humanity, that progress, save in a limited sense, is impossible. As Reinhold Niebuhr reminds us,[4] the increase of opportunities for good is accompanied by an increase of temptations to evil. For example, modern science puts into our hands both the means of happiness and the instruments of destruction. This does not free us from the responsibility to improve our situation by choosing the greater good or the lesser evil available to us in each situation. But it does limit severely the success we can hope to attain by social action, since collective egoism such as that of the national state is even more destructive than individual selfishness. In short, the root of the trouble is in our own selfish wills, individual and collective, rather than in animal impulses

[3] Chas. Beard, *The Republic* (New York: Viking, 1943), Chapter XXI.
[4] *The Nature and Destiny of Man* (New York: Scribners, 1941-1943), Vol. II, pp. 164-169.

or faulty social institutions; and it cannot be overcome without a radical change in human desires and interests.

However, if this pessimism about man as sinner is balanced by faith in his possibilities as a spiritual being, as it is in the Christian view, it is consistent with a realistic belief in the possibility of progress. It becomes clear that progress is *possible* though not inevitable and automatic, but that its *cost* is far higher than modern men have thought. If progress is to be achieved, it must be the fruit of moral effort and sacrifice. The growth of scientific knowledge, the increase in production, the very attainment of liberty under democratic institutions—all these gains of our civilization will remain precarious so long as the power of individual and collective egoism is not broken or at least greatly weakened.

This means that economic arrangements and political machinery for world organization, important as they are, will be futile unless they are accompanied by a kind of education which disciplines the will and broadens the sympathies of men. The family must nourish the social sympathies, the church must extend their range, and the school must direct them through knowledge into effective action. Moreover, the family, church, and school must combine to stimulate the desire of individuals for communal rather than competitive values, i.e., values which unite rather than divide men. As long as economic values are prized above moral and spiritual values and as long as their unlimited acquisition is regarded as legitimate, individual egoism will continue to make a real sense of community among us impossible. Finally, egoism and greed might be overcome in the individual by fostering the still more dangerous egoism and will to power of the group, as we have witnessed in totalitarian states. It is necessary, therefore, to emphasize the humanitarian and Christian conception of the natural unity of all mankind and to instill a deep conviction of the possibility of a world community. These, and nothing less than these, are the moral conditions of dependable progress.

Thus, neither extreme pessimism nor naive optimism should be the last word. Progress is not inevitable, but it is possible. Men are by nature egoistic, but they are also social beings craving harmony with their fellows and moral beings demanding justice for all. A perfectly harmonious and just world community may never be attained, but an approximation to it is possible. Doubtless, this is a more modest idea of progress than that which dominated the nineteenth century, since it asserts only the possibility of progress and acknowledges that the evil in human nature will prevent the attainment of perfection and will make every step forward a costly one. But it is enough for men who have renounced romantic dreams without losing their faith in humanity.

AMERICA'S DESTINY: NATIONALISM OR INTERNATIONALISM?

According to Professor Gabriel, as we have seen, one of the main doctrines of the American "democratic faith" has been that America has a mission to proclaim the benefits of liberty to the world. "Liberty, according to a widely accepted version of American mythology," he writes, "had been established by deity in an empty western continent so that, freed from the burdens of European tradition, it might flourish and become an inspiration to the world."[5] This "myth" has motivated some of our greatest leaders. It was appealed to by Lincoln in Philadelphia in the dark days of February 1861 at the beginning of the Civil War. Asking what the principle was which had held the states together since the Declaration of Independence, he said, "It was not the mere matter of separation of the colonies from the mother land, but that sentiment in the Declaration of Independence which gave liberty not alone to the people of this country, but hope to all the world, for all future time. It was that which gave promise that in due time the weights would be lifted from the shoulders of all men, and that all

[5] Gabriel, *op. cit.*, p. 22.

should have an equal chance."[6] This doctrine gave the humble American "a romantic vision in which he could see his inconspicuous efforts after righteousness invested with a world significance."[7]

Was it *only* a "romantic vision"? There have always been those who have thought so and they are to be found among us today. They have scoffed at the "sentimentalism" and "naive idealism" of Americans about foreign affairs. Sometimes they have regarded our sense of national destiny as nothing but an hypocritical pretense of universal benevolence behind which shrewd Yankees could further their commercial interests. At other times, they have attributed to it a strong influence upon our foreign policy leading us into foolish commitments or quixotic gestures of generosity. In either case they have regarded it as deplorable in its effect.

The fact is that our sense of national mission to humanity has not usually been strong enough to lead to an active and positive foreign policy. We have been content to be the "land of opportunity" and "haven of the oppressed," to be admired and imitated by other nations for our freedom. This sense of complacency has been enhanced by our feeling of security, our rich natural resources, our great territory, our industrial efficiency, and other factors. In short, we have a peculiar nationalism of our own, one based upon other grounds than exaltation of the state but none the less very strong. It may take the form of a blatant provincialism that magnifies our past achievements or future prospects in comparison with those of European nations. Or it may show itself in a deep satisfaction with our past achievement and a fear that it would be jeopardized by embarking on the uncharted waters of internationalism. In either case, the conviction that we have built some-

---

[6] *Complete Works of Abraham Lincoln*, Nicolay and Hay, ed., new edition (New York: Francis D. Tandy Co., 1905), Vol. VI, p. 157.
[7] Gabriel, *op. cit.*, p. 25.

thing new and unique tempts us to keep ourselves aloof and reject any limitation upon our freedom of action.

To nationalists like Charles Beard, for example, the real concern of America in regard to foreign policy is her own national interest. They conceive of American freedom as something to be cherished and defended at home rather than something to be spread abroad. This helps to explain the meagerness of Beard's constructive suggestions for our foreign policy. In effect, he advocates[8] little more than agreement among the United Nations during the war "on points of continuing cooperation" and a "brief and simple treaty" to be limited to ten years or more but subject to renewal. The settlement, he says, "should not be accompanied by an elaborate world constitution, full of vague phrases that could be, and probably would be, twisted and turned by governments competing for power."[9] As these cautious suggestions follow a sharp criticism of proposals for a modified League of Nations or a Federation of Nations, it seems clear that Beard wishes the American Republic to retain after the war its full freedom of action. It would be a mistake to call this cynicism; it is simply the attitude of one who believes deeply in American freedom but feels little responsibility for helping other nations attain it.

Yet, as we have seen, the "romantic vision" of American democracy as a beacon light for the world springs both from the Christian and classical traditions and from the democratic nationalism of the nineteenth century. It would be difficult to find a belief more deeply rooted. From Christianity comes the belief in the unity of humanity and the dignity and value of all men, irrespective of race or color. From the late classical writers comes the idea that natural rights belong to men as men and are therefore universal. The exponents of the Rights of Man in the eighteenth century had no thought that the right to "life, liberty, and the pursuit of happiness" was an exclusive

[8] Beard, *op. cit.*, Chapter XX, p. 329.
[9] *ibid.*

possession of Frenchmen or Americans. According to the Stoic theory of natural law which influenced their thinking, all men as rational beings are equal. Therefore natural rights belong to all men. In so far as these Christian and Stoic ideas have entered into democratic theory, they have given it a strong universalistic tendency. Nationalism in its nineteenth century democratic form, moreover, is not only compatible with internationalism; it demands it for its fulfillment. To Mazzini, who gave the noblest utterance to this democratic nationalism, duties to humanity come first, duties to country second. This means that true patriotism is meaningless without humanitarianism: it is service to humanity through service to one's own nation. Will anyone deny that these beliefs—the dignity of *all* men, the natural rights of men as *men*, the claims of *all* humanity—still have power over the thoughts and wills of Americans?

It is, of course, possible to argue that, while the American democracy of yesterday was universalistic in its hopes, the democracy of today and tomorrow must be purely national. But it is difficult to see how democracy can maintain itself as a dynamic faith if it renounces the conviction that it is the highest form of social organization and as such is normative for all peoples who have reached political maturity. Once this conviction is lost, the preference for democracy becomes irrational and its moral superiority over its rivals disappears.

Therefore, we must hold fast to our earlier sense of national destiny as a beacon light for the world, unless we intend to renounce our faith in democracy as the norm of government. Moreover, since the events of the last few years have shown that security cannot be taken for granted, this sense of national destiny must, in our time, involve an active and creative rather than a passive and defensive foreign policy. Such a foreign policy may seem to many to be fraught with the perils of imperialism. In reality, it has nothing in common with imperialism in respect to either goal or method; it is its antithesis. Its goal is a world community of peoples with equal rights rather than an empire. Its method is collaboration rather than domination.

Indeed, participation by America in an international organization is the only real alternative to American imperialism in the twentieth century. To suppose that a great nation like America, fully aware of its insecurity as well as its power, will be content to play a passive role as a mere spectator of world events which concern her so vitally is utterly unrealistic. To suppose that an energetic and creative nation, with a genius for economic organization and a pride in her political achievement, will not wish to help shape the world of the future is to fail to understand America for what she is. By her wealth, her military power, her political prestige, her impulse to build, her pioneering spirit, America along with the other Great Powers must assume a role of leadership in the world of tomorrow, whatever the risks. The only question is, will she imitate the pattern of aggressive, imperialistic domination followed by the Great Powers in the nineteenth century, or will she follow a pattern of leadership more consistent with her past understanding of her national destiny and with the twentieth century need for a world community?

The answer to this question depends upon the answer to two other questions: What is nationalism and what is the source of its demonic power in the modern world? Is there anything in American experience which offers grounds for hope that America can avoid the evils of nationalism and learn to assume international responsibility?

The first of these questions can be answered briefly. Nationalism may be good or bad. In its nineteenth century democratic form, as we have seen, it is compatible with devotion to humanity and may furnish a strong incentive for its service. The dangerous element in nationalism is not the sense of nationality and loyalty to the nation which has nourished one's life. It is the elevation of one's nation to the status of the ultimate and absolute object of devotion. What are the causes of this pseudo-religious element in modern nationalism? The most obvious is the fact that the national state which arose on the ruins of medieval feudalism has been the strongest unifying force in the modern world and has bestowed great economic and cultural benefits upon its citizens. But there is also a spiritual cause: the weakening of the religious and moral forces which had bound together all western nations into a common civilization. The Reformation destroyed the unity of Christendom, rationalism attacked its faith, and economic individualism undermined its social ethics. As a result, the national state in Germany, and in a measure elsewhere, became to countless people who looked to it for security and opportunity a "mortal god," a substitute object of religious devotion.

The second question, with respect to the American attitude toward nationalism, cannot be answered so briefly. On the one hand, our nationalism has been only partially corrupted by the "religious" exaltation of the national state. We have been prevented, by our traditional preference for a weak central government and by the diffusion of power in our federal system, from attributing all the blessings of our national life to the state. Moreover, we have had a lively sense of the value of voluntary associations such as the church and school in our cultural life and the place of individual enterprise in our economic life. In so far as we have taken pride in our political system it has been centered in our liberties rather than in the state as the protector of those liberties. There has been in recent years a centralization of political power and an increased dependence upon the federal government for security. But we still think of the state as our servant rather than as our master and are little inclined to worship it. Doubtless the youth of our nation has something to do with this. Also, the diversity of races and cultures in our melting pot has prevented the cultural tradition of any one of the mother countries from becoming the tradition of all of us. This is one of the main reasons for our relative indifference to the past and our primary concern for the future. May it not also be true that our experience as the melting pot of races has prepared us to lead the way from nationalism toward a new international order?

Thus there has been a conflict in our ideals between a narrow nationalism and a more generous sense of national destiny. This conflict must now be resolved. If the argument of this chapter is valid, the preservation and extension of our democracy, as well as the peace of the world, require the abandonment of our provincial nationalism and the full acceptance of our international responsibility. In the political sphere this will involve a definite commitment to a policy of concerted action and voluntary assignment of certain functions to an international organization. This assignment of functions must be made with the expectation that it will be permanent, if the international organization is to have sufficient authority to function effectively and hence to endure. Whether this should be spoken of as a limitation of the external sovereignty of national states or whether some other term should be used is largely a matter of terminology. National sovereignty in internal affairs is obviously necessary, since there must be within each state a central authority for the making and enforcement of law. But the claim of any national state to exercise absolute, unlimited "freedom of action" in its relations with other states rests not upon moral right but upon the appeal to naked force. It is time that this amoral doctrine of national irresponsibility be renounced once and for all by democratic states like our own.

THE BASIS OF WORLD ORDER: JUSTICE AND FORCE

If there are no historical forces which doom our hope of progress, and if our sense of national destiny dictates active leadership in establishing world order, we must next inquire into the basis of any international organization which is to be consistent with our dominant ideals. The traditional conviction of Americans that all human laws must be in conformity with an eternal and unchanging moral law will help us to answer this question, since the majority of Americans have not lost their belief that there is such a law and that national policies as well as individual acts must be in conformity with it if they are to stand.

Because of this belief, Americans will approve a world organization only if they are convinced that it rests upon a foundation of *justice*. This means, in the first place, that it must safeguard as far as possible the vital national interests and individual liberties of all peoples. The experience of the generation between the two world wars, it is true, has shown that the claim to national self-determination cannot always be taken as an absolute. The attempt in the Treaty of Versailles to follow the principle of self-determination resulted in too many economic and other problems to be repeated without qualification. But the belief of Americans in the political independence of peoples wherever possible is still very strong. That is why we are suspicious of imperialism and of any colonial administration that does not prepare the people under it for self-government as rapidly as possible.

Justice requires, in the second place, the settlement of disputes between nations either on the basis of law or by political adjustment of conflicting claims. We have been made vividly aware of the difficulties in the way of establishing and enforcing international law, but we believe that these difficulties can and must be gradually overcome. Equality of all nations before the law and the need for a World Court to determine and apply it are taken for granted by almost all Americans who reject isolationism.

In the third place, the belief that justice requires the freedom of all nations and the orderly settlement of all disputes constitutes one of the strongest arguments for an ultimate solution of the problem of peace in universal terms. Americans who think primarily in terms of justice rather than force are deeply suspicious of any attempt to impose peace by agreement among the Great Powers alone, except as a temporary necessity following the war. Just as they conceive of just government at home as involving the representation of all the citizens, they do not see how the interests and rights of small nations can possibly be accorded fair treatment unless they are represented along with the Great Powers in an international organization.

But Americans are also practical enough to realize that leadership in any international organization must be taken by the Great Powers, since these alone (at least for some time) will have the military and other resources necessary to enforce its decisions. Though our belief in justice will make us shun any world system which seems to be based upon force alone, we realize that a world order which is to be effective must be backed by force. The crucial question is, what do we conceive to be the proper function of force and its relation to justice?

The role of force in a democracy is necessarily a *subordinate* one. Force in a democracy is an instrument of justice under law. All of the major traditions which have shaped our thinking are in agreement on this point. Classical thinkers from the time of Plato have insisted that right is not determined by might but by moral reason, in the interest of the weak as well as the strong. From the Sophists to Nietzsche and the Nazis this view has been disputed, but it has been dominant in western political theory. The Christian tradition goes still further. At its best, it has insisted that in matters of morality and religion coercion is wrong, and that even in politics power is a temptation to pride and tyranny. Thus, democracy is heir both to the classical conviction that power is a means to justice rather than an end in itself and to the Christian fear of power in the hands of proud men.

At the same time, the *necessity* of power to restrain lawlessness and protect the rights of men has been almost universally recognized in our democratic theory. It is true that romantic notions of the natural goodness of men have sometimes led modern liberals and humanitarians into a sentimental optimism which thinks force can be dispensed with in the family and the school and all but eliminated in the state. There is also a kind of Christian perfectionism and pacifism which has led certain sects to underestimate the power of egoism in man and to think that aggressors can be disarmed by love without recourse to force. Against sentimentalists and pacifists alike, therefore, the necessity of force must be more strongly asserted. We have learned that mere resolutions outlawing war, together with sentiments in favor of peace, can never restrain aggressors. We have also learned that discussion of differences in democratic fashion around a table may lead to appeasement of tyrants, rather than to justice, when the power is all on their side.

Thus, the best classical, Christian, and democratic thought is agreed both that force should be subordinated to justice and that force is necessary to restrain evil men and nations. Political wisdom lies in a proper *balance* between these two sides of the truth. In the generation between the world wars, the necessity of force for international justice was minimized in the democracies. In the future, however, there is a real danger that the other side of the truth, i.e., the subordination of force to justice, may be forgotten. Despite our democratic tradition, our history has been marked time and again by the use of arbitrary power. In our treatment of Indians, Negroes, the defeated southern states, striking workers, Mexicans, and others we have been guilty of hasty and violent action. At the turn of the century, we embarked for a time upon a career of imperialism, the evil effects of which are only slowly being overcome by our recent Good Neighbor policy. Moreover, we have as great pride in our military power when aroused as in our peaceful intentions when we are not at war. Finally, the shock to our sense of security by the open challenge of the Axis powers might give rise to a twentieth century militarism and imperialism far worse than nineteenth century isolationism.

GEORGE F. THOMAS

The crucial question, therefore, is, How can we maintain our traditional belief that force should be instrumental and secondary to justice at a time when we are being tempted as never before to think that security must be based upon power alone? Since the power of even the strongest state by itself has been shown to be inadequate for security, many political "realists" are arguing that an alliance of the Great Powers offers the only solution. But if our previous argument is valid that justice for all nations is possible only under an international organization based upon liberty and law, we cannot accept such a return to power politics. It would mean an abandonment of the moral principles on which our whole democratic faith rests. Whatever may be necessary in the transitional period after the war, therefore, the only way in which the demands of justice and the necessity for power can ultimately be harmonized is by means of adequate military forces acting under the authority of an international organization.

THE MORAL BASIS OF PEACE

It seems obvious, however, that if we are to escape a narrow and defensive nationalism and share leadership in an international organization backed by military power, there must be a change in the moral attitude of our people. As the aggressive nationalism of our present enemies rests upon a vicious glorification of the state and its power as the absolute good, our own self-sufficient nationalism rests upon a denial of moral responsibility to all who are not members of our own nation. As the remedy for the former is the return of the state and its power to a subordinate position in the scale of values, the remedy for the latter is an extension of the scope of our moral responsibility and obligation beyond our national boundaries.

Bergson has pointed out[10] that there are two different sources

[10] Henri Bergson, *The Two Sources of Morality and Religion*. Translation by R. A. Audra and C. Brereton (New York: Holt, 1935), Chapter I.

of morality. The first is the social "pressure" of a limited group upon its members. This gives rise to a kind of morality which is concerned solely with the solidarity and survival of the group. It not only requires no obligations to members of other groups; it actually deepens hostility to them and serves as a powerful weapon against them in time of war. It is obvious that this "closed" morality is still dominant in the dealings of modern national states with one another. The second kind of morality, which Bergson names "open" morality, is quite different. It has its origin in the intuition of prophets into the unity of humanity and in the reverence for all life which springs from this discovery. It is universal in scope, since it is motivated by aspiration for the harmony of all life with all life.

Only the acceptance of a universal "open" morality of this kind by all the peoples of the earth would make perfect world community possible. But one's faith in the moral perfectibility of man would have to be unclouded by any recognition of the egoism in human nature to believe that universal brotherhood can be fully realized within the limits of history. This should not lead us into pessimism, however, as if peace could be attained only in heaven. For the realistic idea of progress I have defended permits us to believe that a world organization can be *initiated* on the basis of the imperfect sense of community already possessed by the leading powers of the world, and that a deeper sense of world community can be developed within it as a protecting and supporting framework.

There are two facts that encourage us in this belief. The first is that a perfect sense of community is not necessary for the establishment of government. Non-moral factors such as economic interdependence and the necessity of security for survival may be sufficient to initiate the process. Nations as well as men may learn to "live" together before they learn to "live well" together. The second is that political order provides favorable conditions for further moral development. World order will make the extension of moral obligation beyond national boundaries more natural. One of the main reasons for the tenacious hold of "closed" or national morality has been the fact that until recently the largest political unit has been the national state. Given a political organization that is potentially world-wide, the limitation of moral responsibility to the members of one's own nation would tend to become unnecessary and unnatural. At the same time, the various kinds of international collaboration which would arise under the favorable conditions of world security would deepen the sense of world community. As the nations learned to share common interests, they would be brought together in a deeper unity. Thus, it is not necessary to wait for a perfect world community before laying the political foundations of world order; indeed, an indispensable condition of progress toward world community is the laying of these political foundations.

But a deepening of the sense of community between the nations is indispensable for the *ultimate success* of any international organization. Justice among the nations is impossible without their mutual respect and good will. For justice involves restraint upon the self out of respect for the rights of others, and respect for the rights of others presupposes concern for their welfare. Many political "realists" question this and maintain that a stable world organization can be based upon the mere enlightened self-interest of the nations. On this view, if each nation would only recognize that *its own* self-interest requires that it respect the rights of other nations, no real concern for *their* interests would be necessary. This doctrine of national egoism, which asserts that in all its policies the state must be motivated exclusively by national self-interest, is false. The theory that individuals are wholly egoistic in their motives is refuted by the remarkable capacity of human beings for love and friendship in peace and sacrifice in war. The ground upon which the theory of national egoism has often been based, therefore, is the claim that the rulers of states in their motives must be utterly different from private citizens.

But why should this be supposed to be true? The dualism which is thus implied between the morality of the state and the morality of its members often rests upon an artificial separation of the state from its citizens. But it is only in the totalitarian theory that the state is regarded as a mystical entity above its citizens and with a will of its own. According to the democratic theory, on the contrary, the state is nothing apart from its members and its will is the will of its members. If the totalitarian theory is false and the democratic theory true, the idea that the rulers of states must follow moral principles different from those of the majority of its members must be firmly rejected.

It is, of course, true that the representatives of the people in a democratic state must be guided by moral principles acceptable to the majority. As representatives, they cannot and should not follow moral principles which go far beyond those of the majority, and if they do so their policies are almost certain to be repudiated. Under the conditions of modern nationalism, national self-interest has hitherto been the principle followed most often in foreign policy by both the majority of the people and their representatives. But the recognition of this fact in the past need not mean the acceptance of it as inevitable for the future. It should simply stimulate those who see the falsity and danger of national egoism to strive for a change in the moral principles which guide the majority and their representatives. The political leaders of the people can do much to point out the need for this change; but non-political institutions such as the churches and the schools have perhaps the greatest responsibility for bringing it about in the hearts and minds of the people.

But national egoism owes its strength, also, to the fear that the only alternative is its opposite extreme, national altruism, according to which it is necessary to disregard the national interest in the interest of other nations. The answer to this is that the rational alternative to national egoism is not a national altruism that disregards the interest of one's own nation, but a national policy of *mutuality* that is based upon consideration of the interests of other nations *as well as* one's own.

This assumes, of course, that interest in the welfare of other nations is not a mere disguised form of interest in the welfare of one's own, but is an end in itself. To deny that such an interest is possible is to deny every feeling of sympathy for the sufferings of the people of other lands and every desire for their happiness. It is true that interest in the welfare of another nation is seldom or never as intense or vivid as interest in one's own. For this reason, methods must be found for enlarging the scope of sympathy and responsibility by education, as we have said. In principle, however, the same difficulty arises in personal morality, since one feels sympathy for family and friends more intensely and vividly than for others outside one's inner circle. But this difficulty leads no respectable moralist to deny that one has duties to these others. It is also true that interest in the welfare of another nation for its own sake is usually, perhaps always, accompanied by interest in it as a means to the welfare of oneself and one's own people, e.g., the tourist or student in a foreign country may be genuinely interested not only in its welfare but also in what it can teach him. But this should not disturb us. The interdependence of nations, like that of individuals, makes reciprocity between them inevitable, each using and being used by the others. According to one of Kant's formulations of the categorical imperative of morality, a person should always be treated as an end in himself and never merely as a means. This principle does not prohibit the treatment of persons (or nations) as means to our own ends of prosperity, security, and culture, so long as they are also treated as ends in themselves.

Thus, the rejection of national egoism does not require the acceptance of national altruism in the sense of devotion to the welfare of other nations without regard to one's own, but a relationship of mutuality between the nations.

AMERICAN IDEALS AND THE PEACE

It is obvious, however, that mutuality requires national restraint and may require a measure of national renunciation. This fact must be faced squarely and honestly. Refusal to recognize that peace can be achieved only at a cost has exposed many advocates of peace to the charge of sentimentalism. If sentimentalism is defined as lip-service to ideals without any serious effort to realize them, the charge is often just. Anyone who does not will the means, does not really will the end.

On the other hand, defenders of nationalism have often exaggerated the cost of peace and thus frightened timid men and women into the isolationist camp. The answer to these nationalists is that the cost is justified by the greater good it will make possible both for our own and for other nations. In personal life we are all aware of the necessity of sacrificing or subordinating lesser goods in order to attain greater ones. The moral life presents everyone with this necessity since it requires him to choose between the different values and modes of life which are open to him. If he chooses the higher in preference to the lower, he necessarily rejects or at least subordinates the lower. In doing so, he distinguishes between the immediate and the ultimate good, the short-run and the long-run good. He is willing to sacrifice the immediate but lower good, because he envisages the higher good which can come only if he makes that sacrifice. Nations are not exempt from this moral law. They, too, must give up some things to attain others.

For example, as we have said, America will have to renounce that absolute "freedom of action" in her foreign relations which is only a euphemistic phrase for irresponsibility. As a young nation, at once conscious of our power and reluctant to commit ourselves permanently to any settled form of life, this will be very difficult for us. For it will involve not merely a willingness to abstain from any arbitrary foreign policy but also a positive and continuing attempt to collaborate with other nations. Again, it will be necessary for us to consider the effects of proposed economic policies upon the employment and prosperity of other nations and to abstain from any policy which would enrich a minority of Americans but only at the cost of great suffering to other peoples.

In considering the benefits for all nations that would result from these sacrifices, emphasis has usually been placed on economic prosperity and military security. But, important as these economic and military advantages would be, they are by no means all. Peace is not merely a negative condition, the absence of war; it is a positive opportunity for continuous progress in the arts and achievements of civilized life. It provides an opportunity for unbroken family life and for the cumulative efforts of schools and other institutions to foster the moral and spiritual development of personality. It opens up possibilities of friendship between the nations and enables different peoples to contribute their own unique values to the world community. Thus, when we speak of the long-range advantages of international organization, we should not forget that these advantages include cultural and spiritual values.

The alternative to national egoism, therefore, is not a national altruism that disregards the interests of our own people in the desire to "play Santa Claus to the world." It is a practical idealism which is based upon concern for *both* the welfare of other nations *and* the long-run interests and aspirations of the American people. If it were not, it could not hope to win acceptance. Since each nation represents an important achievement of human values, moral right justifies its government in safeguarding its vital interest, and any international order that is to endure must respect that interest. What is required of us, therefore, is not a *choice* between international good will and national interest, but an acceptance of the claims of *both* as valid and a faith in their ultimate coincidence. International good will and national interest, like justice and force, must be reconciled if we are to have peace. It will not be easy to reconcile them. Indeed, if an international organization is established, the stubborn egoism and narrow sympathies of human

AMERICAN IDEALS AND THE PEACE

beings will continue to operate and will make it a very imperfect thing. But this gives us no excuse for abandoning the task. It should only make us more aware of the need for humility about ourselves and for all the intelligence and will we possess. If Americans will only accept the responsibility that history has thrust upon them, they can share leadership in the building of a world community that is at once the primary task of all nations in the twentieth century and the fulfillment of our own deepest ideals.

Acknowledgments

FROM first to last, this book has been a cooperative undertaking, and I am very glad of this opportunity to express my sincere appreciation to all those who have helped us to complete it. A special word of appreciation is due President Harold W. Dodds and Princeton University, without whose encouragement and financial support this volume could never have been attempted, and to Professor Ralph Barton Perry of Harvard University (who founded the Universities Committee on Post-War International Problems), for his inspiration and counsel. Professors T. M. Greene and Frank D. Graham, my colleagues of the Editorial Committee, have earned my profound gratitude for their constant advice and their tireless work of review and revision. Furthermore, I wish to express my appreciation to the Princeton Theological Seminary, the Divisional Program of the Humanities of Princeton University, and the School of Public and International Affairs for secretarial assistance and many other services. Dr. Frank Aydelotte, Director of the Institute for Advanced Study, Mr. Alexander Loveday, Director of the League of Nations Economic, Financial and Transit Department, and Professor Dana G. Munro, Director of the School of Public and International Affairs, have been of great assistance, both in the founding of the Princeton Group and the promotion of its activities. The staff of the Princeton University Press has also been of invaluable assistance in many ways. I am extremely grateful to those members of the Princeton Group who have sent in written criticisms of one or more chapters of this book, some having read the entire manuscript. These members are: Frank Aydelotte, David F. Bowers, Kingsley Davis, Edward Mead Earle, Christian Gauss, Theodore M. Greene, E. Harris Harbison, Martin Hill, J. L. Hromadka, Dudley Kirk, Alexander Loveday, John A. Mackay, Charles R. Morey, Frank W. Notestein, Paul Oppenheim, Joseph R.

ACKNOWLEDGMENTS

Strayer, and all the co-authors of this book. In addition, a number of scholars not members of the Princeton Group have read parts of the manuscript, giving us the benefit of many valuable suggestions. Among these are: Professor Ralph Barton Perry of Harvard University, Professor Arthur O. Lovejoy of Johns Hopkins University, Dr. Margaret Joseph of the League of Nations Economic, Financial and Transit Department, Professor John H. Herz of Howard University, Dr. Walter Schiffer of the Institute for Advanced Study; and Professors Hadley Cantril, Clifton R. Hall and Alpheus T. Mason, all of Princeton University. To A. C. Davidonis are due special thanks for his services as secretary of the Princeton Group.

Finally, I wish to thank all members of the Princeton Group who, in spite of their many commitments, have so generously collaborated during the past year and a half in carrying on the work of the Group, especially by participating in round-table discussions, or by giving their help as authors or critics, or both. A list of the members of the Princeton Group follows:

PRINCETON GROUP FOR THE STUDY OF POST-WAR INTERNATIONAL PROBLEMS

FRANK AYDELOTTE, Director, Institute for Advanced Study

DAVID F. BOWERS, Assistant Professor of Philosophy, Princeton University

JEROME S. BRUNER, Research Associate in Public Affairs, Princeton University

WILLIAM S. CARPENTER, Professor of Politics, Princeton University

GILBERT CHINARD, Professor of French Literature, Princeton University

KENNETH H. CONDIT, Dean of the School of Engineering, Princeton University

JOHN C. COOPER, JR., Vice-President, Pan American Airways System

ACKNOWLEDGMENTS

EDWARD S. CORWIN, Professor of Jurisprudence, Princeton University

GORDON A. CRAIG, Assistant Professor of History, Princeton University

A. C. DAVIDONIS, Instructor in History, Princeton University

KINGSLEY DAVIS, Associate Professor of Public Affairs, Princeton University

HAROLD W. DODDS, President, Princeton University

EDWARD M. EARLE, Professor of Economics and Politics, Institute for Advanced Study

GEORGE H. GALLUP, Director, American Institute of Public Opinion

CHRISTIAN GAUSS, Professor of Modern Languages, Princeton University

JEAN GOTTMANN, Formerly Member, Institute for Advanced Study, now Associate in Geography, Johns Hopkins University

FRANK D. GRAHAM, Professor of Economics and Social Institutions, Princeton University

THEODORE M. GREENE, Professor of Philosophy, Princeton University

E. HARRIS HARBISON, Associate Professor of History, Princeton University

MARTIN HILL, Economic, Financial and Transit Department, League of Nations

PHILIP K. HITTI, Professor of Semitic Literature, Princeton University

J. L. HROMADKA, Professor, Princeton Theological Seminary

ERNST JURKAT, Visiting Research Associate, Office of Population Research, Princeton University

EDWIN W. KEMMERER, Professor of International Finance, emeritus, Princeton University

DUDLEY KIRK, Research Associate, Office of Population Research, Princeton University

ACKNOWLEDGMENTS

MIROSLAV KRIZ, Economic, Financial and Transit Department, League of Nations

ALEXANDER LOVEDAY, Director, Economic, Financial and Transit Department, League of Nations

FRIEDRICH A. LUTZ, Associate Professor of Economics, Princeton University

JOHN A. MACKAY, President, Princeton Theological Seminary

DAVID A. MCCABE, Professor of Economics, Princeton University

R. J. MCMULLEN, President, Hangchow Christian College, Zakow, China

CHARLES R. MOREY, Professor of Art and Archaeology, Princeton University

OSKAR MORGENSTERN, Professor of Economics, Princeton University

DANA G. MUNRO, Director, School of Public and International Affairs, Princeton University

GERHART NIEMEYER, formerly Assistant Professor of Public and International Affairs, Princeton University, now head of School of Citizenship, Oglethorpe University

FRANK W. NOTESTEIN, Director, Office of Population Research, Princeton University

RAGNAR NURKSE, Economic, Financial and Transit Department, League of Nations

PAUL OPPENHEIM, Princeton, New Jersey

WINFIELD W. RIEFLER, Professor of Economics and Politics, Institute for Advanced Study

ROBERT SCOON, Professor of Philosophy, Princeton University

EDGAR SMITH, Attorney-at-Law, Princeton, New Jersey

HAROLD H. SPROUT, Associate Professor of Politics, Princeton University

JOSEPH R. STRAYER, Professor of History, Princeton University

GEORGE F. THOMAS, Professor of Religious Thought, Princeton University

JOHN B. WHITTON, Associate Professor of Politics, Princeton University

J.B.W.

Index

Abyssinia, Italian attack on, 103-104, 111
Aggression, 32, 76, 94, 111ff., 125-126, 179, 183, 185, 189
Agriculture, 132
Aid to Britain, 153-154, 157, 180
Air force as international police, 106-107
Alliances, 21ff., 93, 184, 191
Alternatives to world-wide collaboration, 21
American ideals, and the peace, 6-7, 178ff., 198ff.
American Institute of Public Opinion, 179
Anglo-American Alliance, 26ff., 27ff., 191
Aristotle, 6
Armaments, reduction of, 43, 93-94, 186
Armed isolation, 24
Asia, nationalism in, 40
"Assembly of Governments," 65
Atlantic Charter, 181
Austinian theory of law, 174
"Austrian School," 171-172
Autarky, 128, 133ff., 192

Bailey, Thomas A., 10n.
Bajpai, Sir Girja Shankar, 63n.
Balance of power, 23, 34, 52ff., 93, 184
Ball-Burton-Hatch-Hill Resolution, 148, 166
Bayley, C. C., 14n.
Beard, Charles, 204n., 208
Beard, Charles and Mary, 11n.
Beer, Max, 86n.
Bemis, Samuel F., 12n.
Bergson, Henri, 216, 217
"Big Three," 36, 37ff., 42, 43-44, 47, 49, 63
Boxer Revolt, 153

Brecht, Arnold, 47n.
Bricker, John W., 20n.
British Exchange Equalization Account, 137
Brown, William Adams, 21n.
Buell, Raymond Leslie, 24n.
Butler, Harold, 79n.

Cabinet, U.S. Government, 148
Canning, George, 28
Carr, E. H., 18, 28n., 104n., 112
Cartels, 129ff.
Cecil, Lord Robert, 70
"Central Conference," 62
Chambers, Frank P., 14n.
China, 27
Christianity, 199ff., 213ff.
Churchill, Winston, 28, 108, 181
Clausewitz, 115
Colgrove, Kenneth, 153n., 160n.
Committee on Foreign Relations, 148, 149
Commodities control, 132
Communism, 27, 41, 46
Concert of Europe, 71
Conciliation, 42ff., 48ff., 98-99
Confederation, 79
Connally, Senator, 148
Connally Resolution, 167
Constitutional amendment on treaty-making, 150-151, 197
Constitutional Government, 145
Control of power, *see* Limitation of power
Corrective measures, 5, 87ff.
"Court of Justice," 65
Cram, Lucile Cardin, 160n.
Creel, George, 12
Crowe, Sir Eyre, 42n., 57n.
Culbertson Plan, 106

Daniels, Josephus, 13n.
Darwin, Charles, 200

INDEX

Declaration of Independence, 206
Democracy, 209
Destroyer Deal, 153-154, 157
Determination of aggressor, 111ff.
Determinism, 201
Dinko, Tomašić, 45n.
Dominance and sovereignty, 187ff.
Dumbarton Oaks Conference, 22n., 79, 107

Earle, Edward Mead, 23n.
Economic causes of war, 88-89, 139ff., 193
Economic discrimination, 124
Economic reforms, 5, 88-89, 126ff., 185ff., 221
Economic sanctions, 103-104, 125, 128-129
Economist, 192
Education and peace, 84-86, 189, 192ff., 205
Egoism and peace, 202, 204
Eire, 121n.
Employment and peace, 126ff.
Enemy countries, treatment of, 187
Equity Tribunal, 84
Étatisme, 117-118
Exchange rates, 135ff.
Executive Agreements, 151ff.
"Executive Council," 73, 81, 95, 110, 111

"Farewell Address," 23, 119
Fear as goal of national policy, 39
Federalist, 144, 151, 162
Federated Europe, 47
Federation, 47, 53ff., 79
Fenwick, C. G., 173n.
Field v. Clark, 158
Force, monopoly of in world authority, 76ff., 100, 111
Force, role of, 49, 100, 104, 214
Foreign Debts Commission, 159
Foreign policy, people's version, 182ff.

Foreign policy and public opinion, 84-85, 177ff.
Fortune Poll, 179
Fourteen Points, 16
France, 72, 74, 118n.
Freedom and peace, 121
Free trade, 120ff., 125, 134
Fullbright Resolution, 148, 164-165

Gabriel, Ralph, 198, 199, 206
"General Assembly," 81
Germany, economic policy, 122, 123ff.
Germany, international position, 40
Germany, relations with Russia, 28
Germany, relations with United States, 180
Gibbs, Sir Philip, 15
Gold standard, 137, 140
Gonsiorowski, 78n.
Gooch, G. P., 42n., 57n.
Good-Neighbor Policy, 100, 215
Grant, C. P., 14n.
Great Britain, economic policy, 117ff., 120, 124, 137
Great Britain, international position, 38ff.
Great Britain, relations with Soviet Russia, 39
Great Britain, relations with United States, 26, 41, 191
Great Powers, 4, 22, 30, 31, 35ff., 48ff., 50, 52ff., 53, 62, 68, 69ff., 71, 72, 73, 74, 81, 191, 198, 210, 214, 216
Griswold, Whitney, 22n.
Grotius, Hugo, 68, 76, 173

Habana Convention, 70n.
Hacker, L. M., 22n.
Halifax, Lord, 92n.
Hamilton, Alexander, 148, 151, 162-164
Harding, Warren G., 11, 12, 17
Hay, John, 151
Hay-Pauncefote Treaty, 173

INDEX

Hayden, Ralston, 147n.
Hitler, Adolf, 37, 58, 73, 104
Holmes, Justice, 143, 174
Hull, Cordell, 6n., 8, 9, 16, 19, 25, 76n., 114, 158
Hull-Lothian Agreement, 153
Hungary, 16

"Idealism" and "realism," 6, 179, 219ff.
Imperialism, 121, 209ff., 215
Individual, role of in international order, 55-56
Individualism, 117ff., 199, 202
Indivisibility of peace, 7, 70, 81, 92, 206ff.
Inequality of nations, 53
Institute for Advanced Study, 2, 226
"Interim measures" and determination of aggressor, 112
Internationalism, 178, 206ff.
International administration, 60, 66
International arbitration, 60, 84, 95ff., 185
International bank, 138
International community, 217ff.
International economic controls, 20-21, 88-89, 141
International federation, 47, 53ff., 79
"International government," 61
International investment, 138ff.
International law, 36, 50, 74, 90ff., 171ff.
International law and sovereignty, 74ff., 171ff.
International Law of the Future, 69, 70, 77n., 92, 103n.
International legislation, 50, 90ff.
International monetary authority, 136ff.
International organization, acceptability and effectiveness, 5-6; agencies and activities, 61ff., 79ff., 184ff., 212ff.; fundamental principles of, 57ff., 69ff.; and Great Powers, 37ff., 52ff., 73-74; membership in, 61ff., 80; and prevention of war, 57ff., 87ff.; to adjust national policies, 58ff.; welfare agencies and activities, 61, 94
"International Peace Center," 84-85
International police force, 102, 105ff., 185, 186ff., 190, 191
International welfare agencies, 61, 94
Intervention, 76, 100, 111
"Irreconcilables," 17
Isolation, 17, 22ff., 26, 119, 179, 181, 182ff., 194, 215, 221

Japan, 28, 128
Jay, John, 29, 144
Jay Treaty, 147ff.
Jefferson, Thomas, 119, 120, 131
Jessup, Philip C., 108n.
Joint and several responsibility, 81
"Just" and "unjust" wars, 76, 173
Justice and force, 6-7, 212ff.
Justice and peace, 6-7, 213, 218
Justiciable disputes, obligatory settlement of, 91, 95ff., 213

Keeton, G. W., 32n., 35n.
Kelsen, 171
King, Rufus, 144
Kirk, Grayson L., 36n.
Knox, Frank, 166
Kocourek, Albert, 174n.
Kun, Bela, 16
Kunz, Josef L., 171n.

Laissez-faire, 137-138
Lansing-Ishii Agreement, 157
Laski, Harold, 174n.
Latin America, 24-25, 100, 215
League of Nations, Abyssinian affair, 103-104, 111; Article 11 of Covenant, 69, 70; economic activities, 141; Economic, Financial

INDEX

and Transit Department, 2, 225; Greco-Bulgarian incident of 1925, 112; licit and illicit wars, 77; and peaceful change, 50; and peaceful settlement, 97-98, 99; and power, 72; and prevention of war, 48, 112; and public opinion, 12ff., 85, 185; sanctions, 77, 103-104, 109; Secretariat, 66, 80, 83; and *status quo*, 50; and U.S. Senate, 11, 13ff., 143, 149, 165; and Versailles Treaty, 66-67
Lease-Lend, 159, 186
Legal disputes, settlement of, 91, 95-96, 213
Legal measures for prevention of war, 48, 90ff., 95
Leipzig, Battle of, 19
Levitan, David M., 153n.
Lewis, Representative David J., 161
"Licit" and "illicit" wars, 76, 173
Limitation of power, 5, 52ff., 73-74, 102, 214ff.
Lincoln, Abraham, 7, 206
Lippmann, Walter, 63n., 72n.
Lodge, Henry Cabot, 10
Lovejoy, Arthur O., 110, 226

McClure, Wallace, 152n.
McCumber, Senator, 159
McKinley Tariff Act, 158
McKinley, William, 153, 192
Maclay, William, 145ff.
Marx, Karl, 201
Mercantilism, 116ff., 130
Militarism, 36-37
Military sanctions, 105ff.
Minimal economic conditions of peace, 126ff.
Monopolies, 129ff.
Monopoly of force in world authority, 76ff., 92, 100, 111
Monroe Doctrine, 25
Montesquieu, 5
Moore, J. B., 172n.
Moral law, 175, 199ff., 213, 216ff.

Moral principles in international relations, 6, 55, 175, 180, 198ff., 216ff.
Morris, Robert, 146
Moscow, Declaration of, 8, 20, 111, 154
Most-favored-nation clause, 120, 125

Napoleon, 19, 73, 120
National destiny, 200, 206ff.
National interest, 179, 208
National mission, 199
National Opinion Research Center, 179
National power, 33ff.
Nationalism, 30, 40, 118, 120, 126, 178, 202, 206ff., 210ff., 221
Neo-Mercantilism, 123, 134
Neutrality, 92, 103n., 179, 183, 184ff.
New York Times, 150
Nevins, Allan, 22n.
Niebuhr, Reinhold, 46, 73, 204
Normalcy, return to, 10ff., 194ff.

Obligatory settlement of disputes, 91, 95ff., 213
Office of Public Information, 193
Office of Public Opinion Research, Princeton University, 179
O'Neal, Ed, 178

Peace, and economic policy, 5, 88-89, 139ff., 185ff., 193, 221; and education, 84-86, 189, 192ff., 205; and force, 49, 214; and freedom, 121; and free trade, 120ff., 125, 134; and monopolies, 130-131; and the press, 195-196; conditions of, 126ff.; methods of, 48ff.
Peaceful change, 50, 87ff., 96ff.
Peaceful settlement of international disputes, 48ff., 60, 65, 88, 91,

INDEX

95ff., 185, 212, 213; and League of Nations, 97-98, 99
Pepper, Claude, 17
Permanent Court of International Justice, 60, 65, 82ff., 91, 95, 213
Perry, Ralph Barton, 1, 226
Pessimism and American policy, 202ff., 217
Poland, 16
Political disputes, 96ff.
Positivist theory of law, 174-175
Power in international politics, 6, 52, 72, 104, 214
Power, limitation of, 5, 52ff., 73-74, 102, 191, 214ff.
Power politics, 6, 32ff., 34, 52
Preferential trade, 135
President and treaty-making, 143ff.
Press and peace, 195-196
Prevention of war, economic measures, 88-90, 185ff.; by international organization, 57ff., 87ff.; and League of Nations, 48, 112; legal measures, 48, 90ff., 95; and public opinion, 181
Preventive measures and peace, 87ff.
Price stabilization, 138
Princeton Group for the Study of Post-War International Problems, 1, 3, 226
Princeton Theological Seminary, 2, 226
Progress, belief in, 200ff., 205
Propaganda, 195
Public opinion, education and, 84-86, 189, 192ff., 205; and aid to Britain, 180; and alliances, 184; and American participation in world affairs, 182ff.; and balance of power, 184; and *fait accompli*, 84-85, 179; and foreign policy, 177ff.; and Germany, 180; and collective action, 178-179; and ideological doctrines, 180; and international post-war leadership,

187ff.; and isolation, 179ff.; and League of Nations, 12ff., 85, 185; and peace, 1, 5, 17ff., 64, 82, 84-85, 99; and peaceful settlement of international disputes, 184, 185; and practical internationalism, 181-182; and reduction of armaments, 186ff.; and self-interest, 179ff.; and sovereignty, 187ff.

"*Quis custodiet?*", 109-111
Quota plan for international police force, 105, 106-107

Radio and peace, 82-83, 86
Rappard, William E., 103
Raw materials, 128ff.
"Realism" and "idealism," 6, 179, 219ff.
Regionalism, 53-54, 63, 86n.
Reparations, 186
Republican Platform, 165, 168
Responsibility of United States, 104, 176, 188, 200, 210, 223
Responsibility, joint and several, 69, 81
"Restrictive Measures" to promote peace, 94ff.
Richards, James P., 20n.
Rippy, J. Fred, 13n.
Roosevelt, Franklin D., 13n., 181
Roosevelt, Theodore, 25, 153
Rule of law, 6, 48ff., 68ff., 113-114, 213ff.
Rush-Bagot agreement, 153
Russia, 27, 39ff., 44; relations with Czechoslovakia, 39, 44-45; relations with Germany, 28; relations with Great Britain, 39; relations with Poland, 39; relations with United States, 5, 39, 41, 156; relations with Yugoslavia, 39; recognition by United States, 156

Sanctions, 102, 105ff.; and League

INDEX

of Nations, 77, 103-104, 109; and public opinion, 186-187; decision as to application of, 110; and war, 112ff.; enforcibility of, 109-111
Schnepper, M. B., 160n.
Scholars, American, and the peace, 2
Schwarzenberger, G., 32n., 35n.
Secret Treaties, 15
Secretariat of League of Nations, 66, 80, 83
Secretariat of new world organization, 66, 83
Security, *sine qua non* of peace, 5, 38, 68, 93-94, 125, 142; and limitation of sovereignty, 75-76; security alone inadequate, 68
Self-corrective treaty-making powers, 150ff.
Self-defense, 78
Self-interest, 179ff., 218
Senate, control over treaties, 17, 143ff., 196-197
Senate, and League of Nations, 11, 13ff., 143, 149, 165
Smaller powers, 28, 44, 53, 54, 63, 68, 73, 81, 118
Smith, Adam, 117, 118, 119n.
Smuts, Field Marshal, 72, 165
Sovereignty, 5-6, 56, 74-76, 187ff., 190, 212, 221ff., 170ff.
Sovereignty, and dominance, 187ff.
Spartacist uprising, 16
Spengler, 201, 203
Spheres of influence, 42
Sprout, Harold and Margaret, 13n.
Spykman, N. J., 25n.
Stalin, 41
Stassen, Harold E., 80n.
State, concepts of, 210
Statesman, role of, 48
Status quo, 33, 50, 64
Strayer, Joseph R., 84n.
Superstate, 57
"Suppressive measures," 101ff.
Supreme War Council, 108

Sutherland, Justice, 156
Sweetser, Arthur, 160n.

Taft, Senator, 168
Tariffs and world peace, 89, 133ff., 186, 192
Teheran, Conference of, 8, 20, 166, 184
Temperley, H. W. V., 42n., 57n.
Temporarily mobilized force as international police force, 107ff.
"Third Chamber," 82
Third Internationale, 46
Tinkham, Representative, 161n.
Total peace, 7
Treatment of enemy countries, 187
Treaty-making authority, 17, 143ff., 196-197
Two-Thirds Rule, 149, 150, 158ff., 169, 196-197

Unemployment, 126ff., 137
United Nations, 8
United States, economic policy, 88, 124, 134; and peaceful settlement of disputes, 95-96; international position, 41ff.; relations with Germany, 180; relations with Great Britain, 26, 41, 191; relations with Soviet Russia, 5, 41, 188; responsibility of, 104, 176, 188, 200, 210, 223; security of, 21-22, 25, 26ff., 41ff.
United States v. Belmont, 156
UNRRA, 159

Vandenberg, Senator, 160
Verdross, 171
Versailles, Conference of, 10, 12ff., 66
Versailles, Treaty of, 66, 160, 210
Vienna, Congress of, 19

Walsh, Senator, 159
War, causes of, 58, 139; "just" and "unjust" wars, 173; and mercan-

INDEX

tilism, 116; and monopolies, 131; prevention of, 48ff., 57ff., 88-90ff., 95, 112, 181, 185ff.; and revolution, 48
Washington, George, 23, 24, 119, 120, 145-146, 147, 148
Wealth of Nations, 117, 118
Welles, Sumner, 23n., 70, 101, 189
Willkie, Wendell L., 75
Willoughby, W. W., 174n.
Wilson, Woodrow, 10, 11, 12, 14, 15, 16, 93, 145, 192
Wolfers, Arnold, 54n.
"World Council," 64